PRAISE FOR

make serious money
on eBay UK

"To sell successfully on eBay, you have to create a picture of
yourself as a seller that will make buyers trust you and place big
bids. In *Make Serious Money on eBay UK* expert Dan Wilson
explains how to stand out from the crowd."
Daily Telegraph

"Written with wit, insight and a wealth of experience."
Manager

"Fancy becoming a millionaire without leaving home? ... It is
possible to make extra cash by selling almost anything and, with
a worldwide market and low overheads, a third of all new
businesses are now set up on the net. If you want to get in on
the action, new book *Make Serious Money on eBay* by
Dan Wilson tells you how."
The Sun

"Some of the tricks of trading on eBay... revealed for the first time
by an insider. His advice is timely."
Sunday Mirror

"Get in on the craze that's sweeping the technological world with
this guide. Learn how to dig up the best bargains and how to
market your own treasures, all while keeping your personal
details secure."
Good Book Guide

D0452982

make serious money on eBay UK

Build a successful business online

and profit from eBay, Amazon

and your own website

New and Updated Edition

Dan Wilson

NICHOLAS BREALEY
PUBLISHING

London • Boston

This revised Second edition first published by
Nicholas Brealey Publishing in 2011
Reprinted with corrections 2012

3-5 Spafield Street
Clerkenwell, London
EC1R 4QB, UK
Tel: +44 (0)20 7239 0360
Fax: +44 (0)20 7239 0370

20 Park Plaza, Suite 1115A
Boston
MA 02116, USA
Tel: (888) BREALEY
Fax: (617) 523 3708

www.nicholasbrealey.com
www.wilsondan.co.uk

First edition published in 2007
Second edition published in 2009, reprinted in 2010

© Dan Wilson 2007, 2009, 2011
The right of Dan Wilson to be identified as the author of this
work has been asserted in accordance with the Copyright, Designs
and Patents Act 1988.

Parts of this book were first published in previous editions of
Make Money on eBay UK.

ISBN: 978-1-85788-540-8

British Library Cataloguing in Publication Data
A catalogue record for this book is available from the
British Library.

Printed in the UK by Clays Ltd.

Contents

1

Welcome

This is the latest incarnation of a book I first wrote in 2004. I've brought it completely up to date and added a whole host of new information for this 2011 edition, but my message about eBay is exactly the same as it's always been: anyone can make money from eBay. That's the focus of this book.

I've been associated with eBay for more than a decade. I was part of the team that founded eBay here in the UK. eBay started off as a niche collector's site in the USA in 1995 and by 1999 it had come to our shores. Of course, now it's a household name and millions of people visit the site every month. It's the no. 1 ecommerce destination for shoppers in Britain.

The past ten years have seen dramatic changes on eBay. It started as an auction site for collectables and antiques. The first eBayers were fans and enthusiasts using the site as a great big online swapshop or car boot sale. Nowadays, eBay is so much more. The collectables are still popular, but now you can get anything you can think of on the site. You can buy clothes, cars, CDs, furniture, household goods and millions of other items. And, of course, it's no longer restricted to auctions, you can buy things instantly using Buy It Now. Secondhand isn't the norm any more either. Many items on eBay are brand spanking new and you can buy from businesses big and small as well as individuals.

The size of eBay

But despite its fame and familiarity, lots of people don't have a real sense of how big eBay really is. To give you an idea of its scale, try to imagine a real-life market of the same size. If eBay UK were a market it would have 16 million visitors every month. There would be 10 million items up for sale from millions of people. Nearly 200,000 businesses would be trading. Total sales each month would total hundreds of millions of pounds.

Globally, eBay is even bigger. It operates in more than 40 countries and has more than 300 million members across the planet. Quite simply, it is the biggest marketplace in the world trading billions of pounds' worth of merchandise every year. Even so, there's still room for you.

I worked for the company until 2006, when I took the leap to become a freelance consultant and writer concentrating on ecommerce, internet marketing and social media. My unique perspective as a former member of staff, independent commentator and trader in my own right means that this book is an authoritative and honest account of how *you* can get involved and buy and sell on eBay.

The eBay lifecycle

Most people on eBay follow a similar pattern as they get to grips with the site and gradually come to know all the quirks and foibles and how it works. I call it the eBay lifecycle. If you recognise yourself as one of the following types you'll find something in this book for you:

Dazed and Confused eBay is daunting to newcomers and you might not know where to start. The book will guide you through your first baby steps and help you get up and running.

Cautious Buyer You've bought a few bits and bobs, you want to buy some more things and maybe make a big purchase, but you're worried about safety and getting ripped off.

Keen Buyer You've cracked buying and parcels arrive daily. Now you want to start selling to clear out the clutter and make room for more eBay bargains.

First-Time Seller You've taken the pics and taken the plunge. Having conquered eBay's cumbersome selling form, your first item has been sold and you've got a happy customer.

Hobby Seller As a proficient seller, you've sold dozens of items and understand the power of the eBay marketplace. You think that you could make a go of selling on eBay to generate a decent income.

Business Seller You're selling hundreds of items a month and turn over a very respectable amount of money. You know that you can make your operations more efficient and you want to sell more and increase your profit margins.

eBay Top-rated Seller You're living the eBay dream. Your eBay operations run like a Rolls-Royce and you're operating at capacity: there's nothing more you can do on eBay because you've outgrown it and need more customers.

Multi-Channel Seller You're juggling multiple balls. Your eBay operations are ticking over, you're successfully trading on Amazon and you're using Google to drive sales on your own ecommerce website. You're an ecommerce guru.

The eBay opportunity

eBay is the single biggest business opportunity in Britain today. So if you're a businessperson looking to develop your business, boost your bottom line and increase your profitability, eBay should be on your list. While ecommerce is growing at a phenomenal pace, British small businesses have been slow to get in on the act and stake their claim. But if you aren't on eBay, you're missing a trick.

The site's own figures show 178,000 UK-registered businesses selling and buying on eBay. This is more than in both Germany and France, but it's a tiny proportion of the 4.3 million small businesses that exist in Britain, according to the Federation of Small Businesses (FSB). So you haven't missed the boat: you can still be a pioneer and among the first to profit from the changing shape of business in Britain. In addition, more and more individuals are turning their hobby selling into a second income. In the US more than 1 million people make their primary income, or a significant secondary income, using eBay.

eBay provides a low-investment, low-risk gateway for entrepreneurs interested in getting their share of ecommerce. It offers unique access to a readymade global marketplace populated by 200 million buyers, as well as off-the-peg tools to help sellers promote, manage and develop their sales.

Ecommerce is still in its infancy and many businesses have yet to take even baby steps towards the new online opportunity. eBay is your ecommerce nursery. It's how you get started. Once you are proficient you can branch out and start selling on other sites and via your own website. Your first strides on eBay could be the beginning of a whole new business adventure.

Beyond eBay

Primarily this book focuses on conquering eBay, but it has an important secondary purpose. If you want to build an eBay business, that's great. But there's so much more to ecommerce than eBay. The final part of this book looks at diversifying your operations and embracing Amazon, Google and other marketplaces, and it shows you how you could be profiting from your own web shop. You can use eBay as your springboard to ecommerce success.

Why eBay is amazing

I've been trading on eBay since 1999; in fact ever since there was an eBay.co.uk to use, I've been on it. I also worked for eBay as an employee until 2006. I have more than 1000 unique feedbacks. If I was a contestant on *Mastermind* my chosen specialist subject would be eBay.co.uk. I know eBay inside out.

When I started working for the company in 1999 hardly anyone in Britain had heard of it. To be honest, even I hadn't heard of it before I applied for the job and boned up for the interview. Some of my friends told me I was mad working for an internet start-up that was bound to go bust. I think some people thought I was working for a porno site. And sometimes, in those early days, working for eBay was a chaotic experience: it was a young company breaking new ground, based in an office above a furniture shop in London. There was some uncertainty that we Brits could be converted to this American phenomenon.

Nowadays eBay is an established household name and it's hard not to open the papers or switch on the television or radio without seeing or hearing about the site. Everyone has heard of it and my friends are continually asking me for trading tips and advice. But in all the time I've known eBay, the two things that make it special for me have remained constant. I am still amazed by the diversity of the people who use the site and the astonishing variety of items available.

Just as I was writing this section of the book, I went off for a ramble on eBay to see what I could find to demonstrate the huge range of items for sale. There was a life-size cardboard cut-out of Jack Bauer from *24* and I could, if I wanted, fill my house with others of Vicky Pollard, Justin Timberlake, Darth Vader or Noddy. I could buy from a selection of Rolls-Royce Silver Shadows: a real one for tens of thousands of pounds or a toy one for much less (although some of these collectable models aren't cheap!). I was tempted by a blue police box like Doctor Who's Tardis, although the description was very clear that it didn't actually travel through time and space, which was a disappointment. But maybe I'd be better off with a narrowboat? I could have bought a holiday home in Liguria, a signed P. G. Wodehouse book, Peter Kay's suit or a Yoda costume for a dog. Where else can you find such a wonderful and amusing assortment of things? Of course, eBay isn't just about the weird and wonderful – most of the stuff for sale is everyday gear available for great prices – but it's the crazy items that I find most endearing.

The other attraction for me is the diversity of the people who use eBay. It's not restricted to any particular group of people or section of society. Cherie Blair is a well-known eBay buyer, and celebrities like Jamie Oliver, the Duchess of Cornwall, David Bowie, Sadie Frost and Stevie Wonder are said to use the site. But the majority of people are just like you and me: eBay members are ordinary folk from all over the country doing all sorts of jobs. The one thing they have in common is a shared interest in eBay and most of them have a fun story to tell about their trading. If you want to start a conversation with an eBay member, all you need to ask is 'What's your feedback score?' and soon you'll be jabbering away nineteen to the dozen. Fellow members will often tell you about a fabulous bargain or a particularly lucrative sale. They like to boast about glowing feedback they have received or amazing sellers who have provided brilliant service.

Of the people I meet, the ones I like best are those who have changed their lives by selling on eBay and making money in a way they never imagined possible. I've met single mums who make ends meet through eBay selling and retired people who help their pensions go further by clearing out their clutter. Others have chucked in their day job and make a living by selling on the site. And for most of them it's been a step up: they are making more money than ever and they have the pleasure of working for themselves.

So that's why eBay is amazing: there's nothing else like it in the world. You can trade all sorts of things with all sorts of people. You can make money and buy bargains from the comfort of your own home and also get your hands on items you never imagined you would find. I hope that once you've read this book and started making money on eBay you'll be as enthusiastic about it as I am.

What this book will do

Time and again I've met people who want to buy and sell on eBay, they're just a little scared that they'll mess up or find it all a bit tricky. 'What I need,' they say, 'is someone to take me through it, to show me how it works.' The first part of the book is about just that: mastering the basic skills and giving you the knowledge you need to get started on eBay. Once you have learnt how eBay works, you can use it to make money. The second half of the book is bursting with advanced help and advice for people who want to trade on eBay, Amazon and elsewhere.

Whatever your ambition or aim, this book has been written with you in mind. I've tried to make it easy to understand by avoiding internet jargon and technobabble. I presume no past experience and you don't need to be a technical wizard. It's all explained in plain English.

And even if you're already an experienced eBay seller, this completely revised book has all sorts of great stuff for you too. I've included some 'deep dive' topics that really deconstruct the best practices of making the most of eBay. For instance, there's a big section on item titles that I'm certain even the most successful, seasoned and cynical eBay seller will learn something from.

There are plenty of books out there about eBay. This book has two unique features that you won't find in any other tome on the market. First, it's based on the experience and knowledge of someone who has been close to eBay for more than a decade as both an employee and a trader. Secondly, it brings you a digest not just of my own personal expertise but also of the comments and information given to me by all the eBay sellers I've met over the years. I've met thousands of people over the past decade who are making money on eBay. They often have pearls of wisdoms and clever tips they want to share: you'll find the 'wisdom of the crowd' throughout this book.

As with anything in life, if you want to get the most out of something you've got to bring a little something to the party. All I ask of you is an open mind, a willingness to try new things and a great big cup of confidence. You might not think you've got what it takes to make serious money on eBay, but I'd be very surprised if you were right. Be optimistic, be ambitious, be willing, be keen to experiment and you greatly enhance your chances of success.

Case study: Britain's first eBayer
eBay user ID: gf-attic

Graham discovered eBay in 1996 just about a year after it had been founded. He was one of the first Brits to start selling on the site and he's still at it today. He's a Powerseller who specialises in selling antique sewing machines and other collectables. But what was eBay like back then?

"eBay was more of a cosy club. The whole concept of auctioning items online was a great novelty and provided thousands of words of interesting comment on the various news groups. Back then the vast majority of items offered for sale were collectables and used computer equipment. I also remember being able to give feedback, both positive and negative, on a whim. The first item I sold was to an American antiques store and I'm so pleased to say that the same company is still buying from me today."

There was no eBay.co.uk back then and Graham traded on eBay.com. In fact he still lists on the American site in US dollars because that's what his buyers like: the vast majority of his buyers are in the United States. "I realised very early on that it takes a great leap of faith for someone to send money to a country they've never visited, to a person they don't know, for an item they haven't seen. So we've got to make it easy for our buyers."

Graham is attracted to the worldwide customer base that eBay still offers him. He had previously sold and restored antiques with an outlet in London but eBay's arrival on the scene was timely: the antiques business collapsed in the mid-1990s and Graham considered leaving the trade altogether. "The advent of eBay allowed me to stay in the game but working in an entirely different way. I've lots of complaints about the way eBay has evolved into a relatively faceless giant. But it was there when I needed it. It saved my bacon."

It's that worldwide audience that makes eBay a particularly effective way of selling rare items. "If I am offering a super-rare Edison phonograph, the chances of the world's two top collectors strolling through my shop door are remote in the extreme." The audience and the auction also help Graham shift things he might otherwise not sell: "I deal over a large range of collectables. And while I have expertise in certain areas, others are a closed book to me, and I would have no idea how, in a shop, to write a price ticket. With eBay auctions I don't need to. I can put on a reserve that covers my costs and let the market sort out the correct final figure."

But Graham told me that "there's more to eBay than just making money". It's also about meeting like-minded people and making friends and Graham has certainly done that. "Last October I spent 10 days in Scotland showing round a couple of long-term customers who are now great friends. One's from the USA and the other from Australia. Next year we will meet up in Washington and the year after in Sydney."

Trade safely

Of course there is fraud on eBay. There is fraud in every market-place on the planet. From the souks of Marrakech to the great auction houses in London and New York, at every car boot sale and street market, there are dodgy dealers who want to hoodwink you and rip you off. It's true on eBay too: there are some bad apples.

Every now and again you see a newspaper article about someone who fell for a scam or who sent money to a seller but didn't receive the item they paid for. Some people are put off eBay because they have heard that it's an unsafe place to trade where people get ripped off. Unfortunately, what these articles don't tend to do is put the story in a broader context or help you avoid making the same mistakes.

One of my aims with this book is to give you the tips and information you need to avoid the fraudsters and trade safely every time. You'll find a great deal of information dedicated to trading safely later in the book. For example, I bet you don't know that if you buy an item on eBay that's protected by the PayPal Buyer Protection Programme, you can claim back up to £500 if you don't get the item you wanted. Well, you can. All this, and more, is right here in this book.

Remember this: you don't need to be a victim. You can protect yourself by using your common sense and the protection programmes and safety features that eBay has in place. I've bought hundreds of items on eBay. In fact, I check eBay first whenever I need something. I've bought furniture, vintage vinyl, Cornish pasties, CDs, DVDs, videos, antique prints, hats and computer equipment and I've only had two problems over the years: once when an item was lost in the post, and the second when some razor blades I bought turned out to be phoney and as blunt as a butter knife. I sorted both out and got my money back.

Tips and Inside Information

This book is designed to be a handbook you can have at your side as you navigate eBay for the first time, as well as a reference book for the more experienced and accomplished eBayer. If you see a section billed as Inside Information, that's where you'll find thoughts and comments from me about a certain eBay topic. These 'opinion pieces' are informed by my experience working for the company and are entirely personal. You might disagree!

If you see something billed as a Tip it's a snippet, fact or aside related to the chapter you're reading. Think of these as handy shortcuts.

Inside Information
Get the latest eBay news

I've crammed as much information as possible into the pages of this book. But as with anything on the internet, there's always something new to say and changes to report. That's why you can keep up to date with the latest eBay developments on my website at www.wilsondan.co.uk/ebay.

Whether it's a change to the eBay site, my latest view on this or that or just an update I think will be of interest, you can find out what's going on. It would be great to see you: why not pop by? Also, if you want to get in touch, you can contact me directly via my website. I'd love to hear from you.

Community and commerce

eBay is about so much more than just trading. One guy was really glad he was able to find help from other community members. He used the site from his garden shed and late one night he managed to get himself locked in. Unable to attract the attention of any neighbours, he posted a message on the eBay Community Boards including the phone number of his local police station and his address, hoping someone would call the coppers so they could come round and release him. When the police arrived they told him they had been alerted by a call from an eBay member in America.

Odd as it may sound, some people also find friendship and love on eBay. One lady I heard about sold a comic on the site and was surprised to discover it had been bought by a woman who lived just down the road. Needless to say, the seller popped a few doors down to deliver it and they were delighted to discover a shared interest in Japanese Manga. Despite their proximity they had never spoken, but soon they struck up a firm friendship.

At eBay Live! (eBay's annual Community Conference in the USA) in 2004 a couple who had met on eBay were married and there are some examples of people who have found love closer to home. One regular on the UK chatboards actually moved to the US to live with a man she met on the site and they are now married. Another pair have recently moved in with each other after meeting on the discussion boards. I spoke to one woman who met her boyfriend after she sold him a rare punk record. They lived in the same town and both thought they were the only punk fans in the area until their transaction; they now plan to get married. And they say romance is dead.

Inside Information
What is the eBay community?

I was the Community Manager at eBay for three years. But what do I mean by community? You're going to see the word a lot in this book, so it's worth being clear on what it means from the start.

Community as a word isn't used in Britain with quite the same ease and enthusiasm as it is in America. If you think about it, in the UK community is often used in not-so-positive ways. Think of the community charge, care in the community or community service.

But on eBay it's an overwhelmingly positive word and concept. In fact, it is eBay. You can't have eBay without the eBay community. It just wouldn't work.

On eBay the community is all the buyers and sellers on the site as well as the staff that eBay employs to maintain the marketplace.

But it's not just about the fact that we're all on eBay happily doing our own things in isolation. The power of community is that we're all looking out for each other. Being part of any community is about realising that your actions can have a positive effect on other people.

The other strength of being part of a community is that members are in charge of what is bought and sold. eBay as an organisation doesn't direct the trading on the site. Prices are set by buyers and sellers. It's those in the community who do all the buying and selling. eBay doesn't hold any stock itself. eBay doesn't say 'a sprocket is worth £4', it's only worth £4 if is someone is willing to bid that much.

So for employees, thinking in terms of a community is vital if eBay is to survive and prosper. The former CEO of eBay, Meg Whitman, encourages staff to keep the community 'front and centre' in their minds. Employees must be respectful of the needs of buyers as well as sellers while they go about their jobs and make sure they look after everyone on eBay so that the vibrant trading environment is preserved.

This is why eBay takes the views of the community seriously and consults members and traders more fully than most other companies. You can see the community interacting every day on the discussion boards and staff like to keep an eye on these so they can get a feel for what those in the community are saying.

And you should take the community seriously too as you get started on eBay. Your eBay trading experience and success are dependent on other members of the community. If you check someone's feedback you are checking the views of other members; one day you might go to the discussion boards for advice, which will be freely given by other members; you'll be buying from other members of the community too and selling to them. All that binds eBay together is the power of the community.

As the eBay community we're all in this eBay thing together: you, me and more than two hundred million other people too. We are the eBay community and that's kinda cool.

2

A Brief History of eBay

eBay today has more than 300 million members worldwide, millions of items for sale and thousands of people making a living from selling on it. It is astonishing to think the site was only started in 1995 and began as a labour of love in a spare bedroom.

Pierre Omidyar looked like a stereotypical geek with his ponytail, glasses and goatee beard. He was an early convert to the new technology of the internet and worked as a computer programmer in Silicon Valley, California. In his spare time he created his own computer programs and chatted with other net heads in newsgroups and chatrooms. But he was by no means a loser. He was keen to explore the possibilities the internet would offer as it became more widely used.

In the mid-1990s the internet boom was just beginning and pioneering businesspeople were desperately trying to make millions from the new technology. Pierre stands out as a very different figure.

The legend goes that one evening over dinner at home Pierre's fiancée Pam mentioned that it was difficult to find people to trade Pez dispensers with. The couple had recently moved from Boston to California, where Pam lacked a circle of fellow collectors with whom to trade the plastic sweet dispensers.

Spurred on and keen to solve the problem, Pierre set up eBay so that Pam could interact and trade with other Pez enthusiasts online. That is the touching tale of how eBay was born, although it isn't the whole truth.

Like so many others in California, Pierre was excited by the new potential of the internet. And like the other entrepreneurs in Silicon Valley, he was looking for the 'big idea'. Pierre was different because he was interested in the way the internet could transform how people traded with each other. He wanted to apply his programming skills to an old problem in a whole new way: he wanted to create the perfect marketplace.

How Pierre broke the mould

Even though the Pez story of eBay's creation isn't the complete picture, it does colourfully illustrate the revolutionary way in which eBay broke the mould. Other pioneering ecommerce businesses were striving to establish traditional businesses online. Amazon was applying the usual bookselling formula and offering bargains because it didn't have the expense of shops, for instance.

But eBay isn't a retailer. Pierre wasn't simply trying to create an online shop and sell lots of things to a willing online public. He was creating a marketplace where other people could come together to trade with each other. eBay wasn't set up so Pez could sell directly to Pam; rather, the aim was to provide a venue for people like Pam to buy and sell with each other.

The idea of creating a marketplace is hardly a new one. Trading is an innately human activity. However, the fact that the idea could be revolutionised by the internet intrigued Pierre. The biggest attraction for him was that the normal rules no longer applied. An online marketplace could have a potentially huge impact, not least because geography no longer mattered. On the internet information can cross the planet in the twinkling of an eye.

The perfect market

Pierre's expectation was that over time the number of people who would have access to the internet would be huge. Internet aficionados were a fairly small bunch in 1995, but as the number of households with personal computers grew the web's use was bound to expand.

More exciting was the fact that the rules of the 'real world' didn't have to apply. Pierre could start from scratch and create an unfettered marketplace. Existing marketplaces (stock exchanges or the oil market, for instance) benefited bigger players and established traders. Prices and conditions were fixed to favour vested interests. It was rarely possible for outsiders to compete fairly.

Pierre's belief was that a marketplace had to be as free as possible to be truly effective. He also believed that prices were better set by buyers rather than sellers. After all, what is a fair market price other than what someone is readily willing to pay? This concept was central to Pierre's affection for auctions.

In an auction sellers are able to set the minimum price they are willing to accept and if someone thinks that is a fair price they will buy. If two or more people are willing to pay the price, or more, they bid against each other until the highest price they are willing to pay is established. The fair market price is set by buyers on the basis of what they think something is worth rather than by outside controls, cartels or vested interests.

Why eBay is called eBay

Over the course of the Labor Day weekend in 1995, Pierre wrote an auction program and added it to his existing website. It was a simple affair allowing people to list items for sale, view the items and bid on them. Pierre's website, which was already called eBay, also hosted pages for Pam and an offbeat tribute to the deadly Ebola virus. Pierre added what he called 'AuctionWeb' to the site that weekend and set about publicising it to other internet users in newsgroups and chatrooms.

Pierre called his first auction experiment AuctionWeb and it could be reached via the address www.ebay.com/aw. In due course AuctionWeb simply became known as eBay – but where did the word eBay come from?

There are all sorts of theories. The most famous myth suggests that because eBay was started in the Bay Area of California, the name stands for East Bay. But the company was actually started in Campbell, near San Jose, which is really the South Bay area, so that theory doesn't hold much water.

Another suggestion harks back to an age when clippers circumnavigated the globe carrying exotic cargoes from faraway places. In those days a bay was a place of safety and security where trade was possible. The *e* in eBay denotes the fact that this safe harbour for trade is online.

The truth seems to owe rather more to luck than judgement. Pierre wanted to call his website EchoBay.com simply because he thought it sounded cool. When he went to register the site he discovered that the name had already been taken by a Canadian mining company. eBay.com was apparently still available so, deciding it was the next best thing, he snapped it up. In an age where multinational corporations spend hundreds of thousands of pounds on focus groups and research to decide which shade of blue they should use in their logo, it is amusing to think that one of the most popular brand names in the world was created on a whim.

Fact: *Pierre claims that he realised eBay was going to be huge when he sold a broken laser pointer for $14.*

eBay takes off

In the latter months of 1995 Pierre spent his time developing the auction website by adding new functions and features and advertising it to other web users. He was astonished by the number of people who started flocking to the site to buy and sell. The most powerful marketing tool was the group of happy users who told their friends about the great new website that let you buy and sell to anyone else online.

In the very early days eBay was free. For Pierre it was just a hobby and he was content to let people trade for no fee, but inevitably his costs started to rise. His internet service provider was concerned by the amount of traffic his site was getting and started to charge him commercial rates for hosting his website. Reluctantly Pierre realised that he had to receive payment for the service, so he created a system meaning that sellers who successfully sold items paid him a very small percentage of the price they got to help him cover his costs.

Pierre was amazed when people readily paid what they owed. Typically they were small amounts, but they all added up to cover his running costs. Soon he was receiving so many payments that he was making a little profit and he could barely keep up with the flood of receipts; many were left unprocessed for days because he was too busy to open the envelopes.

People are basically good

As eBay grew Pierre firmly imprinted it with his own beliefs and philosophy. Inevitably there were sometimes disputes between trading partners, who looked to him to resolve their disagreements. It became apparent that most of the problems were simple cases of misunderstanding. People were reading the worst into the emails they received, convinced that other members were trying to rip them off or do them over.

Pierre encouraged aggrieved traders to resolve problems between themselves, firmly believing that people are basically good. They shouldn't jump to the wrong conclusion and immediately think the worst, but rather try to see the issue from another point of view and seek a mutually beneficial arrangement. His faith was reinforced as he watched complete strangers buying and selling with each other every day. People sent money in the post to others they had never met and received their purchases in return. In comparison to the successful transactions, the number of disputes was extremely small.

In many ways Pierre conceived of eBay as a village, but since 1995 it has grown into a huge virtual metropolis and like in real life this has challenged its founding principles. In a small village you can leave your doors and windows open safely because people are basically good. In a city you can still believe that people are basically good, but you always lock your doors and you may have a burglar alarm. It's just common sense. And eBay's the same. It's got bigger and you need to take the appropriate precautions.

The power of community

Pierre was so confident in his belief that people are basically good that he came up with a way of incorporating it as a feature of the eBay site. He wanted to make the good trades count and show that they far outweighed the bad ones. He created a system that became eBay's greatest selling point and most distinguishing feature: feedback. He invited people on eBay to make comments about their fellow traders. These comments were then crystallised as a record of a member's reputation and conduct on the site. Good trading experiences could be marked with positive feedback. If sellers had conducted themselves efficiently and delivered the item well packaged and swiftly, positive feedback comments were appropriate. For buyers a swift payment would qualify them for a positive.

If a transaction was not satisfactory then negative feedback could be left. For instance, if a seller received payment but didn't send the goods or if a buyer didn't pay for purchases, then negative feedback might be the best course of action. From the beginning Pierre encouraged people to settle their differences before leaving a negative. Feedback was a permanent record of a person's dealings on eBay, so a negative left in haste would remain for others to see.

For Pierre the main strength of feedback was its openness. It allowed traders to make public what they thought. They had to be honest and relate it to their own experience. Moreover, people were discouraged from leaving personal remarks. By keeping feedback factual and relevant it became a useful source of information for other members.

Feedback was about empowering eBay's members so they could help each other. If a member had stacks of positive feedback, other members were encouraged to trade with them. If a member had some positive and some negative feedback, it might pay others to be cautious. People with a lot of negative feedback were simply avoided. But the concept of feedback thrived because people are basically good. It feels good to give a compliment and leave positive feedback, and to this day that forms the central tenet of trust on eBay.

Further evidence that people are basically good came from the generosity members showed each other on eBay's discussion boards. Early on Pierre provided a forum for members to interact that served several useful functions. It meant he could distance himself from the site. Rather than being seen as dictatorial and controlling, he preferred to be hands off and allow the community of users to chart the course of the business.

More importantly, people could help each other solve any difficulties they faced as they traded. A core of dedicated and experienced members frequented the boards and when someone was new or unsure they could ask for help and receive it from another member. Fellow members were generous when it came to offering advice on trading, help with HTML for item listings or information on how to display a picture that showed the item being sold.

One early community member using the boards was Jim Griffith, who advised fellow eBayers under his self-created alter-ego, Uncle Griff. The invented character of Griff was a cross-dressing farmer dominated by his mother and he dished out help and advice in a humorous and self-deprecating way that immediately defused antagonism and put people at ease.

Griffith became the first of eBay's customer support reps in 1996. eBay had started to receive a large number of emails every day from members who wanted help and someone was needed to answer them. Griffith was the obvious choice and he continued to post on the discussion boards and answer emails as well as buying and selling on eBay.

eBay's community ethos is something that sets it apart from most other companies. It remains central to the identity of eBay and how it operates. The community is consulted on decisions and members' comments are fed back to executives on a daily basis. In return, the eBay community is not shy in giving its opinions. When a change to the site is implemented, employees can often be found poring over the discussion boards looking for compliments or complaints.

The eBay phenomenon

By 1996 eBay was already very successful. Not only was it attracting buyers and sellers at an astonishing rate, but Pierre had to hire people to help him maintain the website and its momentum. In the early years eBay was predominantly a site for collectors and collectables and its reputation as a great venue for buying and selling was mainly spread by word of mouth.

It became clear that if eBay was to realise its true potential it would have to become a more professional and conventional organisation. Pierre, alongside his friend Jeff Skoll, had always run the business in an egalitarian way and was attracted to hiring people with a similar countercultural mindset, but he came to acknowledge that a more sober selection of experienced professionals was required to complement them. To begin with, some graduates of the Stanford Business School were engaged to offer marketing expertise, and soon eBay was advertising its service on AOL using banner ads.

The next logical step was to hire a professional chief executive officer to take over the running of the business from Pierre. He was perhaps rare as a founder of a successful company in realising that his skills and ambitions were not best suited to running what was fast becoming a big and complicated organisation. eBay found its CEO in the unusual figure of Meg Whitman, who could not have been more unlike Pierre. She was a Princeton and Harvard graduate from old East Coast stock. She had experience working for some of the biggest companies in America: Procter and Gamble, Bain, Disney, Stride Rite and Hasbro. Even though she didn't have much online experience and was by no means a techie, she saw eBay's potential and brought with her vast marketing experience that would be critical to the company's success. Most important of all, she understood the importance of the community when it came to driving eBay's success.

Soon after Meg came to eBay, the decision was made to go public and offer shares on the Nasdaq stock exchange. At the peak of the internet boom going public was the ultimate badge of credibility for internet start-ups. It sent a message that a company was serious and meant to stay the distance. Equally, issuing shares to the public was a useful way of raising money to continue investing in the company, although in eBay's case this was less important.

Looking back there were lots of companies for whom going public was the peak of their success: many went bust within months.

For eBay the flotation was a tricky proposition. Obviously the business was already profitable and successful and had a million members and millions of items being traded. But it was difficult explaining to stuffy bankers that people are basically good and really are willing to trade with complete strangers on the internet. Was eBay just a fad? Did it truly have a broad appeal that would enable it to grow? eBay was valued at about $715mn on the day before its shares went on the market in 1998. By the end of the first day's trading it was obvious that the market liked the company and thought it would be a huge success. So much so, in fact, that trading was brisk and at the end of the first day eBay's valuation stood at $2bn.

eBay goes global

In 1999 eBay began to take the site to a wider international audience. People from all over the world were using eBay.com to trade wherever they lived. But to succeed, it was necessary to create sites in local languages moulded to the needs of the community members in that country.

The first move was to buy Alando.de, a German online trading site that closely resembled eBay in its community-based approach. Alando had been started by a group of young entrepreneurs barely months before. It caught eBay's eye and Pierre travelled to Berlin to have a closer look. He was impressed by Alando and struck by its similarities to eBay, so he bought the company. The site was rebranded as eBay.de and by the end of the year eBay members could trade in German marks. eBay sites were also established in Australia and Canada.

In Britain there was no site similar to eBay that could be purchased, so eBay.co.uk was created from scratch. I was part of that founding team and I can tell you that we had lots of fun as we worked hard to get the thing going in Britain. There was already a core of UK members who traded on eBay.com in US dollars. Sellers would sell uniquely British collectables and goods to Americans, who in return would pay in cash. In those early days there were thousands of envelopes stuffed with money crossing the Atlantic paying for items that were hard to find in America.

In 1999 people in Britain became able for the first time to trade on eBay in sterling rather than dollars. A UK office was set up to start building the eBay.co.uk site for British traders and to market it by attracting buyers and sellers. In those early days QXL was stiff competition, but the draw of eBay became too much for the ever-growing number of Brits who wanted to buy and sell online, and before long eBay became the number one ecommerce site in Britain. And over the next few years eBay expanded to encompass India, China and many other European sites and is now present in more than 40 countries all over the world.

What's next for eBay?

2005 and 2006 were difficult years for eBay. For a long time it had been the darling of the stock market and could do no wrong. Even once the internet bubble had burst, the company had casually beaten expectations and posted profits that wowed even the hard-nosed capitalists of Wall Street. Boosted by good results eBay's stock price soared between late 2002 and January 2005, tripling the value of the company. But then Wall Street lost confidence and punished some disappointing results by hammering down the share price. Google became the new golden child and eBay languished. Wall Street scepticism was compounded through 2005 and 2006 by what many considered to be unexciting results from eBay. Analysts worried that the company might not have the potential to grow as much as they expected. Certainly in comparison with Google eBay looked a little tarnished, and when it bought Skype in autumn 2005 for $2.6bn commentators were surprised.

The bankers and analysts couldn't see how the expense was justified and doubted that Skype would ever be a profit centre for eBay. Moreover, what did eBay want with an internet telephone company? It wasn't considered a good fit. At the time of writing (July 2009) eBay stock is valued at just $16.30, down from its January 2005 high of $60. In September 2008, eBay agreed to sell Skype to a well-funded consortium.

The stock price may be poor compared to the past, but the lack of investor confidence does illustrate the period of change the company is in and some uncertainty in eBay's future. In 2008, CEO Meg Whitman stood aside for John Donohoe. Meg was well respected and had led the company since 1998, delivering some magnificent profits. Donohoe had worked at eBay for three years, having previously been head of US management consultant firm Bain.

He is credited as the architect of far-reaching changes that have been introduced to eBay in the last few years: massive fee changes, a move from auctions to fixed-price selling, Best Match in search, requiring greater professionalism from sellers and, most controversially, changes to feedback. The Detailed Seller Ratings and the removal of the right of sellers to leave neutral and negative feedback have proved unpopular with lots of long-standing eBay traders.

The past few years have seen dramatic changes at eBay and sellers are well advised to remember that change and development form one of the central aspects of selling on eBay: nothing stays the same for long. But that's the nature of the internet and one of the aspects of ecommerce that makes it exciting. What's next for eBay? It's impossible to say, although for the foreseeable future it's going to continue to be a key online player and remain your ideal first step to selling online.

Success you can share

It might sound as if the story of how eBay began is the story of how a small group of Americans became very rich, but what jumps out from the tale are the millions of people who have made eBay what it is today. All the selling on eBay is done by members; all eBay runs is the marketplace. It brings in buyers and makes sure everything is running smoothly, but the site is only successful if its sellers and their sales are successful. eBay doesn't make a bean unless people sell on its sites, so the company's profits are a reflection of the wider success of eBay sellers.

> **Fact**: *The most expensive item ever bought on eBay was a Gulfstream jet, which sold for $4.9 million. One of Mrs Thatcher's handbags sold for more than £100,000.*

eBay continues to expand into new markets and develop its websites to reflect the needs of traders and help them be more successful. There is a market out there for you to tap. You can share in eBay's success by taking advantage of a unique audience that you cannot reach in any other way.

Now is a great time to get involved with the eBay phenomenon. Never before have there been so many buyers on eBay. eBay has never before been investing so much in advertising and development. You too can join in eBay's success, become a seller and make money from the world's biggest marketplace

3

Get Started

Welcome to eBay. In this chapter I'll take a quick look at what you'll need to get started on eBay. We'll consider the equipment you need and I'll guide you through getting registered and help you get your bearings on the eBay site. If you've already registered and have some eBay experience, you can skip this bit.

Most people have a computer and access to a broadband internet connection, whether at home or at work, and that's all you need. If you don't have broadband and are using a 56k dial-up, you'll find eBay (along with the rest of the internet) rather sluggish. A broadband connection, if you can get one, is money well spent.

- **Email address** You can use any email address to register with eBay, but try to choose an account with plenty of storage that you can access wherever you are. Some people set up a specific email address for their eBay use to keep it separate from their other mail.

- **Mac users** eBay is accessible using an Apple Macintosh. But do note that some of the advanced facilities such as Turbo Lister are not available for Macs.

- **Printer** A printer is not essential for buying or selling on eBay, but it will make your life a lot easier. Why not buy one on eBay? When pricing up a printer, remember that the cost of the hardware itself isn't the most pressing concern. Take the price of refills into consideration too.

- **Digital camera** As a buyer you have no need for a scanner or a digital camera, but when you start selling on eBay, a digital camera is essential. While a mobile phone camera will do, even a basic digital camera will be better. You don't need something top of the range and you can get something very serviceable for as little as £80. Remember to check whether you can also make video footage with it.

The eBay Homepage

eBay UK's web address or URL is www.ebay.co.uk. As with any website, you simply type the address into the browser window, press 'Go' and you are taken to the site.

The homepage has links to everywhere you need to visit on eBay. Further down the page you'll find the categories in which people list their items for sale. If you want to browse the items for sale you can click on the heading you want. The top section is the Navigation Bar, which takes you to other sections of the site. From here you can access My eBay (where eBay provides a list of all your buying and selling activities), the Site Map and the Sell Your Item form. There's also a link to eBay's Help section. On the Navigation Bar at the top of the page you will see the Register button. If you click on this you will be taken to the Registration Form.

Tip: Make eBay your homepage

You can make eBay your personal homepage. This means that every time you log on to the internet the first page you see will be eBay. To make eBay your homepage on a PC, simply click the 'Start' button at the bottom left of your screen. In the Menu, select 'Settings' and click on the 'Control Panel' option. In the Control Panel you should choose 'Internet Options' and a grey box will pop up.

In the space for an address enter 'www.ebay.co.uk' and click 'OK' at the base of the box. Now you'll be taken to eBay every time you log on to the internet.

Register with eBay

You can surf around the eBay site and look at the items for sale without registering, but you can't buy or sell. Becoming a member is straightforward and doesn't take long.

To register with eBay you need to click the 'Register' button in the Navigation Bar on the homepage. This takes you to the Registration Form.

The first step of registering with eBay is to provide your personal and contact details. You need to fill in your name, address and telephone number. You can also add a second telephone number or fax number, but this is not compulsory. Obviously your details are kept confidential and secure. eBay doesn't sell your personal information to other companies or third parties. You can find out more about how eBay stores your information by reading the Privacy Policy.

It is very important that you put in correct personal details and valid contact information. If these details are false you will be

suspended from eBay without warning and have to go through the
rigmarole of confirming your identity by providing domestic bills
and ID like a passport or driving licence, which can be time consuming and irritating.

- **Email address** eBay communicates with its members via
email, so it is important that you provide an email address to
which you have regular access. You need to type it in twice to
confirm it's correct.

- **Choosing a User ID** Once you have entered your personal details you need to select a User ID. This is the name
that you will operate under on eBay and is rather like a CB
'handle' or alias. It's a really good opportunity to show off
and choose a name that reflects your personality or interests.
Take a look around the site at other users and see what kind
of User IDs they have. With so many members on eBay
already there is a strong chance that your first choice of User
ID has already been taken, so you need to be inventive. If the
first User ID you choose is not available, eBay guides you
through selecting a different ID.

- **Password** You also need to choose a password. You should
select a password that is easy for you to remember and impossible for other people to guess. You can't use the word 'password' or your User ID as your password. Don't opt for
anything obviously relating to you either, such as your name
or your partner's name. Try to use a mix of letters and numbers and also include lower- and upper-case letters. You can
make the password easier to remember by using numbers as if
they are letters: 'z00k33pEr' or 'Mi11icent'. You can find out
more about keeping your password safe later in the book.

- **Secret question** At the bottom of the registration page
you also need to set your secret question. This is a question
that only you know the answer to. In the event that you
forget your password, eBay requires your secret answer to reset
it. The questions include 'What street did you grow up on?'
and 'What is the name of your first school?'

- **Confirming your registration** When you have completed
all the sections on the Registration Form you are taken to the
next page, where you are asked to accept and agree to eBay's
User Agreement and Privacy Policy. You can print these out

Register with eBay

Register today to bid, buy or sell on eBay.

Already registered or want to make changes to your account? Sign in.

Want to open an account for your business?
Business sellers should register with a business account. Learn more about business registration.

Tell us about yourself - All fields are required

> ℹ️ Your privacy is important to us. eBay does not rent or sell your personal information to third parties without your consent. To learn more, read our privacy policy. Your address will be used for posting your purchase or receiving payment from buyers.

* Indicates required field

First name *

Last name *

Street address *

Town / City *

County *
-- Select County --

Post code *

Country or Region *
United Kingdom

Primary telephone number *
( )
Example: (020) 12345678.
Required in case we need to contact you about your account

Email address *

Re-enter email address *

Choose your user ID and password - All fields are required

Create your eBay user ID *
[Check availability]
Use letters or numbers, but not symbols. Learn more about creating great user IDs.

Create your password *
caSe sensiTive. Learn about secure passwords.

Re-enter your password *

Pick a secret question *
Pick a suggested question...

Your secret answer *
If you forget your password, we'll verify your identity with your secret question

Date of birth *
--Day--   --Month--   --Year-- YYYY
You must be at least 18 years old to use eBay.

---

eBay user agreement and privacy policy

For added security, please enter the verification code hidden in the image.

14 94

Refresh the image | Listen to the verification code

☐ I agree to the following:
- I accept the User Agreement which is the terms and conditions that apply to my use of eBay, and have read the Privacy Policy.
- I may receive communications from eBay and I understand that I can change my notification preferences at any time in My eBay.
- I am at least 18 years old.

[Continue]

so you can peruse them more easily. Once you have agreed to the terms, you are sent an email. This email is eBay's way of checking that the email address you have provided is correct. When you receive the email, click the 'Confirm Registration' button inside. You will be taken to eBay and will then be a fully registered eBay member ready to use the site.

• **Anonymous email addresses** eBay takes safety very seriously and one way it protects the people who are buying and selling on the site is to require a credit or debit card from anyone who is registering with an anonymous email account such as Hotmail or Yahoo!.

If you do want to register using an anonymous email account, you need to provide credit or debit card information. Don't worry: your personal details will be kept confidential and your card will never be charged without your consent. eBay just wants to know that you are who you say you are.

• **What if my email doesn't arrive?** If you register on eBay and you don't get the confirmation email immediately, sit tight. It can take up to 24 hours to arrive. If after a day you haven't received it, it is wise to request that eBay sends it again. You can do this via the Confirm Registration link on the Site Map.

If you have to ask for your email again, the chances are that your email provider is to blame. You may have your email account security settings set so high that you can only receive emails from senders pre-approved by you. If your security settings are in order and you still haven't received the email, you should contact your email provider or internet service provider for advice.

Tip: User IDs

Your User ID is a key part of your eBay personality. Take a moment to think about what you want your User ID to be and what you want it to say. Don't forget that as a buyer, and more importantly as a seller, your ID says something about you and can influence people. A good User ID will attract other eBay members, but one with dodgy overtones might well put people off trading with you.

Some people like to choose a User ID that reflects a part of their character or represents something they aspire to or admire. Some select a favourite character from a soap opera or film. Others opt for a pun, but some are very professional and go for a name that is relevant to their buying or selling interests. Just take a look around eBay and you can see all sorts of IDs for all sorts of people.

If you have an idea for an ID and want to see if it is already taken by someone else, you can use the Member Search facility to check it out. Hit the 'advanced' link at the right of the search button at the top of every page. On the advanced search page on the lefthand side you'll see options to help you 'Find a member'. Search for your desired User ID to see if it has been taken.

PART I

BUY ON eBAY

Tip: Whizz ahead

If you're already a competent buyer on eBay, there's no need to read the next few chapters. They're a helpful introduction for people who are totally new to the site. If you reckon you're a whizz at spending money on eBay and want to learn how to make money instead, skip ahead to Chapter 10.

4

What Can You Buy on eBay?

The answer is just about anything. To start with there are new and nearly new goods. eBay is great for CDs, DVDs and videos. You can often pick these up for far less than you would in the shops. Clothing is also a very popular purchase. Many sellers take pride in offering clothes at a fraction of what high-street vendors charge. Try eBay both for cutting-edge items that are hard to find in the shops and for vintage or retro clothing. You can also get hold of designer labels at good prices.

eBay also has hundreds of thousands of different household items such as DVD players, fun items like iPods, computer-related gear (both hardware and software) and just about any sort of appliance you can imagine. Many of these are brand new or nearly new. Lots of people sell unwanted gifts or things they don't really need. Every year after Christmas eBay is the first stop for lots of people who want to sell that pointless gift from Auntie Maud, so that's a great time to pick up a new item at a bargain price.

Secondhand, antique and collectable

When eBay started in the US in the 1990s, it was immediately seized on by collectors. It was the perfect marketplace for collectables: collectors in Maine could get together with others in California and buy and sell. In the early days Beanie Baby enthusiasts dominated eBay and it quickly became the place that people crazy to get their hands on a new bear would visit.

Collectables are still hugely popular on eBay. Just have a browse through the Collectables section to see the breadth of items for sale. You can buy old theatre posters, cigarette cards, football programmes, porcelain, enamel advertising signs and glass bottles. If you are building a collection, the chances are that eBay will have something you are looking for.

It is also an excellent place to get your hands on antiques of all kinds. Whether you fancy a Victorian oil painting or engraving, a Regency table or some exquisite silverware, it can be found on eBay. Many reputable antiques traders operate on the site and are happy to organise postage and insurance at very competitive rates.

Oddities and curios are also an eBay speciality. If you want to get an antique eyebath, a taxidermy mongoose, a bottle of water from the Princess Diana Memorial Fountain or a smutty postcard, eBay has them all by the dozen.

Local, national, international

The icing on the eBay cake is the option buyers have to trade with sellers all over the world. Not only can you buy from sellers in the UK, but from just about every country in the world. This means that you can source goods from faraway places that might otherwise be out of reach.

And if you want to stay local, you can. You can choose to buy from British members only and you can select sellers from your immediate area. Buying locally is convenient and straightforward. This is ideal if you want a bulky item that would be expensive to post or something perishable that needs to be sent quickly.

Not just auctions

eBay is most famous for its traditional auction format where buyers place bids against each other and the highest bidder wins. But it isn't just about auctions. You can use the 'Buy It Now' option too. This is where you buy an item at a price specified by the seller. You don't bid against other bidders and you don't have to wait until the auction ends. If you want to make an immediate purchase you can use this feature.

Inside Information
But I want to make money, not spend it!

> *Hold your horses. The simple fact is that people who jump straight
> into selling don't tend to make a success of it. You need to learn about
> the eBay marketplace and the features it can offer you before taking
> the plunge. Without doubt the best way to learn about eBay is to
> experience it as a buyer.*

Your first purchase

Once you have registered on eBay, you are ready to start buying.
Even if you are approaching the site as a business opportunity and
plan to become a full-time seller, it is essential that you understand how eBay works from a buyer's point of view. It's only by
being able to please customers that you'll make a success out of
selling.

When buying your first item, it's really advisable to choose
something safe and easy so that you can learn the process. Don't
rush in and bid on an exotic item from Ghana. Choose a cheaper
item located in the UK to gain confidence. Once you are happy
with how eBay works for buyers, the sky's the limit. You can get on
with buying cars, antiques, holidays and other big-ticket items
when you are an experienced buyer.

Inside Information
People really are basically good

> *If the doom-mongers had their way there would be no such thing as
> eBay. It shouldn't work. It's based on a belief that people are basically
> good and they will be as good as their word. Who, apart from some
> idealistic tie-dyed ageing hippie, would believe that you could send
> money to a complete stranger and in return you would receive the item
> you have bought?*
>
> *The majority of transactions that occur every day on eBay are suc-
> cessful for buyer and seller alike. Think about it: eBay couldn't sur-
> vive unless almost every trade was successful and safe – it would be
> out of business. To date over 6 billion transactions have taken place
> on eBay, and if that isn't proof that people are basically good I don't
> know what is.*

Trust is manifested in eBay's feedback system. A member's feedback score is all the reviews that other members have left after a trade. These comments are totally open and available for everyone to see. Feedback is a person's eBay reputation and something members take very seriously. It is the number one factor that builds and reinforces trust on the site.

When you are finding your feet as a buyer, go with someone you trust. Take a look at the seller's feedback. Check out their item descriptions. Look at their About Me page. You'll be amazed how many lovely people there are out there. On eBay there are many more nice people than nasty ones.

Choose a kind seller

Try to find a seller who will help you through your first purchase. Most sellers on eBay are individuals who are happy to guide you if you are unsure or need a nudge in the right direction. It is worth telling a seller that you are taking the plunge on their item. Most sellers will be delighted to assist an eBay newbie and many will go out of their way to be helpful and friendly.

Fact: *The word 'eBayer', meaning someone who uses eBay, was added to the Collins English dictionary in 2005.*

Be prepared

Don't forget to be prepared. Once a listing is over many sellers like to get moving quickly, so you need to be ready to pay and receive the item. Make sure you are able to pay using a method acceptable to the seller. It might also be worth opening a PayPal account prior to placing your first bid. To register with PayPal, go to www.paypal.co.uk; there is more on this later in the book.

5

Find an Item You Want to Buy

There are millions of items for sale, so finding an item you want to buy can be a little daunting. This chapter will show you how to find the item you want with speed and ease. There are two ways of finding items on eBay: browsing and searching.

Browsing on eBay reflects how you would use a department store. If you wanted a new lamp you would go to the lighting section of the homeware area of the shop. The same is true on eBay. You would go to the Home and Garden category and look in the Lamps section. Or if you were after something antique you would go to the Antiques section. Browsing is the way to find an item if you know what you want but are flexible about the style, brand and type.

Searching offers a more focused way of finding items. If you have a brand, specs, dimensions or a particular item in mind, you can use eBay's search engine to search the items for sale in the same way you would use Google to search the internet.

Browse

The items for sale on eBay are divided into categories. Sellers choose the categories in which they want their items to appear when they put them up for sale.

If you want to browse eBay there are two ways to get started. On the lefthand side of the homepage you can find the full list of top-level categories. Simply click on the category you are interested in, such as 'Collectables' or 'Video Games', and you are taken to the Category Index page of that category. From there you can start browsing lower-level categories, leading you to the item you want to buy.

You can also browse by clicking on 'Buy' in the Navigation Bar on most pages. This link leads you to a full list of top-level categories and the next level down. To find a Scrabble set, for example, you go for the category 'Toys & Games' and on the Category Index page you see a heading 'Games' with a subheading 'Board/Traditional Games'.

When you click on the 'Board/Traditional Games' link you are taken to a list of all the items in that category. There are almost certainly some Scrabble sets in this section, but because this is a big category you'd have to look through dozens of pages to find them. It would be much quicker to use the further list of subcategories in the lefthand column and narrow down the results. In this case 'Scrabble' is probably the best choice. Don't forget that not all sellers will have had the good sense to put their Scrabble set in the 'Scrabble' category, so it could be worth having a look in 'Other Board/Traditional Games' too just in case.

Browsing is a great way of discovering the enormous array of items for sale on eBay. It is also ideal if you know you want to buy something but don't have a concrete idea of the exact item you're looking for.

There's a full list of eBay categories at http://listings.ebay.co.uk.

Search

eBay also has a search engine that will take you directly to items if you have a keyword or phrase. If you want to find a Blur-related single and it doesn't matter whether it's on CD, tape or vinyl, or if you're interested in Peter Cook and want to see all related items, then searching is the more efficient way of finding an item. When you put a keyword or phrase, such as 'Wedgwood', into eBay's search engine, all items with that word or phrase in the item title are returned for you to look through.

You can use the search engine for single words or combinations of words. If too many items are returned to you and you want to enter a more specific term (say 'Wedgwood plate' rather than just 'Wedgwood'), simply click 'Back' on your browser and start again.

Tips: Searching

There are a number of tricks you can use to make the eBay search engine work for you and find the items you really want. If you put

Refine search

▼ Categories

Toys & Games (5,105)
Action Figures (4,492)
Games (319)
More ▾
DVD, Film & TV (4,197)
DVDs (2,645)
Videos: VHS (1,011)
TV Memorabilia (514)
Film Memorabilia (251)
More ▾
Collectables (17,563)
Trading Cards/ CCG (9,653)
Science Fiction (5,971)
Photographic Images (941)
Autographs (552)
More ▾
Books, Comics & Magazines (6,253)
Fiction Books (2,514)
Magazines (1,510)
Audio Books (829)
Comics (461)
Non-Fiction Books (351)
More ▾
See all categories

▼ Price

£ ___ to £ ___

▼ Condition

◯ New
◯ Used
◯ Not specified
Choose more...

▼ Seller

Specify sellers...

Preferences

▼ Buying formats

◯ Auction
◯ Buy It Now
Choose more...

▼ Show only

◯ Completed listings
◯ Free P&P
Choose more...

▼ Location

◯ UK Only
◯ Worldwide
Choose more...

▶ Distance

Customise preferences

🛒 Matching eBay Shops

Hill's Cards-Great Trading Car. . (1,138)
hewmuchisitmate (600)
Sisko Stuff (683)
Time Tradingpost Vortex (482)

See all matching eBay Shops

Best sellers

UNDER £20

Hornby

Pokemon cards   Medals

Zippos   Cigarette cards

| All items | Auctions only | Buy It Now only |

34,953 results found for **doctor who** [Save this search]

View as: List ▾ [Customise view]   Sort by: Best Match ▾

		Price	Postage to BN1 3FU, UK	Time Left
Featured Items				
	NEW DOCTOR/DR WHO 4 COMPLETE SEASON/SERIES 4 DVD SET *FREE SHIPPING-1-3 DAYS FOR DEL-DISCOUNTED OFFER*	*Buy It Now*	£18.95 Free	3d 7h 32m
Optimise your selling success! Find out how to promote your items				
	DOCTOR WHO COMPLETE SERIES 3 NEW SEALED DVD BOX SET	1 Bid	£15.00 Free	<1m
	COLLECTORS CARD BINDER FOR MATCH ATTAX DR WHO ETC NEW	*Buy It Now*	£2.69 +£1.79	29d 2h 31m
	Radio Times 6-12 Mar 1999 Julia Walters/Red Nose Dr Who	0 Bids	£0.99 +£2.75	2m
	WII - DOCTOR WHO. NEW & SEALED GAME	*Buy It Now*	£5.99 Free	26d 1h 4m
	Doctor Who - The Edge of Destruction	3 Bids	£2.60 +£3.00	3m
	Dr Who Top Trumps Specials-NEW	*Buy It Now*	£0.99 +£1.27	7d 10h 54m
	Doctor Who - The Macra Terror	3 Bids	£2.60 +£2.00	3m
	Doctor Who - Series 1 CompleteNew and Sealed BBCDVD1770	*Buy It Now*	£15.00 Free	9d 3h 35m
	Doctor Who - The Three Doctors	1 Bid	£1.00 +£2.00	3m
	Doctor Who - Series 3 - Complete (DVD) Sealed UK R2	*Buy It Now*	£16.99 Free	23h 37m
	Doctor Who - The Space Pirates	1 Bid	£1.00 +£2.00	3m
	Doctor Who - The Time Monster	0 Bids	£1.00 +£2.00	3m
	Doctor Who - The Smugglers	1 Bid	£1.00 +£2.00	3m
	Dr Who Tardis Mouse Mat /Pad Brand New Sealed RRP £6.99	*Buy It Now*	£1.99 Free	6d 6h 6m
	Doctor Who - The Happiness Patrol	0 Bids	£1.00 +£2.00	3m
	Doctor Who - The Movie Paul McGann BBC DVD 2007 NEW	*Buy It Now*	£10.82 Free	26d 6h 26m
	Doctor Who - The Mind of Evil	0 Bids	£1.00 +£2.00	3m
	DOCTOR WHO DALEK VOICE CHANGER HELMET DR CHANGING NEW	*Buy It Now*	£7.99 +£3.95	9d 8h 31m

'loch ness monster' in the search engine you will get every item with those words in the title: anything with the words 'loch', 'ness' and 'monster' will be returned regardless of what order they appear in the title. So you might also get a 'Loch Fyne Monster Bundle, Van Ness' alongside 'Loch Ness Monster Legends Book'.

If you are specifically interested in the Loch Ness monster and want to use the search engine to find the exact phrase, you need to enclose your search term in inverted commas like this: "loch ness monster". This only returns items with the words in the correct order. You can do this for any phrase.

If you are more interested in Loch Ness memorabilia but have absolutely no interest in the monster itself, you can instruct the search engine to search for Loch Ness but exclude any results that include the word monster. You do this by placing a minus sign before the word you want to exclude: loch ness -monster.

If you want to exclude a number of words you can do that too. So you might still be after those Loch Ness items but don't want anything to do with the monster and are averse to haggis and whisky too. In that case you would use the command: loch ness -(monster,haggis,whisky).

You can also widen your search by including item descriptions as well as titles. To do this simply click on the 'Search Titles and Descriptions' option underneath the Search box.

Inside Information
Take the Pulse

If you want to find out what everyone else on eBay is searching for, you need to take the pulse. It's easy to find on the homepage or at http://pulse.ebay.co.uk.

Pulse shows you the top ten search terms across the site, the most watched items on eBay.co.uk and also the most popular shops. It's a great way of finding out what's hot and what's not. The most watched items are also a great way of seeing some of the best, funniest or strangest items on eBay at the moment.

By choosing to drill down to a category of interest you can find out the most popular items in the Baby category or the Stamps section and get a feel for trends in even the smallest categories on the site.

How search is ordered

eBay takes a number of criteria into consideration when it presents items at the top of search results. Obviously you can choose to change these results, but as a default you'll generally see search results for 'Items Ending Soonest'. The quality of sellers and the popularity of items are also critical in ensuring the cream rises to the top.

First, sellers have to meet some basic Feedback criteria to get to the top of search results. Sellers with poor Feedback linger further down. Also, if a seller has already sold an item, that's taken into account too. The theory is that if a seller already has a satisfied customer for an item they're selling, that's a good indicator that both product and seller are tickety-boo.

Hunt for bargains

There are bargains on eBay. Some bargains are intentional, coming from sellers who revel in being able to undercut rivals and who offer quality items at a low price. Others are accidental. The accidental bargain is usually being sold by a bewildered seller who can't understand why their treasure hasn't reached the price it really deserves. Typically the seller has made an error in the listing or failed to include something in the title or description, with the result that buyers can't track the item down.

Take note of the following common errors so you know where to look for a bargain on eBay. But make sure you don't commit the same mistakes yourself when you start selling.

Sellers who don't know what they've got

Every now and again you see something on eBay that is rare and spectacular. If the seller doesn't know it is a really desirable object, the title will be vague and the description will lack details. This is where trawling the site for an 'old pot', a 'nice vase' or an 'interesting picture' can reap rewards. 99% of the results will be boring things of no particular interest or value. But one day the poorly titled item will be a treasure.

Bad titles and spelling mistakes

When someone lists an item with a poor title, buyers won't be able to find it. One common mistake is the seller failing to include a keyword that buyers search for in the title. A great example is a US seller I heard about who was trying to break into selling on eBay.co.uk with low-cost mobile phones. He had plenty of buyers, but he couldn't understand why his items weren't getting similar prices to his competition. It took his British friend to point out that on this side of the Atlantic they aren't often called 'cell phones'.

Another common mistake is misspelling the keywords in the item title. One buyer who completed his comic collection by getting his hands on the very first Beano Annual was thrilled that his seller couldn't spell. He got it for about half of what he would have been happy to pay. The seller was miffed that the item hadn't sold for much more. The buyer cheerfully pointed out that other buyers couldn't find it because the item was described as a 'Beeno Annual'. Look out for a rare 'Darlek Prop', an 'Agatha Cristy first edition', 'David Beckam's Signed Boots' or a 'Royal Dollton Vase'.

Wrong category

People are predictable and get into habits. Some buyers only check in one category for the items they want. While most of the items will be located here, there might be other places where the item can logically be. So if a seller puts the item in a less obvious but nevertheless appropriate category, the chances are that fewer buyers will be competing to buy it, keeping the price down.

It's sound advice to check the category an item is listed in every time you are about to place a bid, just to be sure. I heard about a guy who thought he'd got himself a real bargain. He was looking for one of those old-fashioned wooden filing cabinets and was amazed to find one for less than a tenner with really low postage. Desperate not to let the bargain go, he placed a bid immediately and paid quickly in case the seller changed their mind. He waited anxiously for the cabinet to arrive but felt like an idiot when it did turn up: it was four inches tall and meant for a doll's house. If he had checked the category, he'd have known to expect miniature furniture that had been photographed in its correspondingly tiny surroundings rather than in the seller's opulent Edwardian townhouse.

Do the legwork

There is no fast track for finding bargains or a way of searching for items that have been listed badly. You've just got to hunt them out and second-guess the other bargain hunters out there. Not only will you pick up a few really good bargains, you'll soon know eBay.co.uk inside out.

Inside Information
Helpful sites for bargain hunters

The eBay community is infinitely inventive and creative. If there's a gap that needs filling, someone will rush forward with an amazing idea. When it comes to finding bargains there are myriad sites that can help. Many are specifically set up to search eBay for misspelt or incorrectly categorised items.

Here are three of the best:

- **www.fatfingers.com** *Very easy to use, just type in your search term and the aptly named FatFingers will seek out the misspellings.*
- **www.goofbay.com** *A bit more fun than FatFingers but it does much the same.*
- **www.auctiontrax.com** *Auctiontrax can do everything that the other sites do but it can also do your bidding automatically and manage your snipes (last-minute bids). Well worth checking out.*

Listings pages

Whether you are browsing or searching for items, you will be presented with a page of listings that looks very much like the screenshot overleaf.

A Listings Page shows the items in the category you are browsing or the results from the search you have made. It displays the titles of the items for sale. They have been crafted by sellers to attract the attention of buyers: they are the short summaries that aim to catch your eye.

Whether you are browsing or searching you can sort the results or narrow them down by using the options on the Listings Pages. The results default to 'Time: Ending Soonest', but if you want to change the order of items you can choose from 'Newly

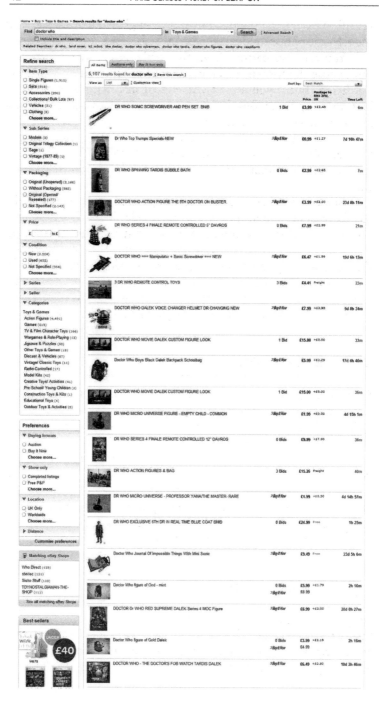

Listed', 'Price: Lowest First' and 'Price: Highest First' by selecting the relevant option under the 'Sort by' tab.

You can also narrow down the results in two ways. First, you can choose the format of the items you see. You automatically see 'All Items', but if you are only interested in Auctions or prefer to buy instantly using Buy It Now, you can opt to see only those items by clicking on the relevant tab.

Choosing a category is also a good way of getting closer to the item you want. If you select the most relevant category from the list on the lefthand side, you will only be shown items listed there.

Sometimes when you are searching or browsing eBay you also see the Product Finder on the lefthand side of the Listings Pages. This is a useful way of boiling down the results until you find the item you want. The category you are rummaging through determines the options the Product Finder provides you with. In the DVD category, for instance, you are able to search items by Genre and Region. In CDs you can choose to search only albums, EPs or singles, or if you prefer you can select a musical style such as Indie or Rock.

Decide whether to buy an item

Once you have found an item you like the look of, you need to decide whether it is exactly what you want and whether the price is right. You also need to make sure the delivery and postage costs are suitable for you. These are just the sort of things you would need to do if you were buying from a mail-order catalogue or another ecommerce site.

There is one extra thing you need to do on eBay to make sure that you have a satisfactory and safe purchase: check out the seller. eBay provides buyers with information about sellers that is worth looking at before you take the plunge and place your bid.

Find out more about the item
If you click on an item title when you are browsing or searching eBay you are taken to the View Item page. This is a page constructed by the seller that tells you about the item for sale. It is your opportunity to find out all about the item and decide whether you want to place a bid.

• **Item details** The top of the View Item page displays the item title you've already seen on the Listings Page. The top of the page has all sorts of vital details about how long the listing has to run, how much the bidding currently is and where the seller is located. If the seller has included a photo it will be shown in miniature on the lefthand side. You will also be able to see where the seller is willing to send the item.

There are two other things worth knowing about at the top of the View Item page. Both are on the righthand side. At the top you can see a text link 'Add to Watch List in My eBay' and just below you can see the Seller Information Box. These features will be dealt with later in the book.

• **Item description and picture** If you scroll further down the page you find the description and most probably a bigger picture. This section is where the seller fully describes the item they have for sale. A good seller will have taken a few moments to provide all the relevant details needed to persuade you to place a bid. Typically you find information about the item's condition, contents and anything else the seller wants you to know in the hope of nudging you towards a bid.

• **Postage and payment details** If you like the item description and are tempted to place a bid, it's a good idea to check that the postage costs are reasonable and you are happy to cover them. Typically buyers pay for carriage of the item, so you need to keep the additional charges in mind when you are deciding how much to bid. Sellers can detail the cost of postage within the UK and also what it would cost to send the item overseas.

On this part of the View Item page the seller can also include extra details about getting paid and state their returns policy if they want.

• **Payment methods accepted** Before you get to the bottom of the page you see one last section where the seller makes a quick note of how they are willing to be paid. Make sure you can pay the seller before you bid. A good seller will offer a selection of payment methods to help buyers.

Seller info

████ (252 ☆) 100%

Ask a question
See other items

Find out more about the seller

If you like the item and you want to place a bid, you now have to make sure you like the seller. It only takes a moment and is time well spent.

On the top righthand side of the View Item page you can see the Seller Information Box. This section contains a précis of the seller's reputation on eBay. For starters you see the seller's feedback score in brackets by the User ID: this is a tally of the feedback they have received from unique members. Obviously a higher number indicates a greater number of successful trades. But you shouldn't just consider this number in isolation, which is why you can also see what percentage of positive feedback the seller has received.

The Seller Information Box tells you when the seller registered with eBay and where they are located. If a seller is situated in a different country from the item, you should be a little more cautious.

If you want more information from the seller about the item you are looking at, click the 'Ask seller a question' text link.

Feedback

One of eBay's unique strengths, and your most valuable trading tool, is feedback. Every time you trade on eBay as a buyer or seller you have the right to leave a comment about your trading partner. The comments members leave for each other are public and available for scrutiny by anyone who wants to look. These comments can help you judge whether or not you want to trade with someone.

Think of feedback as a personal recommendation. When you are looking for a plumber or builder, you sound out friends and relations for good experiences. eBay feedback serves exactly the same purpose: it allows you to get the inside information on a seller or buyer from people who have had firsthand dealings with the person in question.

As explained above, the number that appears in brackets beside the User ID of every member is their feedback score. This number is your at-a-glance gauge of a member's trading history and eBay reputation. As a buyer you can leave three types of feedback: positive, negative and neutral. The type of feedback you leave will depend on the nature of the experience you have with another member. A positive comment adds one to a member's total, a negative deducts one and a neutral leaves the total the same.

The feedback score is a useful ready reckoner, but when you are trading on eBay you want to find out more. eBay provides you with fuller information in the Member Profile.

Member Profile

To access the Member Profile, click on the feedback number in brackets. A Member Profile gives you a much more detailed insight into a member's trading history on eBay.

On the Member Profile the types of feedback a member has received are clearly displayed. It is obvious if a member has received negative comments and what percentage of the member's feedback has been positive.

You can get a clearer view of a member's feedback by sorting it depending on whether it was left by a buyer or a seller. You can also choose to take a look at the feedback that the member has left for other members.

Most importantly, you can view the actual comments others have left. These are the personal views of other members and can be very enlightening. When you are trading on eBay you should always take the time to examine the Member Profile. Mostly you discover that a member is honest, fair and reliable, but sometimes you decide that the seller isn't someone you want to do business with.

Recent Feedback Ratings (last 12 months)	1 month	6 months	12 months
Positive	24	270	282
Neutral	0	0	0
Negative	0	0	0

Detailed Seller Ratings

There's even more information available to you when you're buying. Have you seen the orange stars on the Member Profile? These are called Detailed Seller Ratings and they're a way for buyers to give their opinion on different aspects of a seller's performance. You can use them to judge how honest and complete a seller is at describing their items, how good they are at communicating and how they perform on despatch time and costs. Needless to say, the higher the better. A 5-star score is the top mark and you should be looking for scores of more than 4 across the board.

Inside Information
Buying safely

> *When you are shopping online generally, being safe is about min-imising the risks and behaving sensibly. If you imagine that eBay is a big city, in fact a huge city of more than 200 million people, most of the citizens are completely law abiding and trustworthy. You need to exercise the same caution you would in a big city you don't know well. There are some shady characters and some dodgy streets, like in any city, that you probably want to avoid after dark. If you do go there you wouldn't wave your camera around, wear expensive jew-ellery or have your wallet poking out of your back pocket, because that's asking for trouble.*
>
> *When it comes to being safe on eBay, the key is paying safely. Use methods of payment, such as PayPal, that offer you protection and peace of mind. Take the time to research the item and seller and trust your instincts. If you take the precautions, do your research and pay safely, the chances are you'll never have a problem on eBay. There is more on payments later in the book.*

Safe trading checklist

To make sure you are keeping yourself secure, here are five ques-tions to ask yourself before you bid on something:

• **Do you know what you are buying?** Never place a bid in haste and make sure you are bidding on what you think you are bidding on. Read the small print and make sure the item is what you want. It's always worth researching expensive items thoroughly using the internet and other sources so you make the right purchase.

• **Do you trust the seller?** As a buyer you have lots of sources of information to help you make a sound judgement. If you don't get the information you need to make a choice, then think about finding another seller. Your first step is feedback. Take a few minutes to check out the other items the seller has sold. Do they have a track record of selling items similar to the one you want to buy? Have they got happy customers? If the seller has an About Me page, read it. Business sellers are required to publish their contact details, which can be a reassurance. If you want to make sure, feel free to contact the seller directly.

• **Is the seller truthful?** While you may be very happy to buy from abroad, be wary of sellers who claim to be in Britain but are in fact in another country. Not only is it against eBay rules to claim you are in the UK when you are not, but it can be a hallmark of a dodgy seller. Double check the seller's location. If the postage seems very high and the price of the item very low, be wary too.

• **Can you pay the seller and get your money back if you need to?** A dodgy seller doesn't have the items they are claiming to sell. They want to trick you into sending money you can't retrieve. Do not pay using cash or instant money transfers such as Western Union or MoneyGram. Paying by PayPal, especially if the seller is guaranteed under the PayPal Buyer Protection scheme, is the best and safest method.

• **Can you return the goods if you aren't happy?** Many good sellers allow you to return the goods you buy on eBay. Check out the seller's returns policy at the bottom of the View Item page to see if you can return what you buy if you want to. You may have to pay return carriage or send the item back within a set period of time, but it's good for peace of mind to be able to do so. Certainly if you are buying something of high value, you want to know that you can send it back if you want. If a seller doesn't take returns, you might want to try finding one who does.

6

Place a Bid

Once you have decided you like the item and the seller, you are ready to place a bid. Placing a bid is very easy, but you can maximise your chances of winning the item by understanding how the eBay bidding system works.

Inside Information
Why you can buy cheaply on eBay

> I bought my vacuum cleaner on eBay. If I'd bought it in the shops I would have paid £80 and dragged it home on the bus. On eBay I paid £50 including delivery direct to my door. I put the £30 I saved towards a handheld digital radio. The model I bought on eBay retails in the shops at £99 and I got mine for £68 all in. Another £30 saved! If I need to buy something, I always make a point of checking out eBay first. I'd be mad not to.
>
> How is this possible? How can sellers on eBay undercut the high street? There are lots of reasons. It won't surprise you to hear that manufacturers and retailers end up with a lot of stock they can't sell. It could be because they have overproduced, taken returns and seconds, or are pushing a new product that means the old model is now surplus to requirements. There are warehouses full of stuff that shops can't shift. What you might not know is that it costs money to get rid of this stuff. For a business, disposing of unwanted goods is expensive.
>
> eBay offers a way of selling such goods, so rather than paying to get rid of them the manufacturers can actually make money. Everyone wins. The manufacturers make something back and the rest of us bag a bargain. As my dad would say, rubbing his hands together like Del Boy, 'Everybody's happy!'
>
> If the manufacturers and wholesalers decide not to sell their over-stock on eBay, they might make it available to eBay sellers. I've met loads of eBay sellers who buy their stock from big names and chains. They buy it by the pallet load and often don't know what they are

going to get. They break down the pallets and sell the stuff on. They buy it cheap, they keep their overheads low and the savings are passed on to the buyer. Sometimes the box may be scuffed or it's not the latest model. But really, who cares? It's a good bit of kit and you've saved money.

Other businesses sell on eBay because it is extremely cost effective. They can avoid the huge costs of maintaining a shop or premises in a prime location. For instance, I met one seller who used to run a costly shop in his local town centre. Now he operates from a converted barn in his village. This saves him money, is much more convenient and provides a pleasanter working environment where he need no longer fear the sudden pounce of a traffic warden. eBay can also help sellers cut other operating costs so they can keep their prices low and stay competitive.

And then of course there's everyone else, the individual sellers. Many of these are people who are simply selling things they don't need any more. Often they are merely glad to get something for the item rather than chuck it away or take it to the tip or charity shop. The constant flow of goods means there's always bargains to be found on eBay. You just need to seek them out.

How bidding works

eBay does most of the bidding work for you. You don't need to sit in front of your computer day and night once you have decided to bid: all you need to do is enter the maximum amount you are willing to pay. eBay then does the bidding on your behalf up to your maximum while you do other things. This is called proxy bidding. If other people have placed bids, eBay ensures that you are the highest bidder for as long as your maximum bid is greater than anyone else's.

Most importantly, eBay won't bid more than is necessary for you to stay ahead of the other bidders. For instance, if you have bid £10.01 for a CD and another bidder has placed a bid of £4.01, eBay won't bid up to your maximum. What it will do is push your bid up to just above the other bidder, making your bid £4.21. If no one else bids on the CD, despite the fact you are willing to bid up to £10.01, your winning bid will only be £4.21.

eBay uses a system of bid increments to control bidding. Depending on the price of the item, the bidding goes up according to the following fixed bid increments:

PRICE	BID INCREMENT
£0.01–1.00	£0.05
£1.01–5.00	£0.20
£5.01–15.00	£0.50
£15.01–60.00	£1.00
£60.01–150.00	£2.00
£150.01–300.00	£5.00
£300.01–600.00	£10.00
£600.01–1,500.00	£20.00
£1,500.01–3,000.00	£50.00
Above £3000.01	£100.00

If yours is the first bid on an item, your bid will be the starting price of the item. If you are bidding on an item that already has bids and your bid is higher than the highest other bidder's maximum bid, then eBay will bid up to the other bidder's maximum plus one increment. If your maximum bid is higher than the other bidder's maximum bid but not a whole increment higher, eBay will automatically bid to your maximum regardless.

Proxy bidding is often a source of confusion to new buyers. In particular, many newbies wonder why they are immediately outbid when they place a bid. Obviously this is because the maximum bid they place isn't as high as another bidder's maximum. The best way to get to grips with how bidding works is to practise and experiment. If at first you don't seem to be winning auctions, don't worry: find another one and just keep on bidding!

How to place a bid

To place a bid you can either click on 'Place Bid' at the top of the View Item page or scroll down to the bottom of the page and enter your bid there. You need to sign in and confirm the amount you are bidding.

Bids are legally binding. If you aren't serious about buying the item then you shouldn't place a bid. Sellers get narked by people who place bids and don't pay up and if you do that you will most likely earn yourself negative feedback. Under some circumstances you are permitted to retract a bid, but if you do this it will be noted on your Member Profile. Be warned that other members don't look kindly on those who retract bids. You can retract a bid via the link of that name on the Site Map.

If another bidder places a maximum bid greater than yours, you will be outbid. When you are outbid you have the option to raise your maximum and regain the item. You can up your bid in the same way as placing a bid.

Bidding strategies

Once you have found an item you want to bid on, there are ways of improving your chances of winning that auction. If you have found an item you want at a price you like, then it's very likely that other people will be bidding too. Experienced eBay buyers can sometimes be at an advantage because they know how the bidding system works. You need to formulate a bidding strategy if you're going to be competing against them.

- **Decide your maximum bid and stick to it** The worst mistake a buyer can make is bidding more than they want to pay. Sometimes people can get carried away because they want to beat the other bidders and their competitive instinct gets the better of them. Once you have found an item you want to buy, decide the maximum you want to pay for it and stick to that. If the bidding goes higher you can either reassess your bid or wait for another similar item to come up. Don't forget to consider the postage costs when you are deciding your maximum bid. Sometimes when you add in the postage the bargain you wanted to bag doesn't look so attractive.

- **Don't bid round numbers** If the maximum you want to bid is £10, then it is advisable not to bid £10.00 straight. The eBay system will favour a bid of £10.01 or £10.03 over £10. A higher bid, even if the difference is only a penny, will take preference over a lower one. In the event of two bids being equal, the earlier one will take preference. Experienced eBay buyers will always bid a few extra pence.

- **Watch an item** Wise men say only fools rush in. If you spot an item you want to buy and have decided how much you're going to bid, it can be worth biding your time if the item has only just started or has a number of days left to run. It's a bit like playing poker: you don't always want to show your hand too soon. By being the first person to bid on an item early on in the listing, you are expressing your interest, which can alert other members or mean that in the long run you are pushing the price up. eBay gives you the opportunity to watch an item (meaning the item is displayed in My eBay and you can keep an eye on it and choose to bid later if you want to). To watch an item simply click the link on the View Item page and the item will be added to your Watch List.

• **Last-minute bidding** For some members the real thrill of buying on eBay is waiting for the last minute and bidding in the dying seconds in the hope of outwitting other potential buyers and bagging a bargain. Bidding in the last minutes of a listing is called 'sniping' by eBay regulars, who find it an exciting way of using the site.

Inside Information
Sniping

Sniping is a controversial issue for many members of eBay and one of those topics that is guaranteed to get a robust discussion going on the Discussion Boards. Snipers believe that keeping their bid secret until the last minute means that the price is kept low and they can beat the other bidders by the smallest amount necessary. The end of a listing on eBay is non-negotiable and if a bid is received in the final moments, there isn't time for anyone else to bid even if they are willing to bid more than the sniper.

Snipers believe that the highest bid should win and they can get the items they want at the price they like. But for the people who are outbid it can seem desperately unfair to be robbed of an item at the last minute by a matter of pence, especially if they were willing to pay more. The options are clear. Either become a sniper, or bid your maximum bid and be happy to accept that you didn't want to pay more even when you are outbid at the last minute.

Buy It Now

Buying on eBay doesn't need to be simply about bidding and using the auction format. You can also buy instantly at a fixed price by using Buy It Now. Clicking 'Buy It Now' ends the listing immediately and the item is yours. The Buy It Now price is determined by the seller and you can either take it or leave it.

This option can be seen on its own on pure fixed-price items or it can be added by the seller to any auction item. If you see an

auction item with Buy It Now, you have the choice to bid or purchase the item instantly. If you want to bid, just treat the item as a
normal auction item. Once you have placed a bid, the Buy It Now
option will disappear. If you would rather use Buy It Now because
you like the fixed price, click the 'Buy It Now' button and you can
buy the item instantly.

Keep track of your buying activities

Once you have placed a few bids you'll know that eBay can get
addictive: it's difficult to keep away from your computer because
you want to make sure you are still the highest bidder. For ease
eBay organises the details of your buying activities in a special section called My eBay.

My eBay is a personalised summary of your trading activities.
You can see at a glance the items you are bidding on, auctions you
have won and those that you have bid on but not won. You can
access My eBay by clicking on the 'My eBay' link in the Navigation
Bar. You will need to sign in using your User ID and password.

- **Your summary** When you log in to My eBay you are
  taken to the Summary page, which gives you a selection of the
  most important information you can find in My eBay. At the
  top, eBay provides reminders about items you need to pay for.
  A bit further down the page you can see news from eBay in
  the 'Latest Announcements' section. If eBay is launching a
  new feature, changing a policy or holding a Free Listing Day,
  it will tell the community about it here.

If you want to go to specific trading information, you can navigate through My eBay by using the links on the lefthand side of the page.

• **Your buying information** As a buyer all the information you need to keep tabs on your activities can be found by clicking on the 'All Buying' link. In this section of My eBay you can see what you have bid on, whether you are the highest bidder and what you need to pay for. My eBay is a very intuitive and well-organised part of eBay. If you want to find out what a symbol or icon means, just position your mouse pointer over it and some explanatory text will pop up. If you want to find out where a link goes, simply click on it. You can always go back to where you started by clicking the 'Back' button on your browser.

• **Save your favourites** As a buyer there is a second helpful section of My eBay that you can use to make your trading easier. If you click on the 'All Favourites' link, you'll find a great resource to help you store information about your favourite searches, sellers and categories.

• **Customise My eBay** eBay offers you the opportunity to customise how the information in My eBay is displayed. Within each section you can use the double arrow icons to change the order in which the information appears. If you want something nearer the top you can use the up arrows, and if you aren't as interested in something else you can move it towards the bottom of the page. You can organise My eBay to your liking by clicking on the 'Customise' link at the top right of the page.

• **Information for sellers** As you develop your eBay trading and move on to becoming a seller, you'll find that My eBay is indispensable. When you are a buyer it helps you organise your purchases by giving you information on what you have bought and for how much. For a seller My eBay is the nerve centre of activity: it lets you know how the bidding is going on items you are selling, which of your buyers have paid and which of your sales you have despatched.

Sellers in other countries

One of eBay's greatest attractions is the opportunity it opens up for buying items from other countries. eBay has established web-sites in 39 countries and your eBay.co.uk registration allows you to buy on any eBay site just as you would in the UK.

There are obvious benefits to buying items from abroad. Sometimes an item is considerably cheaper than in Britain. Electronic accessories are often much cheaper when purchased from the US (although check that the item is the correct voltage for the UK). Designer clothing is much cheaper in Italy. eBay also makes it easier to buy items from abroad that simply aren't avail-able in the UK. Collectables, stamps, books, magazines, comics and records that would otherwise be unobtainable can be snapped up with ease.

Buying from abroad shouldn't be a chore if you follow a few simple steps:

• **Make sure the seller will send the item to the UK** If you are searching for items on eBay.co.uk and what you want shows up as located elsewhere in the world, the chances are that the seller will send the item to the UK. To double-check, sellers indicate where they are willing to send the item to on the View Item page. If a seller doesn't say they are willing to ship to the UK but you are very keen on the item, you could ask the seller if they would make an exception. With the reas-surance that you are keen and able to complete the trans-action, they might broaden their horizons.

• **Make sure you can communicate with the seller** If you are buying from a seller in the US, Canada or Australia, lan-guage won't be an issue. However, with other European coun-tries and sellers in Asia or South America it can be a barrier. Many overseas sellers do indicate that they are willing to con-duct the sale in English, but if it isn't clear it is best to contact the seller to ensure you can communicate. Obviously, if you speak their language, trading won't be a problem.

• **Make sure you can pay** For international traders the number one source of problems is payment. Despite modern technology, paying for items across borders can still be time-consuming, expensive and slow. So if you do bid on an item located overseas, make sure you can meet the seller's payment terms.

If the seller accepts PayPal then there won't be a problem because you can pay them with speed and ease. If they don't accept PayPal you will find other options on the View Item page. Remember, money orders and cheques sent overseas can attract high conversion fees and many sellers expect you to meet those costs. If you need to send small amounts of money overseas, cash can be the easiest if not the safest option.

• **Make sure the postage costs are acceptable** International postage can be expensive so to avoid a nasty shock, make sure you have an idea of the postage costs before bidding. Some sellers note international rates in the item description. If you are in any doubt, send the seller an email and ask for an estimate before you bid. If you aren't in a hurry to receive the item, remember that surface mail is much cheaper than air mail.

• **And don't forget Customs** Items sent to the UK from outside the European Union are sometimes liable to customs charges. Not every parcel is stopped and assessed, but if it is and a charge is levied then it is your responsibility to pay it. You should bear this in mind when you bid. You can find full details on the HM Revenue and Customs website: www.hmrc.gov.uk.

Buying successfully checklist

• **Check the item details and pictures** Make sure you know what you're buying and that the item is right for you.

• **Is this the best deal?** Before you bid, it can be worth checking out whether there is a seller with a better deal.

• **Read the terms and conditions** Some sellers have their own rules: make sure you can comply with them.

• **How long until the item ends?** Is the item newly listed or about to end? Remember that most bids aren't placed until the last hour of an auction.

- **Are the postage costs reasonable?** Check the cost of carriage and avoid sellers who profit from inflating their postage costs.

- **Where is the item shipped from?** The price may look good, but if the item is coming from outside the EU you may have to pay import duty.

- **Can you pay?** Check out the payment methods and make sure you can pay safely and securely. Ensure you can get your money back if you need to return the item.

- **The seller's feedback** Take a few minutes to check the seller's feedback and About Me page if they have one. Is the seller trustworthy?

- **Ask the seller any questions** If you need more details, don't hesitate to contact the seller.

- **If in doubt, don't bid!** There are millions of items for sale on eBay. If you have any doubts, don't bid. There'll be another one along soon, have no fear.

7

Complete Your Purchase

Once you have successfully bought an item you have to pay the seller, receive the item and leave the seller feedback. It's important that you pay swiftly and work with the seller so you can get your hands on the item as quickly as possible.

Pay the seller

Many new members are confused about paying for their first purchase. Paying for an item needn't be a problem as long as you have taken the time to examine the payment methods the seller is willing to accept on the View Item page. If the seller offers a number of payment methods, you can choose the one that suits you best. Obviously, the quicker the seller has the payment the quicker they will despatch the goods.

Checkout

The Checkout process helps you pay quickly and sends the seller your delivery details at the same time. There are two ways to enter Checkout. The first is via My eBay. By clicking on the item title in the 'Items I've Won' section of My eBay, you are taken to the View Item page. After the Listing has ended the page looks slightly different from when you were bidding. Near the top of the page you will see a 'Pay Now' button. Just click on it and you will be guided through the payment process. You are able to choose the payment method you want to use, enter your address so it's sent to the seller, and if you want to pay by cheque you receive the seller's address so you know where to send it. You will also be sent an email with all these details for your reference.

You can also access Checkout via the automatic email that eBay sends you when you have won an auction. You can get started by clicking on the 'Pay Now' button in the email.

The first time you go through Checkout is the most time consuming. Every time you use Checkout in future will be quicker because eBay stores your address so you don't need to add it again and again. If you want to include multiple addresses for your convenience, you can.

How do I know how much I need to pay?

The Checkout facility automatically tots up the price plus the postage and tells you how much you have to pay.

If you are in any doubt about the postage costs or want to clarify anything with the seller, you are best advised to contact them directly. At the end of the Listing you receive an email from eBay informing you that you have successfully purchased the item. This email includes the seller's email address for your reference.

PayPal

On most eBay listings you will see PayPal offered as a payment option. PayPal is a swift and easy way of paying your seller online using your credit or debit card. It is popular with many eBay buyers because you can pay instantly, but your card details are kept secure and confidential from the seller. In fact, PayPal proved so popular with buyers and sellers that eBay bought the company in 2002 so that the two organisations' services could be effectively integrated.

What do I need to join PayPal?

Joining PayPal is very simple. All you require is a credit or debit card and an email address. For ease, it's best to use the same email address you used to register with eBay. PayPal accepts MasterCard, Visa, Visa Delta, Visa Electron, Switch/Maestro, Solo and American Express cards. To register go to www.paypal.co.uk.

Once you have registered with PayPal you can bid on eBay listings displaying the PayPal logo safe in the knowledge that you will be able to pay quickly and easily if you win the item.

How do I pay with PayPal?

The easiest way to pay for an item you have won is by using eBay's Checkout facility. If you use PayPal the seller knows instantly when you have paid because it shows in their My eBay. As you are guided through Checkout you are asked to choose how you want to pay. If you choose PayPal, you are automatically taken to the PayPal site to complete your payment. Alternatively the seller can send you an invoice via email and you can then log in to your PayPal account to pay.

What are the benefits of PayPal for buyers?

The greatest benefit of using PayPal is speed. When you send a PayPal payment the seller has the funds immediately and can safely send the item straight away. Without PayPal you have to send a cheque, wait for the seller to receive it and then wait for it to clear. PayPal speeds up the buying process and doesn't cost buyers anything.

If you use PayPal to pay for an eBay purchase you can also enjoy greater protection and peace of mind. PayPal is a trackable payment method, so you can be reassured that you aren't sending your payment into the blue never to be seen again. If you pay by PayPal and the seller is eligible (see the Seller Information Box), you can also enjoy the benefits of the PayPal Buyer Protection Programme.

PayPal is terrific for international trading. You can use your British debit card or credit card to pay sellers from all over the world and PayPal takes care of the currency conversion.

Inside Information
Why PayPal is bloody marvellous

The beauty of PayPal is security. You can pay individuals using a debit or credit card without having to reveal your personal details to people you don't know. PayPal keeps your details safe, the seller gets paid immediately and everybody's happy. I just wish I could use PayPal for more mundane things like the phone bill and council tax.

The security of PayPal is reassuring, but I also love the speed and convenience. If I bid and win or use Buy It Now I like to pay immediately. Good sellers despatch the item a day or two later and another day or so after that I have the item I bought. Often buying on eBay is quicker than ordering online with other companies because sellers take such pride in shipping items speedily.

Unless the item is really rare and I have no choice, I won't bid on

an item if the seller doesn't take PayPal. I just can't be bothered with
the hassle of digging out my chequebook, writing a note, finding an
envelope, applying a stamp and putting it in the post. It'll take a day
or two (at least) and then I have to wait for the seller to bank the
cheque and let it clear. If I'm lucky my purchase turns up a week or so
later.

eBay wants more people to use PayPal. All new members are
required to sign up, all listings must offer PayPal on eBay.co.uk and
in some categories it is the only acceptable payment method.
Increasingly, PayPal is the payment norm on eBay. But all that said,
PayPal isn't perfect and lots of people have stories of frustration and
annoyance.

The thing to remember is that PayPal is quite complicated and not
necessarily very adept at explaining a problem before it suspends your
account. If your PayPal account runs into difficulty, it's likely to be
one of a few problems. If you're new to selling and you hit a limit,
you'll be required to verify your account. This can be time consuming,
but it's easy to do if you log into PayPal. If you're trying to pay and
you can't, nine times out of ten the problem will be that your credit
card or debit card has expired or been replaced. If you get a new card
you'll need to update your details on PayPal too.

PayPal does have a phone helpline you can call if you get into difficulties and I can honestly say that the few times I've had to call it
over the years have been trouble free. You can contact PayPal on
08707 307 191. You can get a security code via the PayPal site for you
to quote for added safety.

For whatever reason, if you don't embrace PayPal you are dam-
aging your sales. Not only could it save you time, it could also be
more efficient than regular trips to the bank and waiting for cheques
to clear and possibly bounce. It's not only me who avoids sellers who
don't take PayPal: I talk to members all the time who 'can't be bothered' when it comes to writing a cheque, or indeed have bank accounts
that don't use chequebooks.

Other payment methods

Every seller has to offer PayPal as a payment method and the
majority of payments you make will be via PayPal. Sometimes, you
might want to pay using another method. For instance, your PayPal
account may be broken, or if you're collecting a big item personally cash is easier, or the seller has requested payment via another
medium.

eBay has rules about which methods a seller is allowed to solicit. The reasons for these rules are largely to protect buyers from unscrupulous sellers and keep them away from potentially unsafe payment methods. You can check out the Acceptable Payments Policy here: http://pages.ebay.co.uk/help/policies/accepted-payments-policy.html.

Don't forget: if a seller is keen to get you away from PayPal it might be because they have nefarious aims. Have those common-sense antennae on full alert if a seller starts making odd requests.

Other electronic methods: Aside from PayPal, there are several online payments services permitted by eBay. These include Allpay.net, hyperwallet.com, Moneybookers.com, Nochex.com, Paymate.com, Propay.com and XOOM.

Cheques and postal orders: You can send cheques or postal orders for eBay purchases and within the UK it's pretty safe and almost entirely trackable. When you do so, don't forget to include a note with your payment so the seller knows who it is from. Include your email address, User ID and the item number.

Credit and debit card payments: Lots of professional eBay sellers have the facility to process debit and credit cards, either online or over the phone. Again, with a reputable seller this isn't unsafe. You're probably doing it every day via other websites. Credit card payments often have additional protection programmes that you might want to make use of.

Bank transfers: Sellers can provide you with bank details and you can transfer your payment directly to their account. Many buyers are uncomfortable with this option and if you are in any doubt about the seller this method should be avoided. There is nothing wrong with paying by bank transfer. Just never do it internationally and absolutely don't use it for high-value items.

Cash: Never send cash in the post: it's not insured and sellers aren't allowed to ask you. But if you're meeting someone in person, you can pay with your finest folding.

Instant cash transfer services: Systems such as MoneyGram and Western Union have been misused by fraudsters on eBay for many years. That's why they're banned. They're untrackable and not designed for use in ecommerce. Avoid.

International payment methods

When it comes to sending money to buyers overseas, payments are harder to track. The horror stories I've heard about sending money to sellers in other countries are reasonably commonplace and sometimes even heartbreaking. In all conscience, I can't recommend anything else but PayPal for international trading. Using any other method is asking for trouble.

Receive the item

As with any distance-buying experience, the most frustrating aspect is waiting for the item to arrive. Many eBay members say that waiting for the delivery is like waiting for a birthday gift or exam results.

Many more times than not, your item arrives swiftly and in exactly the condition you expect. Sometimes the item is even better than described, which is why you often see 'Item better than expected' in feedback comments. If you are happy with the item when it arrives you can go and leave the seller positive feedback immediately. Sometimes, however, your buying experience might be less than perfect.

What if your item isn't what you expected?

The vast majority of sellers understand how eBay works and describe their items honestly. Nevertheless, sometimes items might have been misrepresented, deliberately or accidentally, so you should contact the seller and tell them. eBay will take action against sellers who misdescribe the items they are selling. If a seller misdescribes an item and won't offer you recompense when you tell them, you should inform eBay via the webform in the Help section.

If the item was damaged in the post, you should contact the seller. The cover you can expect depends on the delivery method: if you opted for insured post you have extra cover. You need to work with the seller to make a claim. If the damage was a result of poor packaging, then you have good reason to expect the seller to see you right.

What if your purchase doesn't arrive?

If your item doesn't arrive at all you should follow these steps:

- **Contact the seller** The first thing you should always do if you haven't received the item in good time is to get in touch with the seller. A polite and friendly enquiry usually gets an apologetic reply. In the first instance be patient; don't forget that many sellers are busy people and they may simply have forgotten to send the item. In other cases the Royal Mail may just have let them down and the item might be lost in the post. You should always try to work the problem out with the seller if you can.

- **Contact eBay** If you have sent the money to the seller, contacted them to chase your purchase up and still not received the item, then you should contact eBay. They will chase up the seller on your behalf and you won't be surprised to hear how quickly a tardy seller swings into action when threatened with suspension from eBay. You can report a seller via the 'Help' link in the Navigation Bar.

Buyer protection programme

If your purchase fails to arrive or arrives and isn't what was described, you need to take action. If your seller is uncooperative, then you may need to resort to using eBay Buyer Protection.

Just about everything you buy on eBay is covered by this protection scheme, which will reimburse you in the case of fraud. There's just one key criterion: you must pay with PayPal.

- **eBay Buyer Protection** In the event that something goes awry with a transaction, in the first instance you should contact the seller. If they don't offer a satisfactory resolution, then you should contact eBay via the link below. They will facilitate negotiations with the seller and adjudicate if necessary.

- **Exclusions** There are some exclusions that you should be aware of before you place your bid. Only 'tangible' items are covered. Items such as ebooks, information or software downloads are not covered. You must also make your claim within a specified time after the listing has ended: typically 45 days, although there are sometimes extensions for event tickets.

You can find out further details about the Buyer Protection Programme and make a claim via this page: http://pages.ebay.co.uk/ebaybuyerprotection/index.html

Leave feedback

By this stage you will be aware of the value of feedback as a trading tool: it's how eBay members can judge the reputation of others in an honest way based on other people's experiences.

This is why it is important to leave feedback when you have received your purchase. Your experience as a buyer will be invaluable to other members who are trying to trade successfully. Your positive feedback will encourage others to bid. Your negative feedback may warn them off.

Feedback is vital to sellers. A good seller takes pride in receiving glowing feedback. Better feedback means better sales, and most sellers guard their eBay reputation jealously. Negative feedback can be a warning to sellers that their performance isn't up to scratch and they need to reassess their activities. Negative feedback also serves as a warning to eBay. A seller with negative feedback can warrant investigation and perhaps suspension from the site. You can also leave Detailed Seller Ratings to give more information about your experience as a buyer. These ratings are important to sellers and good ratings are essential. Giving sellers a fair appraisal is vital.

How do you leave feedback?

The easiest way to leave feedback is to use the Feedback link in My eBay. Click on the My eBay link in the Navigation Bar and sign in. Once you are in My eBay there is a 'Feedback' link on the lefthand side and if you click on that you will be taken to a list of all the feedback you have to leave. You can then opt to leave a feedback comment by clicking the 'Leave Feedback' link.

Which type of feedback should you leave?

The type of feedback you leave depends on your experience with the seller. Positive feedback should be left if you are very satisfied with the transaction, happy with your item and pleased with the service you received. If you are not entirely satisfied but found the service and item acceptable, you might want to leave neutral feedback. Many sellers will be very unhappy to receive a neutral: it is considered to be almost as bad as a negative. So if you are thinking about leaving neutral feedback you might want to contact the seller before you do, so they understand why you want to leave a neutral and have a chance to remedy any problems you feel have occurred.

Fact: Everydaysource are the eBay sellers with the most feedback. Search for their User ID to see how much they currently have.

Negative feedback is a last resort

Leaving negative feedback is a serious business, so you need to be sure that it is the right thing to do. You also need to give the seller a chance to change your mind. Politely email the seller and explain why you are dissatisfied. Keep your email calm and factual and try to outline your thoughts clearly so they can understand exactly why you are dissatisfied. Don't forget that sometimes an email can seem very cold and the words can easily be misunderstood. A problem may be solved more simply by giving the seller a call.

If you have contacted the seller and you are unable to resolve the problem between you, then you are clear to leave negative feedback. Take a few moments to decide what it is you want to say, and don't resort to personal insults or vitriolic comments.

Don't forget that other members can see the feedback you leave. It can damage your own eBay reputation if you look like the kind of member who leaves negative feedback in haste and anger. As a buyer sellers might cancel your bids, and as a seller it could cost you sales.

If you have never left negative or neutral feedback before or have a rating of less than 10, you have to take a special test to make sure that you have done everything you can to avoid leaving negative feedback. In some cases you'll be required to contact the seller before you can leave a negative.

Leaving Detailed Seller Ratings

Almost as important as the kind of feedback you leave is the kind of DSRs you provide. DSRs are incredibly important to sellers. They enjoy greater prominence in search and sometimes get fee discounts if they're providing a top-notch service.

As usual, being honest is vital but it's best to avoid being harsh. Don't forget that if a DSR bobs below 4, that's very bad news. So when it comes to leaving a DSR and you're totally satisfied, give a 5. The item is exactly as expected, arrived as promised and postage was reasonable: it's time for top marks. Obviously if you're dissatisfied then use your discretion, but if you're satisfied, be generous.

Feedback tips

Ensure that you're making the most of feedback and helping the rest of the community. Here are some feedback tips.

Make sure your feedback comments are useful

Feedback is about helping other people. On one level by leaving feedback you are building your own eBay reputation by encouraging reciprocation. But the major value of feedback lies in what you are offering to the community as a whole. By leaving positive, negative or neutral feedback you are telling other eBay members about your trading experience. Your comments will help them make successful trading decisions. Your duty as an eBay member is to be honest and helpful. Make sure that the comments you leave, regardless of whether they are good or bad, help other people when they are looking at them. Be factual and objective and relate what you say directly to your experience.

Feedback cannot be retracted

Only in the rarest of circumstances will eBay totally remove a feedback comment. So if you say something in feedback you should expect it to remain part of the other member's profile forever. This is one reason you should be cautious and never leave feedback in the heat of the moment, however tempting it might feel to get your revenge.

If a seller feels aggrieved, they can request that a feedback comment be amended. You'll be contacted by eBay and required to enter into a negotiation with your seller. This is a fairly rare occurrence, as sellers have only limited amend requests.

Feedback isn't compulsory

Sometimes you leave feedback and it isn't reciprocated. This is an unfortunate fact of eBay life. If you have left positive feedback for another member and have not received it in return, you should feel free to drop the other member an email and ask them to reciprocate. Obviously approach them politely, tell them that you'd really appreciate the boost to your rating and nine times out of ten they will return the favour. But if you ask and they don't, while it is obviously annoying, there isn't much you can do. And obviously if you keep on pestering them demanding feedback, they might even retaliate with a negative.

Fact: *More than one million feedback comments are left on eBay every day. Seven billion have been left since eBay began.*

Top rated sellers?

The newest category of eBay-approved sellers you might see are Top Rated Sellers. You'll identify them by the rosette eBay gives them in search results and on View Item pages.

It's all a bit confusing. eBay will steer you towards Top Rated Sellers in search, but what about PowerSellers and private sellers? How good is a TRS? And of course, none of the above overrides good old-fashioned feedback and shining DSRs. What does it all mean?

The simple fact is that Top Rated Sellers are usually larger retailers who are accredited by eBay. eBay is sticking its neck out to recommend people it trusts. That's good news: you're unlikely to be ripped off. Top Rated Sellers are bona fide and screened so you can buy from them in absolute confidence. But it doesn't necessarily mean they're going to offer you the best deal.

I say keep looking out for those good, small sellers with illustrious feedback records. Typically individuals or tiny enterprises, they're the most personal people to trade with and are likely to offer you great products, great prices and even better service.

8

Buy Safely

One of eBay's core values is the belief that people are basically good. And for the most part the truth of this maxim is borne out in the everyday trading activities of eBay members all over the world. People are trading all the time with people they have never met, sending money to strangers and receiving items in return that they have not seen or handled before. eBay is based on trust and the vast majority of purchases and sales go without a hitch, leaving both buyers and sellers satisfied.

Despite the many good and decent people out there, it is nevertheless the sad truth that some people set out to do bad things. eBay has systems in place to detect such people, punish them and remove them from the marketplace, but you can protect yourself further by being vigilant. Your greatest tool to avoid being one of those who get ripped off is your own common sense.

Inside Information
The 'man in the pub' rule

> If you wouldn't take a risk in real life, you shouldn't do it online either. For instance, imagine a man you'd never met before came up to you in the pub and said he would sell you the Harley Davidson you had always dreamt of owning for £5000. You wouldn't give that man £5000 there and then and wait until he returned with the bike, would you?
>
> You would want to ensure you were protected, verify the bike was real and confirm that it was exactly what you wanted. Most likely you wouldn't hand over the money until you collected the bike. That's just common sense. The same principle applies on eBay.
>
> I can't make this point strongly enough: using your common sense when trading on eBay will ensure that you stay safe. If a seller wants you to pay using a service you aren't comfortable with or have never heard of, don't use it. Someone who wants to rip you off doesn't want

you to pay using a secure service such as PayPal. If they attach odd terms and conditions such as using a particular escrow service other than Escrow.com, eBay's recommended escrow partner, you should be wary. Especially with high-value items, make sure you can get your money back if you need to.

Over the years I've seen a number of people ripped off or scammed on eBay, but those who are still represent an astonishingly small percentage of the total transactions that occur worldwide. What makes me angry is the fact that most scams like these are totally avoidable if you take a moment to engage your common sense before you get out your wallet.

Feedback is your friend

Feedback is your most vital tool when deciding whether a certain seller or buyer is the kind of person you want to do business with. The Seller Information Box on the Item Description page gives you plenty of information, but you need to unravel it.

Look for a positive feedback score of 98% or above. Remember that a high total isn't automatically a guarantee in itself. If you want to find out about a seller, or if you are curious about a buyer, you should click on the feedback total to find out more about their eBay history.

But Feedback is so much more than a percentage and a total. The Detailed Seller Ratings let you know how swift, honest and conscientious a certain seller is (DSRs aren't applicable to buyers). You're looking for scores between 4 and 5 across the board.

You'll find the DSRs on the Member Profile. Here you'll find so much more detail about a member's previous activities on eBay and more information to use to form a judgement. If there is any negative feedback on the profile, you want to find out what it is for. A person with 1000 feedbacks has clearly had many successful trades with many different members, but a closer examination will reveal whether a trader has received complaints. A few negative feedbacks here and there are pretty much inevitable for members with a lot of feedback, but sometimes even excellent feedback totals conceal members with less than enviable reputations.

If you are looking into a seller, you can check the items they have sold recently and examine the feedback left. If a seller has already received good feedback for an item similar to the one you want to bid on, then you can probably bid with confidence.

Feedback tips

When it comes to feedback it's easy to take false comfort from the fact that a seller has 20,000 positive feedbacks or to judge them too harshly because they only have 99.7% positive. Every Member Profile tells a story and as with any source of information, over-simplification can render the information misleading.

A bumper feedback total and a very high percentage can actually disguise a seller who is selling many thousands of items a month and yet leaving several hundred buyers a month unhappy. Equally, one unfair negative left for a seller with only a few hundred feedbacks can be a disproportionately big blot on their copy book.

If you really want to unleash the power of feedback, it's worth moving beyond a quick glance and digesting the information in detail to help you make the right decisions.

- **Repeat feedback** When you see a feedback score by a member's User ID, the number is a tally of the unique members who have left a positive comment. It doesn't tell you how many buyers have gone back again and again to buy from the same seller, and if people do go back for more that's a good sign. To see how many repeat buyers a seller is getting, go to the Member Profile and look for 'All positive feedback received'. If this number is higher than the unique score it means the seller has repeat bidders. Obviously, if the repeat score is very high it means that people keep going back to the seller to buy.

- **Check items being sold** What's the feedback for? You need to check that the feedback is for selling and hopefully for items like the one you want to buy. Click on the item numbers by the feedback comments to see what the feedback is for.

- **The DSRs have it** Don't forget to take a closer look at a seller's Detailed Selling Ratings (DSRs) to get a real flavour of how good the seller is. Those stars you see should be as close to 5 as possible. So if you're buying a rare antique, say, you want to know how full and honest a seller's description is. If you're in a hurry, fast despatch counts.

Buying tickets safely

One of the most controversial issues involving eBay regards event tickets. It's a topic that excites lively, opinionated debate. I'm totally in favour of the sale of tickets on eBay (some people call this the secondary market), having bought and sold tickets for both above and below the face value myself. I'm not a tout and I've seen some great gigs too.

But if you are buying tickets, it's time to really exercise your eBay nous. Here are some tips:

- **Feedback really says it all** You should be able to identify a reputable ticket seller by checking feedback. Unless it's really glittering, avoid.

- **Business sellers are safer** If you want the full raft of consumer protection, then buy from a business registered seller. The death of Michael Jackson ably demonstrated that sometimes private sellers don't understand what they are legally required to do when it comes to refunds of cancelled gigs.

- **Pay properly and that means PayPal** eBay extends the 45 days' protection for a claim on ticket sales.

- **Shop around** That can mean side-stepping eBay and going to a specialist site. Seatwave.com and Stubhub.co.uk are respected services dedicated to selling only tickets.

- **Don't forget** eBay sometimes bans the sale of some types of tickets and requires an obligatory charity donation for charity tickets sold, so make sure you're not breaking any eBay rules because you won't be protected.

Tip: Returns
   eBay has made it very easy to administer returns from a buyer perspective. You can simply log into the Dispute Console in My eBay and start the 'Easy Returns' process. eBay requires business sellers to offer returns.

Tell-tale signs: Spot those dodgy listings

What I want to say about spotting a dodgy listing is 'You just know'. But that's not necessarily very useful. If your antennae start twitching, if something just doesn't seem right or feel right, then move on. You should trust your instincts because even if you're not right, you can always find another item you want to buy.

But there are some elements that betray a dodgy seller. Sometimes when you see things from the list below it's the clue you need to back off. While none of them alone is necessarily enough to categorically say 'That's dodgy', if a listing has two or more danger signs the chances are it's best avoided.

Obviously, some areas are more risky than others: mobile phones, plasma screen televisions and other electrical goods are prone to attracting fraudsters more than, say, stamps or Beanie Babies. If you keep an eye out for the following features in listings then you will be safer.

- **Check the location** There are three places where the location of a seller and the item they are selling is provided. Make sure they all tally: there aren't many legitimate reasons for a seller and their item not to be located in the same place. On the View Item page it states the Item Location at the top of the page and in the Meet the Seller section too you'll see which country the seller is registered in: these should match. If the Item Location is stated as something like 'We despatch all over the world' or 'Straight to your door', avoid.

The location of the seller is also recorded on the Member Profile page on the righthand side. Check that this is the same as on the View Item page by clicking on the seller's feedback number by their User ID.

Fraudsters can be found all over the world, but on eBay be especially careful and secure when sending payments to Indonesia, the Ukraine or Romania, where criminal gangs are active.

- **Postage costs** Inflated postage costs are often a sign of a dodgy seller, so make sure you take a close look at the carriage costs. Sometimes, of course, profiting from postage is the aim of pricy postage. But sometimes it can reveal that a seller isn't being honest about their location. People may tell eBay that the items for sale are in the UK when in reality their stock is located elsewhere, often in the Far East. If postage seems very expensive, don't bid.

- **The price** Lots of sellers will happily start off an auction listing at a penny. It gets them lots of interest and usually the bidding carries the price up to a realistic level. But if you see a Buy It Now listing at a surprisingly low price, especially a price substantially lower than other similar items on eBay, then it's a good bet that this is a dodgy item. If it seems too good to be true, it probably is.

• **The seller invites you off eBay** If a listing says 'Contact me to buy this item' or 'Don't bid, call me', then avoid it like the plague. Not only is this against eBay's rules, it's an invitation to get ripped off. If a seller wants to defraud you then it's easier for them to do that if they get you off eBay and turn the sale into a private transaction. There's no recourse to eBay, no eBay feedback and no PayPal Protection if you take a transaction off eBay. So don't fall for it.

• **Payment methods** Fraudsters don't want you to be able to track them down. They don't want a paper trail and they don't want you to be able to get your money back. That's why they might ask you to pay with cash (sometimes coming up with a strange reason for them only being able to accept your finest folding) or an insecure service like Western Union that is untracked. In general, too, they don't really want you to use PayPal. So those alarm bells should be ringing if a seller wants cash or an international money transfer and definitely doesn't want you to pay with PayPal.

• **Dodgy English** I'm certainly not saying that all scammers on eBay are foreign or indeed that the Brits are universally squeaky clean, but it often seems to me that a great deal of the eBay fraud suffered by UK buyers is perpetrated by sellers from overseas. One way you can spot such a listing, even if the location says the seller resides in the UK, is from the quality of writing in the description.

The native language of many scammers is not English; indeed they may not speak English at all. So to compile their listings they have to use a computer translation program. While these are great, they are by no means 100% accurate. In fact they can be humorously wrong. I once saw a listing for a car that told buyers to 'Twist my gas helmet hemisphere' – I kid you not.

If you see very flowery but basically wrong language that doesn't make much sense, it's likely that it's automatically translated. If you're already suspicious, bidding should be a no-no, especially if the seller claims to be in the UK.

• **The seller is in a rush** eBay does have all manner of mechanisms and safety checks that go on in the background but sometimes they can take a while to kick in; after all, checking the many millions of items that get listed every week is a huge job. One way the fraudsters will attempt to get round this is to try to get a transaction over and done with as quickly as possible. Take particular care when you buy items with an auction duration of only 1 day.

• **Strange requirements** Do they want you to send the cheque to their friend in Nigeria? Do they require you to meet them in person to hand over the goods? Are they cagey about details when you communicate with them? If a seller asks you to do anything odd, that doesn't inspire confidence.

• **No photo** There really isn't much of an excuse for a seller not to include a picture on their listing. Mobile phones with cameras are widespread and digital cameras are much more readily available than they used to be. If a listing hasn't got a picture or only has stock catalogue pictures that could have been plucked from a manufacturer's website (especially if the item is something expensive), that's not a good sign.

• **Breaking the rules** If a seller is breaking eBay's rules in their listings it's not unfair to assume that they might be lax in fulfilling their obligations to you. So if you see a seller who has miscategorised an item to get more attention, puts irrelevant keywords in the title, is soliciting cash or a Western Union transfer or is breaking other eBay rules, then it's probably best not to do business with them.

Inside Information
Buying from China

The emergence of China on to the online stage has happened quickly and forced internet companies to change their world view. There are now more than 100 million Chinese people using the web (and that's growing all the time) and big online businesses want their share of the action. eBay's interest has meant that Chinese sellers (as well as those from other Asian countries) are often offered up in search and browse results on the site as potential vendors.

In many ways eBay and China are a perfect fit. China is emerging as an entrepreneurial society producing dizzying amounts of consumer products for foreign markets and you probably want a bargain. Buying from China can be a good way of saving money, there's no doubt about that. But I've also heard a disturbing number of horror stories from buyers. So much so that it's fair to say that buying from China probably represents a greater risk than buying from sellers in the UK.

You may think I'm being a bit hard on the Chinese. But the stories I've heard speak for themselves.

You probably won't buy from China accidentally: eBay makes it very obvious where sellers reside and you should always check. But if you are buying from China, you're wise to exercise extra caution.

- **What are you buying?** *Whenever you're buying you need to know what you're bidding on, so make sure you read the description carefully. Examine the pictures closely. Is the offer real and plausible?*
- **Feedback** *As ever, feedback is your friend. When assessing a seller's feedback you should be interested in only one thing: has this seller got a proven track record of sending goods like the one you want to buy to Britain without complaint?*
- **Payments** *As with any international trades, for safety reasons, you should only entertain paying via PayPal. If the seller doesn't offer it, or prefers a different method, walk away.*
- **Postage** *The cost of carriage is often the clue you need to ascertain that all is not well. Look for a very small price combined with a huge postage charge. Obviously postage from China is going to be greater than domestic or European costs, but look out for costs that are artificially inflated. And while it's not just Chinese sellers that profit this way, it does seem particularly prevalent there.*
- **Remember your duty** *Whenever you're buying something from outside the European Union, you become liable for customs duties. It's the buyer's responsibility to pay these, so bear them in mind when you're bidding for a bargain. Trading with China is more sensitive than trading with Australia, say, because of the scale of the imports coming in and the sometimes fraught relationship that the EU has with China. Anecdotally it would seem that items coming from China get more than average attention from Her Majesty's Revenue and Customs. And some of the duties I've heard about have been eye-wateringly enormous...*
- **Fakes and counterfeits** *One of the reasons that trade relations with China are somewhat fractious is the country's attitude to intellectual property: the Chinese don't look as dimly on fakes, pirates and counterfeits as some in the west would hope. It's a reasonable bet that a branded item coming from China at a bargain price will be a fake.*

Pay safely

Paying safely on eBay is the key to trading safely. The safest way to pay is by using PayPal because of the PayPal Protection it has in place. Essentially, PayPal guarantees your money when you buy from eligible sellers. However, not all sellers use PayPal and you should be aware of the potential dangers represented by other payment methods.

You want your payment to be secure and trackable so that you can follow up if a seller disputes receiving it, or get your money back if the item doesn't arrive.

Never pay by cash or an instant money transfer service such as Western Union or MoneyGram. It is against eBay's rules for a seller to offer these as payment methods, because they are untrackable and it is virtually impossible to get your money back if you need to. You will have no recourse if you pay a seller using these payment methods. Not only will you not be protected by the PayPal Protection Programme, but the Metropolitan Police have indicated that they won't investigate fraud cases where instant money transfer services have been used.

Cheques are reasonably safe to send as payment within the UK because they are trackable and banks are required to keep records. In the unlikely event of a problem you will be able to follow up with your bank, and you can also cancel a cheque if you encounter a problem with a transaction before it clears.

9

Find Help on eBay

You'll remember that the idea of getting to know eBay as a buyer was to help you when you become a seller. Getting the hang of using eBay's own help systems before you start selling is also a very good idea. This way, when you need to find something out in a hurry later, you'll be able to keep your swearing to a minimum.

Buying and selling on eBay is a different experience every time you do it. You might have sold a dozen CDs, but you might never have sent one to South Africa. Most problems are easily solved, but for those that aren't you'll need to find help. eBay knows this and provides a help system to support traders. If you get stuck you can contact the Customer Support team. For specialist advice on eBay you can also get in touch with the experts: the eBay community. After all, the chances are that someone has faced the same problem before.

Inside Information
eBay Customer Support

eBay doesn't have a very good reputation in providing customer support. Ask most eBayers and they will tell you that it's often difficult to get the answer you want quickly and the response you will receive will be a stock reply.

To be honest, you're best off trying to get your own answers and to do that you should get to know eBay's Help section. Other eBayers are also a great source of expertise: asking your question on the Discussion Boards is often your best hope.

Don't forget off-eBay sources. I often search Google for information relevant to eBay because it has a better search facility than eBay Help.

The Help section

On the Navigation Bar at the top of nearly every eBay page you can see a link to 'Help'. This gives you access to eBay's dedicated Help pages. There are hundreds and hundreds of pages containing information and advice on all aspects of trading on the site.

Whether you want to know about selling pet food, advice on setting a safe password or information about payment methods, you'll find it here.

How do you find the information you need?

There are three ways of finding the information you need. You can browse for the information by clicking on the topic you want on the Help front page. If you wanted information about selling, you would click on the selling link and be offered a further list of subtopics. You can keep clicking on the links until you get the page you want. You can also search the Help section to find the information you need in the same way you would search eBay for an item you wanted to buy.

Simply enter a search term relevant to the information you want and click 'Search'. So if you want details about eBay fees you would search for 'fees'. Any relevant Help pages that exist will be listed and you can browse them for the information you want. You can also browse the Help pages by using the A-Z list on the left-hand side.

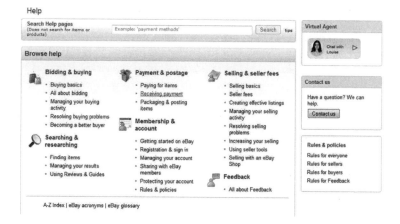

What if you can't find the information you want?

With so much information available and so many questions you might want answered, it is possible that you won't be able to find the answer or that it might not even be included in the Help pages. If you can't find the information you require you will need to contact Customer Support or try out the Community Help Boards.

How to contact eBay Customer Support

You can contact Customer Support in two ways. First, if you are on an eBay Help page and you can't find the answer you want on that page, there will be a link at the bottom to 'Ask a question'. You will be required to sign in and type your query into a text box. Your enquiry is then sent to Customer Support. Typically you receive an email back within 24 to 48 hours.

You can also contact Customer Support via the webform, which can be accessed from the lefthand side of the Help pages. Simply click on 'Contact Us'. On the webform you have to choose the topic of your query from the list available and then fill in the details and send it to Customer Support.

What should you include in your query?

It is very important that you give the Customer Support representative as much information as possible to help them to provide a relevant and full answer. Obviously include your User ID and if appropriate the User ID of the person you are trading with. It is

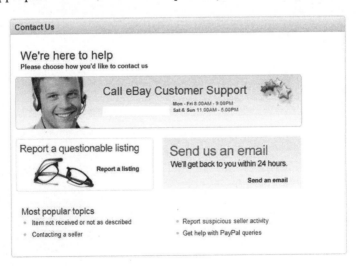

always handy to add the item number if your query relates to a specific transaction. Basically include all the important information relating to the transaction.

Keep your query brief and factual and try to be clear about what you are asking. You might feel angry or upset about a transaction that has gone wrong, but it won't be very useful if you write a long tirade. Just stick to the facts and your chances of getting a swift, correct answer will be higher.

Tip: Use Google

If you want to find help in relation to eBay, you might find it easier to use Google. Start your search 'eBay UK Help' followed by what you want to find out about.

Report violations

If you find an item that is against eBay's rules or you need to report a dodgy buyer or seller, you can also do it via the relevant Help page or the webform.

The most effective way of keeping the eBay marketplace safe and pleasant is to report infringing items and sellers when you spot them. eBay will take action if it receives a report.

Community help

As discussed before, its community is a unique feature that distinguishes eBay from other online companies like Amazon or traditional old-style organisations. The eBay community comprises all the buyers and sellers who use the site. eBay provides Discussion Boards so that community members can discuss their trading, meet friends and enjoy themselves. All registered members can use the Discussion Boards and they offer a unique opportunity to get help from other buyers and sellers.

- **Aren't chat boards just for weirdos?** Some chat boards do have a bad reputation, but the ones on eBay are unusually diverse and friendly. The people who use them are just normal buyers and sellers who enjoy the community atmosphere and being sociable with other people. eBay members become very passionate about their trading and like to talk about their successes and frustrations. eBay offers a common, shared experience, but the boards are not just restricted to eBay-related chat.

• **What are the benefits of using the Discussion Boards?** Sometimes the best person to get help from is someone who understands exactly what you are experiencing. You can find these people on the Discussion Boards. eBay can give general advice about communicating with a seller or filing an alert for a buyer who hasn't coughed up. But if you want firsthand experience from other sellers and buyers, the best people to ask are those who might have faced the same issue before. Other eBay members can give you personal insights and candid responses.

Many eBay members take a real pride in offering help to less experienced traders. They are very keen to give quick and factual replies about all aspects of eBay trading as well as tips and hints. Think of the Discussion Boards as the place to get insider knowledge.

Where are the Discussion Boards? You can find the Discussion Boards by clicking 'Community' on the Navigation Bar and following the link to the Discussion Boards. There are numerous discussion boards for all sorts of trading topics. The discussion boards are an ideal place for new members and experienced traders alike to find answers and advice about all things eBay.

Answer Centre

If the community help boards are too scary for you, try the Answer Centre, which is a more structured and ordered way of getting help from other members. You can get to the Answer Centre by clicking on 'Community' in the Navigation Bar and taking the 'Answer Centre' link halfway down the page.

In the Answer Centre you'll see a selection of topics related to eBay buying and selling. Pick the most appropriate for you and check out the questions asked and the answers given. If your question isn't addressed then just ask it yourself and wait for the answers from other members. You usually find that you get your answer pretty quickly from an expert member.

Announcement Board

One important way in which eBay communicates with the buyers and sellers who use the site is via the Announcement Board. Think of this as eBay's official noticeboard for members. If there is a change in a policy or an enhancement to the website on its way, eBay announces it on the Announcement Board. Also, if there has been a problem with the website eBay will often note it here and inform members of any refunds that are due. The Announcement Board on eBay.co.uk publishes information specific to UK traders.

You should try to keep an eye on the Announcement Board. It is regularly updated and the more you use eBay the more invaluable the information will become. You can also see a digest of recent announcements on the Summary page of My eBay.

The System Status Board should be your first stop if there is an issue or problem with the site. Inevitably with a website the size of eBay, with so many different functions and features, there are sometimes problems. If there is an outage or problem eBay will record it on the System Status Board.

You can access the Announcement Board and System Status Board by clicking on the Community link in the Navigation Bar.

Find help on PayPal

Just like eBay, PayPal has a comprehensive Help section for you to refer to if you get stuck. You can access it by going to the PayPal homepage: www.paypal.co.uk.

In the top right corner you will see a text link, 'Help'. Click on it and you will be taken to the Help Centre.

You have three ways to find the information you want. PayPal lists the questions most people ask on this page, so the chances are that a simple query might be addressed there. If it isn't, check out the categories on the lefthand side and navigate down to the topic you want. You can also search PayPal's Help resources using the Search Box on this page in the same way you would search eBay's Help.

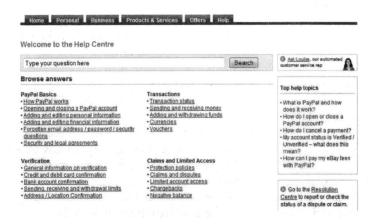

How to contact PayPal Customer Support

You can contact PayPal's Customer Support team via this page by clicking the 'Contact Us' link on the lefthand side at the bottom of the list of categories. You can also contact PayPal via email or by telephone during business hours at the national rate.

Tip: Tamebay

One of the best eBay-related help forums is a blog called Tamebay.com, run by an eBay PowerSeller called Chris Dawson. He really is a fount of all eBay knowledge and is always happy to help. Stop by at Tamebay to get all the latest news and tips.

PART II

SELL YOUR FIRST ITEM

10
It's Time to Start Selling

Once you are a competent buyer on eBay, with a clutch of positive feedbacks beside your User ID, you will want to start selling. Selling on eBay can be a great way to make money and many sellers say that once they have sold their first item they become addicted to the thrill of watching the bids on their listings mount up. Many people are surprised by the sums their items achieve compared to what they might have reached in the local paper or at a car boot sale. There are so many buyers on eBay that there is a much better chance of finding people who will pay a good price to get their hands on the junk gathering dust in your attic.

Embarking on anything new can be nerve-wracking and selling your first item on eBay can feel like a daunting experience. But don't be worried: selling on eBay is a straightforward and easy process.

This chapter will show you how to register as a seller and list your first item on eBay using the traditional auction-style bidding format.

Inside Information
My most memorable sale

The most memorable sale I ever made on eBay wasn't the most lucrative. In fact it was a 78 rpm record that I got just about a fiver for. But the reasons the buyer bought it and the delight he so evidently took from finally getting his hands on the disc make it stand out in my mind.

I'd bought a box of 78s on eBay for a quid with the express purpose of splitting the lot and selling them individually. There were more than a hundred of them and I'd got them for a steal because the lady who was selling them hadn't put much effort into the listing. She didn't live far away and when I went to collect them and had a quick look through the box I was certain there were some gems in there.

One record in particular looked interesting. It had a yellow HMV label on it and was marked 'Private Recording'. I listed it along with the others and fully expected it to make a bundle. It didn't, but some of the others got really excellent prices and I made a huge return on my £1 investment.

The guy who bought the one with the yellow label got in touch quickly and was very keen to come and collect the record in person. He lived nearby and I agreed that he could stop by and pick it up that same day. When he arrived he was visibly thrilled to finally find the record he had been seeking for decades. The pianist on it was his grandfather and to his knowledge there were only two other copies in the world. One was in a university archive in the US. The other was in the British National Sound Archives, and was broken. He now had the third, thanks to me and eBay. It makes me smile every time I think of the story.

Prepare to sell

As the old saying goes, 'Failing to prepare is preparing to fail'. On eBay this couldn't be more true. If you sit down to sell your first item in a spare five minutes without any preparation, the chances are that you won't do it justice and you won't sell it successfully. By taking the time to create your first listing you will not only have one successful sale under your belt, you will also have the knowledge to create successful listings again and again.

- **Choose the item you want to sell** For your first sale don't be too ambitious. Consider it a learning experience that will act as a springboard for your later sales. You may be longing to sell your late Uncle Monty's Victorian grandfather clock or desperate to get rid of those ultra-valuable Ming vases, but try to be patient. Make it easy for yourself and sell something that is simple to list and send. Starting with CDs, DVDs, videos, books and collectables is a good way to ease yourself into eBay selling. Once you have a few successful sales behind you, you will be better placed to make a real success of the big-ticket items.

- **Use your experience as a buyer** Take advantage of the wealth of eBay experience you already have to help you as you start out as a seller. You know what attracted you to the items you bought and what inspired you to trust the sellers you bought from. Perhaps it was their detailed description, the clear photographs or the reasonable postage costs laid out in advance. If you were attracted by certain qualities in a listing then other people will be too. If you think like a buyer when you are selling, you can't go far wrong.

• **Emulate the experts** The resources you have at your disposal as you embark on becoming a seller include other established sellers. Tap into their experience and use it to your advantage. Find a seller you like or admire who is selling the sort of things you want to sell and emulate their style. Ask yourself what they are doing right and why their listings are successful. Use their listings as a model for your own. But be warned that copying descriptions and pictures directly from other listings isn't looked on kindly by other sellers or by eBay.

• **Persevere** If at first you don't succeed, try again. Don't be disheartened if your first item doesn't sell. There can be all sorts of reasons why an item doesn't find a buyer, and it's not always your fault. Look on your first listing as a chance to experiment and gain vital experience. And remember that if the item doesn't sell the first time, eBay gives you a second chance by offering a free relisting. If it sells the second time, eBay will credit one lot of listing fees.

Create a Seller's Account

Before you can list your first item you need to create a Seller's Account. You fill in an online form and provide information that verifies you are who you say you are. eBay requires sellers to provide additional verification in order to maintain the website as a safe trading environment. It will keep your information entirely secure, so there is no need to worry about submitting your personal details.

When you sit down to create your Seller's Account make sure you have the following close to hand:

• **A credit or debit card** You can choose to use a Visa or MasterCard credit card or a Maestro debit card.

• **A statement that corresponds to the debit or credit card** You need to enter the postal address relating to the credit or debit card you use. It's best to have the bill to hand so you can enter the information accurately. If the address you enter doesn't match the one on the bill, eBay will reject your attempts to register a Seller's Account.

Tips: Using another card
> If you don't have a credit or debit card of your own you can use someone else's card as long as you have their permission. Remember, the card will not be charged to pay your eBay fees unless you choose.

You may have already provided credit or debit card information when you registered if you used an anonymous email address. It might seem odd that you need to provide your card details again, but it is necessary.

Primarily, the information provided here is for verification purposes. At the end of the online form you have to choose whether you will use your credit card details for your payments or establish a direct debit instead. There is no fee for setting up a Seller's Account.

Seller Registration
Once you have all the details to hand you can get started with Seller Registration. Click 'Sell' in the Navigation Bar on the eBay.co.uk homepage and on the Sell Hub you need to click 'Sell My Item' and sign in again.

Verify your address
The first step is to verify the information that eBay already holds about you. Make sure that eBay has a valid contact address and telephone number for you.

Once you have double-checked that the details are correct, click 'Continue' at the bottom of the page to go to the next page. If any of the details on the page are incomplete, you will be prompted to correct them before you can continue.

Provide credit or debit card information
As mentioned, you now have to provide details of a credit or debit card. All the information eBay requires can be found on the card

you are using. Some of the boxes on the form are marked 'if available', so if they are not applicable to your card type you don't need to fill them in.

You also need to provide the address associated with the card you are using. Take care when entering the address and the other information, because if the details are incorrect eBay will refuse your attempt to create a Seller's Account, as discussed above.

If you are entering credit card details you also need to provide your Card Verification Code. You can find this printed on the signature strip on the reverse of your card. You only need to enter the last three digits. Once you have entered all your details, click the 'Continue' button.

Choose how to pay your eBay fees

Many people find this part the most confusing. You are required to choose a payment method for your eBay selling fees using the information you have provided. If you want to pay using the credit card you have just entered, you can simply choose that option and your card will be automatically charged on a monthly basis as fees accrue. There is more on fees later in the book.

If you would prefer to pay using a monthly direct debit you can select this option. The bank account you provided eBay with will be debited monthly if you complete the online direct debit mandate. Most sellers pay their eBay fees via PayPal and you can set that up later in My eBay.

> **Fact**: *There is no subscription fee to sell on eBay, unless you open an eBay Shop. The only fees you pay are the ones you accrue when selling.*

If you have any difficulties registering you have two options. First of all, try again and ensure that you have filled in all the details correctly. If you are still having difficulties you are best advised to contact eBay's Customer Support team.

11

Prepare Your Listing

There are five key elements to a listing and you should have them all prepared before you even log on to eBay's Sell Your Item form:

- Category
- Item title and description
- Pictures
- Pricing
- Payment and postage details

When you list something on eBay you enter your details into the online Sell Your Item form. Basically you have to enter all the relevant information you want in your listing so that eBay can build the page for you. If you have prepared all the information you need in advance, you will be able to fill in the Sell Your Item form quickly and easily.

Inside Information
The level playing field

> You can compete with big corporations on eBay because it is a level playing field. This means that whether you are a hobby seller listing one item a month or a multinational corporation shifting thousands of units a week, you are treated just the same.
>
> This is important because it preserves the vibrancy of the marketplace, making it a great place for people to buy and sell. If eBay became dominated by a small group of large retailers it would lose a lot of its charm. So if Big plc lists the same item as Mr Small Trader, they both pay the same fees and are subject to the same rules. And because they compete on a level playing field, their style of selling and how they treat customers count.

In many ways a small seller is more attractive to buyers because they know they can expect a more personal service and most likely a caring human to deal with. Small-scale traders can also be more flexible and nimble than outfits with dozens of employees. Smaller sellers can often provide greater satisfaction to their buyers and possibly be even more successful. On eBay, small is beautiful and the real-world factors that favour established companies are swept away.

Choose a category

As you will remember from your experiences as a buyer, the items for sale on eBay are organised under relevant headings in a category structure rather like in a library. For instance, if you were looking on eBay for a first-edition copy of *The Old Devils* by Kingsley Amis, you would go to the Books category, click on Fiction and browse under First Editions.

There are thousands of categories on eBay.co.uk and this is a mixed blessing. On the one hand it means you are certain to find one that is just right for the item you want to sell, but on the other it might take you a few moments to find it. Choosing the right category is very important because it helps buyers locate your item. If your item is not in the best category, buyers won't be able to find it and you might lose out on a sale.

There are two ways to find the best category for the item you want to sell. The first is to browse the full list of categories. You can do this by clicking on 'Buy' in the Navigation Bar and pretending you are a buyer looking for your item. The second option is to search for an item similar to the one you want to sell and see where other sellers are listing. You can do this via eBay's search engine by using the Search box found at the top right of most eBay pages.

For many items you list, the choice of a category will be very straightforward. If you are listing a calculator the obvious place will be in Consumer Electronics > Gadgets > Calculators. It's not rocket science, but it will take a bit of time for you to get used to the massive choice. Some of your choices will require good judgement. A set of Queen Mum stamps are attractive to royal collectors and also philatelists, which will require a choice. Which category will give you most viewers? That's the thing to decide.

On the Sell Your Item form, if you give eBay an idea of what you're selling you'll get suggested categories for you based on other items listed on the site.

Tip: Sell Your Item form

The eBay form for selling an item is daunting, long-winded and confusing. Lots of people drop out at this point in the process. Just by persisting with the form you are getting yourself ahead of the crowd. But if you really can't face it, eBay has produced a basic version of the form. Just choose the 'Quick Sell' option on the first page of the Sell Your Item form. Don't forget though, this option isn't valid if you're selling a vehicle.

Listing in two categories

You have the option to list your item in two categories if you like. But if you choose to do this, don't forget that your listing fees will be doubled (although not the Final Value Fees). It's not a sure-fire way to success, so think hard about doing this – those extra fees add up. It's better to choose a really good first category and hone your title so buyers find you in Search before you pony up extra Listing Fees.

Create an Item Title

Your Item Title and Description are where you get the opportunity to show off the item you are selling and persuade buyers that it is something they want to buy.

The Item Title is the name of the item you are selling and what buyers see first when they are searching or browsing. You need to ensure that your Item Title is as descriptive and eye-catching as possible so that buyers will be interested enough to look more closely at your item. You only have limited space for your Item Title and to make effective use of the space you need to be inventive and precise.

If you were selling a Harry Potter book, you could just have a title that read 'Harry Potter Book'. But that wouldn't stand out from the thousands of other Harry Potter books for sale. In order to give yourself an edge, you need to think about what makes your item special and then distil the most important details into the short space. Which Harry Potter book is it? Which edition? Is it a hardback or a paperback? What kind of condition is the book in?

If you had a rare, first-edition, signed copy of *Harry Potter and the Chamber of Secrets* in mint condition, the Item Title could read 'Harry Potter Chamber of Secrets 1st Ed Signed'.

Whatever you're selling, the Item Title should consist of words a buyer is likely to search for. Avoid meaningless or vague terms like 'old', 'good', 'nice' or 'interesting', because they are not words people normally use when searching eBay. Stick to factual words that describe the item precisely, such as the brand, its size or type. If it is of an era or style such as Georgian or Art Deco or Retro, include this term as many people will use it to search.

The title is what eBay's search engine will use to make your item available to buyers, so think about how you search for items on eBay and employ that experience to make your item as findable as possible. If a buyer is interested in your Item Title, they will click on it to find out more.

Write a description

Even if you are including photos in your listing, it is vital to compose an Item Description that tells buyers as much about the item as possible. Give as many details as you can about the item and its condition. Again, put yourself in a buyer's shoes and imagine what you would want to know if you were considering placing a bid.

Talk the item up. Leave the buyer in no doubt that this is the item they want and give them reasons to place a bid. Be creative and don't be afraid to be personal. If the item is unusual or rare, explain how you got hold of it. Go into as much detail as you can. People like eBay because they are buying from other individuals and not giant, faceless corporations. Show that you are caring, individual and keen to be as helpful as possible. Taking the time to compile your description is an important way of building trust.

It is essential that your description is full and honest. Don't just include all the plus points; if there is damage or something that affects the quality of the item, mention that too. Failure to disclose something now could result in negative feedback later.

Imagine you have a rare Doctor Who video for sale. A hastily assembled description would read: 'Dr Who Video "Shada". Rare, in almost perfect condition.'

This Item Description would suffice, but a few extra moments honing the description could reap bigger rewards: 'Dr Who video "Shada" BBCV 4814. This classic Tom Baker adventure, also starring Lalla Ward as Romana II, was written by Douglas Adams and is set in Cambridge. Never originally completed for broadcast in 1978 due to BBC strikes, the fragments that do exist have been linked by superb and often bizarre commentary from Baker. This adventure is now considered a classic by Who fans and the 1992 video is highly sought after. The item is in almost perfect condition with a small scuff on the spine of the video and comes complete with the script book as originally released. The video is in the PAL format and is not compatible with American (NTSC) video machines. An absolute must to complete any Whovian's video collection.'

Although you have the option to give further details later, it is wise to include some information in the Item Description about payment and postage. Explain briefly what payment methods you are willing to accept and what the postage costs will be.

- **Preparation** Write your title and description in Microsoft Word (or any wordprocessing software) in advance. This means that when it comes to logging on to the Sell Your Item form you can just copy and paste what you have already written into the right boxes.

- **Know your item** If you don't know much about your item, eBay itself is a good source of information. Search the site for items like yours. Don't forget that there are countless collector and expert websites that can fill in your gaps in knowledge. Use a search engine such as Google to find out more about the item you are selling.

- **Specialist terms** Be careful about misusing specialist terms. Books, records and stamps in particular have a whole host of specialist terms that dealers use to describe items. If you misuse a term and misdescribe the item, you will have an irate buyer on your hands.

- **Keep it basic** Some sellers like to customise their Item Description so it is bright and colourful. Some even include animation and fancy effects. Not only do effects irritate some buyers, they can also take a long time to load if the buyer has a slow connection. It is best to keep your description clear and basic so it is easy for buyers to understand. Don't forget that you don't need to use HTML (web page markup language) to format your description; eBay will do all the formatting for you on the Sell Your Item form.

- **Returns and refunds** It isn't obligatory to have a policy on refunds and returns (unless you are a professional seller).

Some buyers like the peace of mind of buying from a seller who will refund if the buyer is not satisfied with the item when they receive it. It's a good way of building trust; as long as you are honest in your description you will probably never need to apply your policy. Take a look around the site for examples of what other sellers offer.

Tip: Bullet points

Many sellers organise their Item Descriptions by using bullet points because buyers find this an easy way to absorb a lot of information quickly.

Inside Information
Market intelligence for sellers

When you are selling anything, whether on eBay or not, there is a bit of science as well as art to the process. Supermarkets, for instance, spend millions of pounds every year researching the best places to position their wares in store, what goes in which aisle and how much people will pay for certain items. You will need to do a bit of research too to maximise your sales, but you won't have to shell out for it because most of this information is free.

Checking out other sellers and how they sell is perfectly allowable as long as you don't steal their pictures and descriptions. Don't forget that you can search items that have sold successfully to check final prices. Click the 'Completed Items' box in Advanced Search.

eBay Pulse may be an interesting guide for buyers but it is also a vital information source for sellers. You can use it to check whether you are using the most appropriate keywords in your titles based on what people are actually searching for on the site.

One seller I know has been selling bed linen for a while and making a good living, shifting a lot of stock. Obviously, he lists most of his items in the same categories, so he was intrigued to check out Pulse and see what the most popular search terms were in his categories. He discovered that he wasn't including the most popular relevant keyword in his titles and when he added it his sales rocketed. You should do the same to make sure you aren't missing out on a key search term.

Create good photographs

Including pictures in your listing is vital. If you want to get the best possible price, you have to encourage bidders that yours is the item they want and that you are a seller they can trust. One way of really putting a buyer's mind at rest and assuring them that they want your item is to provide a picture.

Inside Information
Bad pictures and hilarious mistakes

Bad pictures can be found all over eBay. Considering how easy it is to create a useful picture and how important a good picture is to buyers, it's astonishing how many really awful pictures you see. I can't claim to be Lord Lichfield, but I always take the time to create a picture that will clinch the deal when I have an item for sale.

Why don't other sellers do the same? I honestly don't know. Maybe they are too busy listing dozens of items. Maybe they just don't understand the power of a good photo. What I do know is that a minute spent creating the perfect image can reap the rewards of more bids and a better price.

When you are taking your picture, however, be careful that you aren't giving away too much: remember the very famous example of the man and the kettle. It was a handsome kettle made of metal and burnished to a gleaming sheen; so shiny was it that in the picture the seller was reflected in the surface of the kettle as if it were a mirror. This would only have been a minor distraction, of course, had the photographer been wearing any clothes when snapping his item ready for sale on eBay. If he hadn't been naked the picture wouldn't have been passed around the internet and seen by millions of people. It's a cautionary tale: make sure you check your pictures for unintentional details.

Needless to say, some people have seen the humorous accidental picture phenomenon and taken it to its illogical conclusion. When someone takes a picture that deliberately includes a reflection of themselves in the nude it's called Reflectoporn. It's difficult to know whether to laugh or cry. I imagine that some people do it for the thrill; others have no idea that their mistake is amusing millions of people. But you do see it sometimes, so keep an eye out.

Why photos are important

Remember that buyers on eBay don't get the opportunity to handle or examine the item they purchase until they receive it in the post, so by providing a picture you are giving them the opportunity to see the item online before they bid. eBay sellers are agreed: pictures encourage buyers to bid with more confidence. If you don't have a picture in your listing you are limiting your chances of a successful sale.

There are a number of ways in which you can capture a digital image to use in your listing. You could use a digital camera or scanner and nowadays you can get hold of one relatively cheaply. Many computer packages come complete with a scanner. If you don't have a digital camera or scanner, try to borrow one if you can because a picture will enhance your listing dramatically. If you only have a conventional film camera you could use that. Many film-developing companies offer a service that means you can get your prints as usual but also receive a set of digital images on CD, which you can then use on eBay.

With such an enormous selection of cameras and scanners on the market it would be impossible here to provide precise guidance on how to produce images with your particular apparatus.

For the purposes of selling on eBay all you need is an image saved on to your computer and ready to upload to the website. For detailed instructions on how to capture images using your digital camera or scanner, consult the manufacturer's manual. To use eBay's Picture Service to host your images you need to save the image in JPEG (.jpg) format.

Perfect your image

Simply including a picture isn't enough. Your picture needs to provide the buyer with information that will be useful.

- **Show your item off** Ensure that the image you produce is sharp and in focus; blurred photos don't impress. Consider what the buyer wants to see. If you are selling a book, for instance, is the front cover what a buyer wants to see or would a shot of the inside of the book be more useful? Will a buyer appreciate a close-up image of the markings or serial number if your item has one? Record collectors often value a close-up of the label on the record itself rather than merely the sleeve. If you are selling an item in its original box, then removing the item is usually best (unless of course it means that the item is worthless because it has been opened), rather than offering a view of a cardboard box.

Photograph your item from the most appropriate aspect, remembering that the obvious picture may not be the most useful. Good lighting can also make a world of difference.

• **Compose a useful image** The setting and background of the image are also important. Avoid photographing your item in a way that distracts from the item or causes confusion. Photograph your item against a blank background, perhaps by using a sheet or cloth. Make sure that your item is the central feature of the picture.

• **Consider using several pictures** If your item is of high value or there are different aspects you want to show, don't forget that you can use more than one image in your listing. You can include a number of pictures so you can show different angles and details as you wish.

• **Digital cameras** You don't need a top-of-the-range digital camera to produce the pictures you need for your listing. Perfectly adequate images can be created with a three or four mega (million) pixel camera. Even a clear, well-composed image taken using the camera in your mobile phone could do the trick.

Name your price

Setting the price you want for an item is a delicate balancing act. Obviously you have the kind of price you want in mind, but equally you don't want to price yourself out of the market.

• **Check the price of similar items** You can get a feel for the price that items similar to yours fetch by checking on eBay. You can search or browse as you would as a buyer to find similar items and keep an eye on them to see how they go. Another option is to do a search for completed items. This will show you the items that have recently ended and you will be able to check the price they sold for.

To search for completed items, click 'Advanced Search' in the Navigation Bar. You can then Search Completed Items in the usual way with keywords and the Completed Items option.

• **Set a realistic price** eBay is a very competitive market-place. There are other sellers out there who may well have a similar item for sale. If a buyer can get the same item cheaper elsewhere, they will. You should set a starting price that is the lowest amount you are willing to let your item go for. Be realistic about the price you set and remember that buyers often bid up an item if they want it badly.

Inside Information
Pricing

Why not price your item a little bit lower than comparable items on the site? You will get more attention and probably more bids. Think about it. If you have included all the right keywords in your Item Title and your listing is returned alongside identical ones, the price will often be the deciding factor when it comes to making a bid. I've found that if I start my items at a slightly lower price than the competition, then in the end I get a better price than them: buyers get carried away and bid more because they are determined to beat other bidders.

Some sellers like to take a gamble and start their item at 99p even if it is worth much more. Their confidence in the eBay system reassures them that the item will find its true eBay value. The low starting price means lower eBay listing fees, but there is a risk. If the bidding doesn't get going, you will have to let the item go for 99p if you only get one bid.

Always think about eBay's fees when you list an item. For instance, if you want to list your item with a starting price of £5 you should list it for £4.99 because the eBay Listing Fee will be 20p rather than 30p. Familiarise yourself with eBay's fees so you can minimise the price you pay to list your item. There's a section all about fees later in the book.

PayPal only categories
In some categories, PayPal is the only acceptable payment method. This is because these categories have a higher than usual fraud risk. The categories include:

- Computing > Software
- Consumer Electronics > MP3 Players
- Video Games > Consoles
- Wholesale & Job Lots > Mobile & Home Phones
- Business, Office & Industrial > Industrial Supply / MRO

Decide your payment and postage details

Including information about how buyers can pay you and how much it will cost to send the buyer the item is vital.

Payment methods

Often when people are new to eBay selling the first question they ask is 'How do I receive the money?' The simple answer is 'It's up to you.' On eBay you are free to determine the terms under which you sell your item and when it comes to payment options you can choose to receive payment in whatever form is convenient for you. Cheques and postal orders are easy to accept, but you can also opt for online services such as PayPal. For bulky items that need to be collected or if a buyer is close by and wants to come and pick up the item, you can accept cash on collection.

PayPal for sellers

As you will have discovered when you were buying on eBay, PayPal is an attractive way of sending payment because it is quick and easy. It is very handy for buyers because there is no cost to them and they don't have to write a cheque, buy a stamp and go to the postbox. As a seller you do incur a charge for accepting PayPal, but many sellers agree that the cost is worth it. Many take the PayPal fees into account when they list their item and incorporate them into the starting price or postage costs. Cashing cheques means a trip to the bank and waiting for clearance, which can take days. An immediate payment via PayPal means you can despatch the item straight away and turn around your sales much more quickly.

PayPal is also a very useful way of accepting payment from overseas. When you are selling on eBay it is worth thinking about whether you are happy to send your item abroad rather than restricting it only to British buyers. The obvious advantage of offering your item to overseas buyers is that there are many more potential buyers. eBay was founded in the USA and has millions of members there; and don't forget its growing communities in Europe and Asia. With PayPal your buyer can pay in their own currency using their credit or debit card and PayPal will take care of the currency conversion.

There are several other online payment methods that you can accept. None is as widely used as PayPal or offers the flexibility of international trading in the same way.

On the Sell Your Item form you can note the payment methods you are willing to accept. Offer as many as you can. The more options you provide, the more flexibility you are offering your buyers.

Postage costs

When you are selling on eBay it is essential to state the postage costs of your item up front. For many buyers the postage costs are the deciding factor: if your postage charges are too high you will put people off.

The more details you can provide for international buyers the better, but at the very least you should state the cost of posting the item within the UK.

Postage and packaging tips

To attract buyers you should keep your postal charges as low as possible. After all, if it is a toss-up between your item and a similar one from another seller, the cost of postage can be the deciding factor.

• **Keep postage costs low** Postage and packaging costs should be exactly that: the costs of protecting the item in transit and the price of the postage. eBay does allow sellers some leeway and lets you include some additional handling costs, although these shouldn't be excessive. High charges put buyers off.

• **Scales and rates** Within the UK, the Royal Mail and Parcelforce are usually the most convenient and cost-effective carriers. It is well worth familiarising yourself with the published rates at www.royalmail.com. Additionally, as most eBayers know, your local post office is able to advise you. Get to know the people there. If you are successful on eBay you will almost certainly be a frequent visitor.

Your other best friend will be your kitchen scales. Once you are armed with the Royal Mail rates you can weigh the items and make a good estimate of the postage costs. Buyers always like to know the price of postage and if you give accurate quotes you will seem like a professional and organised seller. The scales will also ensure that you do not underquote and lose money.

• **International shipping** For items up to 2kg (5kg for printed matter) that need to go overseas, the Royal Mail is also the most convenient carrier. On international shipments you can save your buyers money by making use of the different options available. Surface mail takes longer than air mail, but it is also much cheaper and many buyers are willing to wait if it means they can save money. Also, where appropriate, ensure that your items are sent using the small packet rate because this is cheaper than the letter rate. If you are selling books, comics or magazines you can make use of the preferential rates offered for printed matter.

• **Packaging** Don't forget to factor the packaging costs into your postage charges. It is vital to ensure that the item you send is packaged well and totally protected.

It pays to be inventive with packaging. Buyers don't necessarily want expensive packaging, and are happy to receive a parcel that looks amateurish with an intact purchase inside rather than a very smart package that hasn't protected the item at all.

Many sellers recycle old padded envelopes or boxes. Very strong 'envelopes' can be fashioned from cardboard boxes and brown tape. Consider reusing bubble wrap, packing peanuts or other items you receive your purchases in.

As long as the savings you are making are reflected in what the buyer pays, you won't receive any complaints. However, if you charge for new packaging and then recycle, you might have an irate buyer to deal with because they know you are pocketing the difference.

Tip: Postage

Shop around for the best deal on postage. In 2012 Royal Mail restructured its pricing and as a result you may well find better deals elsewhere.

Listing enhancements

When you are selling an item you want it to stand out from the many others for sale. A listing enhancement is a way to pay for your item to have a greater profile when a buyer is browsing or searching eBay. There are different enhancements available depending on the prominence you want to give the item and what you are willing to spend. The fees for listing enhancements are payable regardless of whether your item sells or not.

There are a few listing enhancements available to sellers.

• **Subtitle** If you want to add more information to your Item Title you can buy a subtitle for 35p. This means that your potential buyers get a bit more detail when they are searching or browsing.

Inside Information
You can't buy visibility

I'm a sceptic when it comes to buying visibility. If you have to, it means something else you're doing is wrong. It could be because your feedback and DSRs aren't up to scratch. In that case, don't spend more money, simply take steps to get better feedback.

Equally, if you haven't fully optimised your listing, it's money wasted again. If you could improve your titles, why spend to get more prominence before you have?

Features on eBay are predominantly there so eBay itself can make a bit more money. Use them sparingly, even experiment a little if you like, but few sellers will make them a central part of their selling strategy.

12

List Your Item

Tip

If you've already sold an item on eBay, you can skip this chapter. It deals with the basics of listing an item.

Preparing your listing before you even log on to eBay is the key to selling your item successfully. Only when you have sorted out a picture and a description and decided all the other important elements of your listing are you ready to list your item on eBay.

Inside Information
Timing your sales

There are no hard-and-fast rules on what will work best for your sales. Received wisdom has it that ending your listings on a Sunday evening is the best plan: lots of sellers start their listing on a Thursday evening so they get two weekends and end on a Sunday evening. But recently sellers I have spoken to seem to think that avoiding Sunday evening altogether is advisable, because so many items end then.

The traffic on the eBay site roughly follows the pattern of the internet in general. There is steady traffic during the day and from 6pm the volume increases dramatically, before tailing off from 10.30pm or so. Friday and Saturday evenings tend to be a bit quieter than other nights of the week.

It's easier to suggest what you should avoid. Try not to have your items ending on a Friday morning between 7am and 9am because this is when eBay tends to do its scheduled maintenance to the site. Although the site is generally operational, some sections of it are not available.

Also avoid clashes with major events, especially if they are related to the item you are selling. The last hour of your listing is when much of the bidding will take place, so make sure it's going to suit bidders. It would be a bit silly to end a listing for a Big Brother-*related item*

*while the eviction is on the television. Equally, if everyone in the
nation is glued to their screens watching a big game, your England
football shirt might not get the bids it deserves.*

*Don't forget international bidders. If your item is likely to be
attractive to buyers in America, you can adjust the timing so it
finishes later in the evening in the UK but in the early evening on the
other side of the Atlantic.*

*As you sell more you start to learn what works for you, so you can
experiment with timings. For instance, I have noticed on my own
sales that workday lunchtimes, especially on Monday, seem to be a
good time. I reckon there are thousands of bored office workers
chomping on their sandwiches and bidding on eBay to alleviate the
post-weekend blues and hoping for a bargain.*

The Sell Your Item form

To list your item on eBay and make it available for people to buy,
you need to enter all the content you have prepared into the Sell
Your Item form. This is a series of online pages that allows you to
build the View Item page that buyers see.

It isn't a difficult process, but it can be a little daunting for
beginners because you are required to answer questions and provide details that you might not have thought of. But don't be
nervous: lots of people list items on eBay and if they can do it, so
can you.

And don't forget, if you do get it wrong you can always go
back and edit your listing or even scrap it and start again.

• **Just take your time** When you are an experienced seller
listing an item only takes a few moments, probably less than
five minutes. But new sellers often say that their first listing
took half an hour or even longer. So don't worry if you feel
like you're making little progress or going very slowly;
everyone was slow the first time. As you become familiar with
the process it gets quicker and easier, so don't be afraid to
take a bit of time and really get a feel for how you list an item.
Have a relaxing cup of tea or glass of beer by your side to
keep you going.

• **How do I find the Sell Your Item form?** You can get to
the Sell Your Item form by clicking on 'Sell' in the Navigation

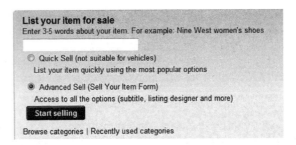

Bar. You need to sign in using your User ID and password. If you haven't registered a Seller's Account you will be prompted to set one up.

Select a category

You will be offered a Search Box and asked to enter relevant keywords related to your item such as 'Bob the Builder pencil case' or 'Prada purse'. eBay searches the site and tells you which categories similar items are listed in. eBay's results are presented to you as percentages. So if eBay makes a suggestion saying that close to 100% of items with matching keywords are found in a particular category, that's a good one to choose.

But don't be blinded by the numbers. If you think the category you have already selected after your research is better, go with it. If the results from eBay are inconclusive (three items with close to 30% each, say) you should rely on your previous research.

If you're sure about the category you want to use you can skip this search. Just click 'Browse for categories' and you'll be able to choose which category you want to use without eBay's help.

Once you have made your selection another list shows you the next level of categories. Keep on choosing and moving from box to box until there are no more options to take. This requires three or four clicks. Once you have made your choice, simply click 'Continue' to go to the next page.

If the category selector isn't visible on the screen this might be because your PC can't view certain types of computer code. You have the option to use the same function in a different format by clicking the link under the category selector.

Before you move to the next page, you can opt to list your item in two categories rather than just one by clicking the 'List your item in a second category' link. This might be a good way to attract more buyers, but don't forget it will double all your listing fees, so only choose this option if you think it's worth it.

Once you have chosen your category, you're ready to enter the majority of the information about the item into the Sell Your Item form. Most of it will already be prepared: item title, item description and a picture.

Create your listing: Enter your description

Describing your item will be a doddle because you have already written your title and item description and have it ready to paste into this page. Simply copy the title from a Word document and paste it into the title space. You can do the same with your description. Just copy and paste the description you prepared earlier into the appropriate space.

You can change the look of your Item Description text from within the Sell Your Item form using the formatting buttons at the top of the Item Description box. Highlight sections or the whole document and change the font, size or colour. You can also alter the alignment of the text and emphasise key details by making them bold, italic or underlined.

If you are a computer whizz and have prepared your description using HTML, you need to switch to the 'Enter your own HTML' tab. If you enter HTML in the normal description field it won't work.

If you want to see how your description will look when it's live on the site, click the 'Preview Description' link near the

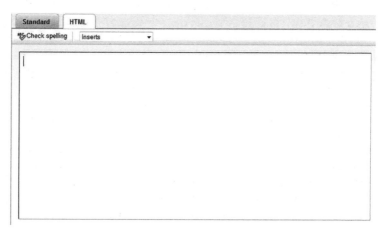

bottom of the page. You'll also have another opportunity to review the look of your listing on the next page.

You need to provide some further information. Some is compulsory (marked by a green star), some isn't, but make sure that you provide as much information as your buyers will require.

Bear two things in mind when you're filling in the Sell Your Item Form. First, your item isn't available to buyers until you submit the item to the site. You can change, amend and edit the listing as much as you like until it's gone live. Secondly, there is a wealth of information and help on the Sell Your Item form. If you need guidance or help, the Help pages are just a click away.

Tip: Green stars

This main page is the most confusing in the Sell Your Item form because there are so many things you can choose from. Remember that if something isn't marked with a green star you don't have to express a preference.

Add your pictures

If you haven't got a picture ready by the time you reach this stage of the Sell Your Item form, it's a bit late to get your digital camera out and take one. If you have one prepared, all you have to do is upload it to eBay.

The first time you upload a picture you need to install a small piece of software from eBay on your computer. This won't take a minute and you won't have to do it again. eBay guides you through the download step by step.

eBay offers all sorts of advanced picture options that can be useful. Its pictures appear in a standard format of 400×300 pixels, which is roughly the size of a cigarette packet on screen. For most items this is more than enough, but sometimes you might want to show your items in greater detail. What you choose depends on what you are selling and how you need to show it off, but for a big-ticket item investing a few extra pence can be well worth it.

If you like you have the option to host your photographs on your own web space. Hosting your own images can take a bit longer than letting eBay do it, but it can be worthwhile. eBay will host one image for free, so if you want more than one you can either pay for them or keep them on your website. eBay automatically crops and edits your pictures, but if you do your own they can be as big or as small as you like. Nevertheless, for a first-time seller eBay's picture service is more than adequate and by far the easiest option.

Other details you need to provide

On this page of the Sell Your Item form you also need to add vital details that will attract buyers and clinch the deal.

- **Price** First of all you have to select your Starting Price. This is the minimum price you are willing to sell your item for. From your general knowledge and research into similar items on eBay, you know what your item might sell for. You enter the Starting Price in the first field.

- **Choose a selling format** You need to choose between the traditional auction format, where buyers bid for your item, and the Buy It Now option, where people don't bid but simply buy your item at a price specified by you.

For your first sale, choose the auction format. This way you'll get a real feel for how eBay works. You can experiment with Buy It Now when you have found your eBay feet. In fact, if this is your first sale you probably won't be able to choose Buy It Now. To use it you need to have 5 or more unique feedbacks or have given eBay your direct debit details. If you're not qualified to use Buy It Now listings, eBay assumes that you want to sell using an auction and you won't have to take any action.

- **Duration** You are also required to select how long you want your listing to last for. You have a choice of 1, 3, 5, 7 or 10 days. How long your listing lasts for has no bearing on fees. You should choose whatever suits you best: 7 or 10 days are the most popular options, but if you are selling concert tickets or something else that is time sensitive a shorter duration might suit you better. It's generally advisable to avoid 1-day listings, because that's just too short a time to attract meaningful bids.

- **Quantity and location** You should also state where you and the items are. No messing about: eBay requires you to be 'factual'.

You can be boring and just say 'London' or 'Middlesbrough', depending where you are. But it can be worth being more specific, like 'Putney, London SW15'. Or you can interest buyers by including something more romantic and attractive like 'The Wild North East of England'. It's up to you, but do be truthful. Misrepresenting the location of your item is against the rules.

• **Post-to locations** Where you are willing to send your item to is up to you, but you should be aware that it also determines who can see your item and the number of potential buyers who can bid. If you choose 'Will Post Worldwide' your item will be available to all eBay members all over the world. If your item is only going to be attractive to UK buyers, or is too bulky to send overseas, then the 'Will Post to the United Kingdom Only' option will be best for you.

You can pick and choose your options here. If you want to ship to the United States and Canada as well as the UK, or just the UK and Asia, it's totally up to you.

• **Payment options** You're in the home strait by the time you have to specify your payment and postage preferences. You should accept PayPal as an absolute minimum and any other payment options that suit you. The Sell Your Item form automatically assumes that your PayPal-registered email address is the same as the one you have given to eBay. If it isn't, you should add your PayPal email address here. eBay will remember it for when you list in future.

If you are willing to accept a cheque or other payment that will be sent in the post, eBay assumes that you want it to be sent to your registered address and tells your buyers that address when the time comes. If you want it to be sent to a different address you need to enter that by clicking the 'Change' link under the 'Seller's Payment Address' heading.

It is best to provide a postage cost for UK-based buyers in the relevant field because it saves you time later. This can easily be calculated and means that a British buyer can make a PayPal payment immediately at the end of the listing if they wish. You can also indicate international postage costs if you like.

• **Payment instructions and returns policy** Even though you have specified how much UK postage is and the payment methods you are willing to accept, it is probable you need to include some extra details to assist your buyers. For instance, you might want to note that you expect payment within 14 days, that you prefer PayPal or that international bidders should contact you for further details about overseas postage costs.

If you are willing to accept returns or offer refunds, this space in the Sell Your Item form is the ideal place to provide your terms.

If you are a registered business seller trading on eBay, you must accept returns under the terms of the Distance Selling Regulations and other consumer law.

Tip: Make it easy to pay

By entering these details now you are making it easy for your buyer to pay at the end of the auction. When your listing ends successfully your buyer automatically receives an email from eBay with all the instructions they need to make their payment. If you don't enter payment details now, you have to email the buyer yourself at the end of the auction.

Promote and review your listing

Once you've provided your item's title, description and images and given information about price, postage and duration, you've finished the bulk of your work on the Sell Your Item form. The next page is where you choose any extras you want to add and have the opportunity to preview your listing. When you're happy you can send your listing live to eBay. You don't pay a bean until you confirm the listing.

Add the extras

The options highlighted so far are the most important. Some are compulsory while others are free and useful. Sometimes you might want to make use of the extras on offer on the Sell Your Item form. Most of them have an additional charge attached, but for the right item and seller they can mean better sales. You'll find these on the Create Your Listing page and the page that follows.

.co.uk

SELL YOUR ITEM   1. SELECT A CATEGORY   **2. CREATE YOUR LISTING**   3. REVIEW YOUR LISTING

Create your listing   🖫 Save for later   ⑦ Help

Categories where your listing will appear Get help

Category ⓐ
Collectables > Trading Cards/ CCG > TV Series > Doctor Who
Change category

Help buyers find your item with a great title Add or remove options | Get help

∗ Title ⓐ

Subtitle (£0.35) ⓐ

Type

Stickers: Options

Sub-Type

Accessories: Options

Genre/ Theme

Genre/ Theme Options

Condition ⓐ

Bring your item to life with pictures Add or remove options | Get help
The first picture is free. Each additional picture is £0.12. ⓐ
Add pictures   Your pictures: 0 | 12 can be added

First picture is
free
Click to add
pictures.

ⓘ Good news! Gallery Picture is free. Add a picture and we'll show your item to buyers in search results. ⓐ

∗ **Describe the item you're selling** Add or remove options | Get help
| Standard | HTML |

🔤 Check spelling | Inserts   ▾ |

Q Preview | Save draft

Listing Designer ⓐ (£0.07)
⬚ Add a theme

Select theme: | New (49)   ▾ |
Select design: | ▴ |
              | Animal Prints   ▤ |
              | Astrology Blue |
              | Baby-Clothes |
              | Baby-Infant   ▾ |
                                    Q Preview

- **Schedule your listing** If you want your item to start, and therefore end, at a particular time but can't be at your computer then, you can choose to schedule your listing. This means you can create the listing and send it to eBay immediately, but it won't be available to buyers on the site until a time you specify. The option to schedule a listing costs 12p and you can do so up to three weeks in advance.

- **Counters** Including a counter is free, so there's no reason not to have one. A counter shows you how many people have taken a look at your View Item page. This can be a great way of gauging interest and letting you know whether you are attracting people to your listing.

- **Listing designer** If you want to give your item a really professional and jazzy look, you can choose a Listing Designer template from the selection eBay has available. This is a graphical border that sets your Item Description off to a tee. Depending on what you are selling you can choose a theme or colour scheme to complement it. Adding a Listing Designer template costs you an additional 7p, so it can be well worth it if you are selling a high-priced item. Sci-fi fans should check out the 'SpaceCows' theme.

- **Private auction** Sometimes people prefer anonymity. If you hold a private auction no one can see the identities of the bidders. This can be particularly useful if you are selling something very, very unusual (which people might want to be secretive about owning) or something people might be embarrassed to be seen buying. Otherwise, don't use this option. It is free, but it can put off buyers who don't understand the reason for keeping identities hush-hush and are scared away by the cloak-and-dagger approach.

Tip: You only enter it once

Much of the information you enter on the Sell Your Item form is common to all your listings. You only need to enter it once and eBay remembers it. Once the information is stored you can make the form easier to navigate by clicking the 'Minimise' buttons on the righthand side of the page. When you do this you won't see the options and your stored details will be used until you change them.

SELL YOUR ITEM   1. SELECT A CATEGORY   2. CREATE YOUR LISTING   **3. REVIEW YOUR LISTING**

Review your listing   🖫 Save for later   ⑦ Help

Select listing enhancements, then review and submit your item.

Make your listing stand out Get help

ⓘ Good news! Gallery Picture is free. Add a picture and we'll show your item to buyers in search results. ⓐ
You need to add a picture to show a Gallery Picture.

Gallery Plus (£0.95) ⓐ
☐ Display a large picture in search results — capture special details or different views for buyers.

Subtitle (£0.35) ⓐ
☐ Give buyers more information in search results (searchable by item description only)

Bold (£0.75) ⓐ
☐ Attract buyers' attention by making the title of your listing appear in **Bold**

Highlight (£2.50) ⓐ
☐ Make your listing stand out in search results with a brightly coloured band

Maximise your listing's visibility
Featured Plus! (£14.95) ⓐ
☐ Upgrade your listing to show up at the top of the same page it would normally show up in search results

Featured First (£44.95) ⓐ
☐ Showcase your listing at the top of search results. Gallery Plus included!

Submit your listing

Once you get to this point you're pretty much ready to send your item live to site and make it available to buyers. This is your opportunity to ensure that the listing you have created is shipshape and Bristol fashion.

All the information you have submitted is available for your review and you have the opportunity to go back and edit it as you wish by choosing the appropriate link on the lefthand side of the page.

Take a moment to examine the listing fees that eBay will be charging you. They are detailed at the bottom of the page and won't be charged until you submit the listing. If you have chosen a feature you don't want to pay for, you can go back and remove it from this page. If you want to include additional features you can go back and add them too.

When you're happy with your listing, all you need to do is click 'Submit Listing' at the bottom of the page and your item is complete. eBay starts to weave its magic and the item will be added to the Search index and the category you chose.

Hello, eBay seller

You've listed your first item on eBay! Now the excitement begins. Usually a listing is available to buyers within a few minutes of your completing it, but sometimes it can take a few hours for it to appear, so don't panic if you can't find it immediately. You'll be able to access it from My eBay or if you want you can search or browse for it like a buyer would.

If you go searching for your listing and you notice that it isn't exactly as you want, you can even edit it when it is live. You can find out how to revise and add to your listing in the next chapter.

Case study: Advice from an old hand
eBay user ID: sean_coolness

Sean got started on eBay by accident. He had a loft full of brand-new but slightly out-of-date computer bits and pieces. A friend had just discovered eBay and recommended that Sean have a go. 'My first listing,' says Sean, 'was for a Pentium Pro PS2 motherboard. It sold very well and made four times more than I expected! That gave me the incentive to start listing away. I haven't looked back since.'

Sean now sells on eBay full time and makes his living from the site. He runs his business using two selling accounts. He has discovered that that it's a good idea when trying to create a good brand to have an ID relevant to what's for sale. That's why he has one ID where he sells motorbikes and a secondary ID where he sells bike accessories and sundries.

According to Sean, 'This actually gives me two completely different types of account. One account is low-volume, high-ticket items, the other is high-volume, lower-value items, so I get to see both ends of the sales spectrum as a seller.' He is also a keen buyer: 'I'm a collector of first-edition books. I have now managed to get full sets by three different authors; that would have been very difficult before the advent of eBay.'

He found it easy to transform his selling from a hobby to a business. He comments, 'I simply listed more to sell more. It's a bit of basic selling really, if you only have five items listed, you can only sell five items. But if you have one hundred items listed, you have a lot more potential for sales.'

He reckons that honesty is the best policy: 'I think the most basic of things that any seller needs to know is one of eBay's core values, be honest! Be honest in your description, in your postage costs, in your location and in any emails. eBay buyers have an amazing knack of rooting out the bad sellers very quickly. In most part by the feedback system, a bad seller's reputation is instantly visible. So be an honest seller. It doesn't matter if the item is marked, broken or stained, all that matters is that you are honest!'

And honesty is also vital if something goes wrong, according to Sean. 'Don't go into a panic when you make a mistake. If you have listed something which has sold and you then discover a problem, don't start telling little porkie pies. Simply communicate honestly with your buyer and explain the issue to them: a vast majority will understand that we are all human and we occasionally make mistakes.'

For beginners, Sean has two nuggets of advice: do your research and be ready to face up to change. Getting to know eBay well before you take the plunge will 'save you a lot of time and money later on. Find out if your widget has a market on eBay and at what price. Learn the sell-through and conversion rates for that widget and work out if there is enough margin in it for you to list that item two, three and even four times! Find out what colours sell best and what times and days are best. It's back to school to do your homework first, but you will save yourself a lot of pain later on.'

And 'be very aware of just how quickly things can change on eBay. Learn to plan ahead, have a strategy and alternatives. You need to be able to adapt very quickly if you want to stay ahead of the game.'

Get more from selling

Depending on what you are selling, there are two other features you might see on the Sell Your Item form when you are listing your item: Item Specifics and Pre-Filled Item Information. Both are useful and free.

Item Specifics

When you were learning about eBay as a buyer, you will have come across the Product Finder on the lefthand side of search and browse listings. For instance, if you searched for 'Paul Simon' in the Music sections, you had the opportunity to narrow down your search by choosing just to look at the CDs found in the results or those that were unplayed and 'Never Opened'.

The Product Finder is not available in every category, but where it exists it is an easy way of locating the item you want to buy. As a seller you should take advantage of it and make sure your item is available to buyers who like to use it.

It only takes a few moments on the Sell Your Item form to add the Item Specifics that the Product Finder needs to locate your items. If this function is available in the category you are listing in, an 'Item Specifics' section will be visible in same section where you add your Item Title and Description.

All you need to do is select the values that best match your item. If you can't find one that matches, you don't need to choose one. In fact, if you don't want to choose Item Specifics at all you don't have to: it is totally optional.

For instance, if you were selling a CD of *Definitely Maybe* by Oasis that you had listened to a bit over the years, you would choose 'Indie/BritPop' as the genre, 'Album' as the format, and the condition as 'Played'.

The choices are slightly different if you choose to use Item Specifics in DVDs, Videos or Automotive or whatever, but the principle is the same.

Pre-filled Item Information

Pre-filled Item Information is available if you are selling all sorts of items, but is probably most useful to sellers of DVDs and CDs. eBay takes a lot of the grubby work out of listing an item by providing you with catalogue information to include in your listing. For instance, if you are selling a DVD and you enter the EAN from the barcode on the back of the box, your item will automatically include details of the film such as the cast, running time, a basic plot description and a stock photograph. For a CD you get the track listing and some notes and reviews.

Obviously this is going to save a bit of time, but it doesn't mean you don't have any work to do. The catalogue information that eBay provides for free is just the common information that every single item of the same kind has. You still need to include information that is only true for your particular item: good and bad. If your item comes complete with extras that others may lack, add those details. If your item has been damaged then you should note that too, just as you would if you were writing your own description from scratch.

Tip: Be different

Using Pre-filled Item Information isn't an excuse for being lazy. It will save you a slab of time, but if you really want your listing to work you need to be clever. For instance, because anyone can use Pre-Filled Item Information, the chances are that there will be items that look very similar to yours. In particular you need to pay attention to the Item Title. This will be provided, but it will be identical to everyone else's. Add to, amend and improve your Item Title so that your item stands out from the crowd.

Selling checklist

- **Everyone has something to sell** Researchers reckon that every household has more than £3000 worth of stuff that can be sold on eBay.

- **Research your item** Find out as much info as you can about the item you want to sell using eBay itself and the internet.

- **The title is vital** 75% of buyers on eBay search for items they want using the eBay search engine. Make sure your title is as descriptive as possible.

- **Choose the right category** Take a few moments to put your item in the right place to help buyers.

- **Write a winning description** Be honest, but talk the item up. Be precise and comprehensive to give your buyers all the information they need.

- **Seeing is believing** A good picture will only take you a few minutes to compose, but it's worth the effort.

- **Postage and payments** Weigh the item so you can accurately estimate postage, and make sure you can accept PayPal.

- **Think like a buyer** When listing your item, think like a buyer to get your description, picture and title the best you can.

- **Time it right** Try to end your item in the evening, using a 7- or 10-day listing to get maximum exposure.

- **Your first sale is a learning experience** Trying anything new is tricky, so don't get disheartened if your first sale doesn't work out.

13

Manage Your Listing

Once your listing is live on eBay and available to buyers, you don't have the luxury of simply sitting back and relaxing until it ends. You still have a little work to do. Taking the time to manage your listing can win you more bids and a better price.

First things first: sit tight and try not to worry. Lots of first-time sellers get anxious when the item they are selling doesn't get any bids in the first few days of the auction. Commonly they worry that they have made an error or that buyers can't find the item. This is usually not the case. On eBay, just like at real auctions, bidders like to keep their powder dry. Rushing in and placing a bid early on is considered by many buyers to be a surefire way of pushing up the final price.

The vast majority of bids on eBay are placed in the final 24 hours of a listing and often you see the bulk of bidding going on in the closing minutes. This can make the first days of a listing seem dull for the seller who worries that no one is going to buy what they are selling. But just because people aren't bidding it doesn't mean that they aren't looking at your listing and deciding whether it is for them.

Inside Information
Selling surprises

Sometimes when you are selling an item you get a surprise - a good surprise. If you don't know much about the item you are selling, it could turn out to be worth much more than you imagine.

Two great eBay selling stories stand out as examples. The first is about a seller in America who discovered a beer bottle in his attic. It was old and dusty, but the seller knew there was a market for collectable breweriana, so he chanced his luck and listed it on eBay, starting the bidding at a dollar.

Little did he know that the bottle he had was something of a Holy Grail among collectors. The bidding got off to a good start. Soon the word was out and he was astonished when the bids were in the hundreds of dollars. Collectors from all over America were emailing him asking for more details. When the auction ended the seller netted $19,000 for a bottle he might otherwise have thrown away.

A similar story involves a seller who put up a fishing lure or fly on eBay. He didn't know that the fly was a very rare example from a well-respected maker: it sold for $32,000.

Closer to home there are some fascinating examples of runaway bidding that have amazed sellers. On the UK Discussion Boards there's a member who bought a record at a car boot sale for 5p and sold it on eBay for more than £500. It isn't uncommon to read about sellers who pick up an item for a quid or two and sell it on for £20, £30, £40 or more.

The moral of these stories is twofold. It proves the old maxim that one person's junk is another person's treasure. The stuff you have gathering dust in the loft may well be the one-off collectables that other people spend a lifetime seeking.

Secondly, it demonstrates that if you're going to sell something you don't know much about, eBay is the place. If the sellers of the beer bottle or the fishing fly had been at a car boot sale they might have raised a few dollars because they didn't know any better. A chuffed collector who couldn't believe their luck would have scuttled off with a very smug grin on their face and the bargain of their lives. On eBay buyers have to battle with each other and when there are lots of bidders who want to buy an item, the seller stands the best chance of getting the price they deserve.

My eBay

You can easily track your listings by using My eBay. To find the item you are selling, click on the 'All Selling' tab in My eBay and a list of the items you are selling will be there for you to examine, just as they are when you're buying items. My eBay summarises whether your item has bids, the current price and the time the listing ends. You can access My eBay by clicking on the 'My eBay' link at the top of most eBay pages and signing in using your User ID and Password.

If you want to take a closer look at the item you are selling, simply click on the Item Title in My eBay and you are taken to the

View Item page. From there you can examine your highest bidder and see what the current price is. By clicking 'Bid History' you can see more details about the bidding activity and all the bids you have received. You can also check out the bidders themselves by examining their feedback, as you would with a seller.

To reassure yourself that people really are able to find your listing and are taking the time to check it out, scroll down the View Item page and see how many visitors you've had. The counter you included in your listing tells you how many people have looked at the item.

If people like the look of your item and think they might want to place a bid later in the auction, they will add your item to their Watch List. You can see how many watchers you have in My eBay.

Respond to emails

However detailed and full your description is, buyers often contact you directly with questions requiring further information or clarification. The emails are forwarded to your registered email address by eBay. Your email address is not disclosed to people who ask you a question. Take the time to answer these questions honestly and quickly, because that gives a good impression and shows you are a good seller.

Sometimes you might get an email from a member asking you to end the auction early and sell the item to them. Sometimes they might make you an offer above your asking price if you agree to sell it to them there and then. The best advice here is to decline politely. Think about it. If they are willing to pay you £20 for something you have listed for £10, it is possible there are people who are willing to match that offer or even go higher. Also remember that if you agree to sell your item 'off eBay' you won't be eligible for protection or help from eBay if the buyer turns out to be a timewaster.

Best Offer and Second Chance Offer

Two features you might like to use are Best Offer or Second Chance Offer. If you list a multiple fixed-price item, then you can invite buyers to make you an offer under the Buy It Now price if you like. Sometimes you get a silly offer that you can't accept, but sometimes you might be willing to let your item go for a few quid less than it's listed at just to shift it.

If you create an auction listing you can make a Second Chance Offer to your under bidders (unsuccessful bidders) at their highest bid. You can do this in My eBay once the item has ended.

Improve your item description

If you receive a question about the item via email, it is possible other people might want to know the same information. You could consider adding the information to your listing. If your item has a bid you can only add information to the View Item page in a separate box. If you don't have any bids you are free to edit the item and add or remove anything you want.

You can add to and amend your listing via the 'Services' link in the Navigation Bar.

Tip: Question and Answer

The Question and Answer feature saves you time and effort. If you are asked a question by a potential buyer, you can opt to publish the question and your answer on the View Item page. You can do this automatically by selecting the 'Display this question and response on my listing so all buyers can see it' option in the email you receive from eBay.

How to cancel bids and block bidders

As the seller you are free to cancel bids for whatever reason you choose. If you don't like a bidder's feedback you are within your rights to cancel their bids. The bidder is free to bid again and it is polite to inform them that you have cancelled their bid and why.

Don't forget that a bidder with no feedback isn't necessarily a bad person: it wasn't so long ago that you had no feedback. Usually a friendly email to a zero-rated bidder assuages your fears that they aren't bidding in good faith. You can block all buyers who have -1 feedback or less if you like. You can also ban any buyer who has had a non-payment strike in the last month or who isn't located in a country you are willing to send your item to. You can also insist on your bidders being registered PayPal members if you want. You can change your preferences in My eBay using the 'Buyer Management' link.

Cancelling bids only removes the bids from one item. In some extreme instances you might want to block a bidder from bidding on any of your items ever again, in which case you can add them to your Blocked Bidder list. This bidder will no longer be able to bid on any of your sales until you remove them from the list. You can add any member to the list regardless of whether they have bid on any of your items or not.

You can cancel bids and add members to your Blocked Bidder list via My eBay.

14

Complete Your Sale

When your item has ended you will hopefully have a buyer. If you have been successful, you need to ensure that your buyer has all the information they need to send you their payment. Once you have received payment you are ready to despatch the item and leave your buyer feedback.

Checkout for sellers

When you listed your item you had the option to include postage costs for the UK and other locations. If you took a moment to include postage details at that stage, you just need to sit back and wait for the buyer to pay. The buyer has all the details they need to make their payment to you. At the end of the listing they will have received an email and you'll find that many buyers just pay up without any prompting from you. When they complete Checkout it is noted for you in My eBay. If they pay by PayPal, you receive an email notification with the buyer's address. All you need to do is despatch the item.

If they want to pay by cheque or postal order, you need to wait for it to arrive and, if necessary, clear. eBay sends you an email as soon as the buyer has completed Checkout that includes the buyer's address and any message they have for you. The buyer should then send you payment in the post.

Contact the buyer

If the buyer doesn't complete Checkout and you don't hear from them, you need to contact them to make sure everything is OK. Buyers and sellers must contact each other within three days of the listing ending, but a good seller should do it sooner than that and preferably within 24 hours. eBay sends you the buyer's contact details in an email at the end of the listing: a quick and friendly email to your buyer usually does the trick. Sometimes a buyer needs clarification or maybe has a specific request about delivery that you may have to resolve. If they are overseas and you haven't stated a cost for sending the item to their part of the world, you have to find out the cost before they can pay you. Sometimes the buyer is new and doesn't know how to complete the purchase, so you may need to be patient and helpful as they find their way.

Whenever you are dealing with a buyer, take the time to communicate clearly. Your buyer doesn't know the person behind the User ID, so make sure your emails do you justice. Most misunderstandings and disagreements on eBay, and online generally, are the result of hastily written emails taken the wrong way.

Despatch the item

Once your buyer has paid, the ball is in your court: you need to send the buyer the item they have bought and paid for. Where possible you should get the item in the post as quickly as you can. Your buyer shouldn't be kept waiting. Obviously taking a few days is fine, but if a buyer has to wait any longer than that they often start asking questions. If you can't despatch your item within a few days of receiving cleared payment, you should contact the buyer so they know what to expect. Buyers are typically very flexible as long as you keep them informed.

It's important to package your item safely and securely. Parcels can get rough treatment as they go through the postal system, so it's best to err on the side of caution when you are judging how well to protect the item. If you are sending your sale overseas, you should pack the item even more securely. If you are sending it outside the EU you need to fill in a Customs Declaration; you can get these at the post office.

When you do send the item, try to give your parcel the personal touch. Including a pre-printed letter that you have signed is good way of making each and every buyer feel special. Some sellers like to include a personal handwritten note or card. Any note you include should thank the buyer for their purchase and encourage them to leave you positive feedback. You should also make sure your buyer is in no doubt that they should contact you if they feel moved to leave a negative. This is your chance to connect personally with your buyer and anything you can do to make them feel good about buying from you should be included. You want to encourage repeat buyers and you want to avoid negative feedback: by coming across as a caring seller you can encourage your buyers to think well of you.

Inside Information
The personal touch

> On eBay you are typically buying from other individuals. The experience you so often get on the site couldn't be more different to buying from a catalogue or ordering from other ecommerce businesses. Frequently, I get handwritten notes from sellers thanking me for buying the item and hoping I am happy and enjoy it. I bought a video once and the seller enclosed a letter about the film and what he thought about it. I replied with my thoughts after I'd watched it and we exchanged a few emails over the following days. It was nice to have an interesting discussion over email, and this experience isn't unique.
>
> A friend of mine bought a nice piece of jewellery from a woman in Scotland. She wanted to treat herself and she spent about £80 on something she could enjoy wearing. When the item arrived, not only was it better than the seller had described but it had been beautifully packed too. It was like getting a present, said my thrilled friend. The seller had also included a handwritten letter, explaining that she was an elderly woman selling her jewellery on eBay. She didn't have anyone to leave the items to and she wanted them to find homes where they would be appreciated. She told my friend how she came to own the necklace and she hoped she would get as much enjoyment from owning it as she had.
>
> Another woman I know bought a pair of trousers for her baby daughter on eBay. When they arrived she was surprised to discover that the parcel not only included the trousers but the matching top as well. The seller explained in a note that she hadn't listed the top on eBay because it was slightly soiled, but she thought she would send it anyway because it seemed too good to go in the bin. The top did have a slight mark, but nothing major and certainly not bad enough to warrant chucking it away. My friend was delighted and needless to say left glowing feedback.
>
> I've heard of sellers who include a sweet or chocolate for the buyer as a treat, but this might be taking it too far. People who include little

*cards and notes of thanks are commonplace. I've even heard of one
seller who includes pictures of her dogs with all her despatches.*

Leave feedback for your buyer

When you are a buyer you can leave positive, negative or neutral
feedback. As a seller you can only leave positive feedback. The decision of when to leave feedback for your buyers is up to you. Many
sellers leave feedback when they have received cleared payment.
The thinking behind this view is that once a buyer has paid in
good faith, they have fulfilled their obligations. Other sellers disagree and don't leave feedback until they get confirmation that the
buyer has received the item and is happy with it.

There are no rules when it comes to leaving feedback for
buyers, so you need to decide your own policy. It is true that
leaving feedback first is a good way of ensuring that your buyer
reciprocates. If you want to build your eBay feedback reputation,
then it probably makes sense to bite the bullet and leave feedback
first.

Tip: Criticising a buyer

If you want to criticise a buyer's performance your only option is to
leave positive feedback but with negative content in the comment
itself.

Inside Information
Dealing with difficult buyers

*I've said it before and I'll say it again: the vast majority of people on
eBay are good and honest. But some are less than perfect and can be
difficult to deal with. You have to summon up a bit of patience when
someone like this turns up.*

*The most annoying type of unreliable eBayer is the person who
bids but doesn't pay. Obviously you can get your Final Value Fee
back, but it's also a pain to chase the buyer and file a dispute. Of the
hundreds of sales I have had on eBay I can put my hand on my heart
and say that not more than four or five bidders have failed to pay.
The most irritating was an American who just couldn't seem to
understand that I was located in Britain, that we don't use the dollar
over here and that postage from the UK to the US was rather more*

than from Utah to Oregon. He refused to pay because he was convinced I was trying to fleece him. It was frustrating but thankfully unique in my eBay experience. I prefer to recall the dozens of pleasant and successful trades I've done with our chums in the US.

Then there are the people who are just difficult to please. I had one buyer - whom I eventually refunded when he sent me the item back - who was adamant that the item I despatched wasn't the one I had listed because it looked slightly different in real life to the photograph on eBay. Needless to say, it was one and the same thing. One buyer sent me a snotty email after he received an old 78rpm record complaining that he was surprised the item had arrived in one piece considering the quality of the packaging. His item had arrived intact and in one piece (as did all the others I sent out), but he simply wanted to have a go.

As my mum would say, 'There's just no pleasing some people.' And that's sage advice on eBay. Stay calm and be polite when you encounter these people and you can't go far wrong.

Unpaid items

Every now and again a buyer doesn't pay. It's an unfortunate fact of eBay life, but by no means a typical experience. eBay recognises that transactions go awry for all sorts of reasons. Some buyers have a legitimate, if annoying, reason for backing out, while others are simply timewasters. The Unpaid Item process means that you can claim back your Final Value Fee for an item that hasn't been paid for (see the information on fees later in the book). It also alerts eBay that a buyer might be unreliable.

• **File an Unpaid Item Dispute** You can file an Unpaid Item Dispute for up to 45 days after the listing has ended. Sometimes you know quite quickly if a buyer isn't going to pay. They might tell you they have made a mistake in their bid or that they can't actually afford the item. In these circumstances you can file a dispute immediately. Even if the buyer is from overseas and has sent you payment in the post, you shouldn't expect to wait more than 30 days for payment. Even if you think payment is on the way, it is worth filing a dispute just to be on the safe side. Filing a dispute doesn't mean you have to follow it through: if the buyer pays up you can retract it.

- **Attempt to resolve the dispute** The next step in the process is to communicate with the buyer and attempt to resolve the situation. The ideal resolution is for the buyer to pay up and fulfil their obligation. When you file your dispute the buyer gets an email reminding them to contact you and pay up. Even if they don't want to pay they are encouraged to contact you and explain why. Many buyers do cough up at this point and all is well.

- **Get your Final Value Fee back** If your buyer responds and you are unable to resolve the issue or you don't hear back from them after seven days, you can close the dispute and get your Final Value Fee back. Details of the disputes you have filed are listed in My eBay so you can keep track of them.

- **But it's only a few pence: why bother?** Even if you are only claiming a few pence from eBay when a buyer backs out, it is worth filing an Unpaid Item Dispute because it helps eBay keep an eye on unreliable buyers. If a buyer gets three strikes for non-payment, they will most probably be suspended from the site unless there are significant mitigating circumstances. By claiming back your few pence you are helping other sellers.

You can find complete details about the Unpaid Item process at http://pages.ebay.co.uk/help/policies/unpaid-item-process.html

- **Minimising unpaid items** There is a useful feature on eBay that can help minimise non-paying bidders: Immediate Payments. On the Sell Your Item form you can choose to require a buyer to pay immediately via PayPal if they win your item. When they bid they have to enter their PayPal details so payment can be taken if they win. This is a good option if you don't want to risk a non-paying bidder, although it does mean that people who don't have PayPal accounts can't bid on your item.

What if your item doesn't sell?

If your item doesn't find a buyer you have two options: give up or have another go. If you want to make money on eBay it's best to have another go, especially if you see similar items to yours selling on the site for a decent price.

• **Consider amending your listing** Is your listing up to scratch? You might need more details or a better picture. Perhaps you could choose a better category or hone the title so that your item is easier to find. Cast a critical eye over your listing, because you may well be able to improve it and encourage bidders to make a purchase.

• **Was the price right?** eBayers can be very price sensitive, so it's worth checking that the price you are asking for the item is realistic. Check out other items for sale to gauge whether you are asking over the odds. And check out your postage too. If that's too pricy, you could be turning buyers off.

• **Relist your item** You can relist your item on eBay via My eBay. Simply click on the Item Title and you see a link to relist the item. eBay walks you through the listing and gives you the opportunity to edit and improve it. If your item sells the second time, eBay refunds one set of Listing Fees.

15

Sell Safely on eBay

Buyers on eBay are at risk of lots of different types of fraud. An item could arrive not as described, or they could be ripped off in the time-honoured way: pay the money and get nothing in return. They can be targeted with spoof emails, tricked by a deliberately misleading auction... the list is endless.

As a seller, you're really only at risk from two things: receiving dodgy payments, and account hijacks or identity theft as a result of phishing or pharming attacks. Dodgy payments are easy to avoid, account hijacks are more complex.

Avoid dodgy payments

Take PayPal and you eliminate a huge chunk of the risk. If you insist on PayPal for international payments, you avoid a whole chunk more.

eBay bans the use of Western Union, MoneyGram and other untrackable systems, so you shouldn't accept them as a means of payment. Even if a foreign cheque appears to clear, payment for it can later be withdrawn, so it is best not to accept these. Make sure that UK cheques clear before you release the goods, and be especially careful with high-value items. The best advice can be summed up in two words: take PayPal.

Protect your accounts

As an eBay buyer and seller you need to take precautions to protect your eBay and PayPal accounts from people who try to take over your accounts and use them for fraudulent activity.

Spoofs, phishing and pharming

You may have heard on the news about fake emails being sent out by fraudsters targeting online banking customers. By tricking people into giving out personal details, they hope to take control of bank accounts for fraudulent purposes. Such a practice is called phishing.

Spoof emails and fake websites are also used in attempts to take over established eBay members' accounts for other people's fraudulent activities. An eBay account with good feedback is a valuable commodity that other people prize. If you have taken the time and effort to build up your reputation, you don't want to jeopardise it.

- **Identifying spoofs** Spoof emails can look deceptively like official eBay or PayPal emails. However, they are in fact pretty easy to distinguish from the genuine article. The purpose of these emails is to trick you into revealing your personal details so that the fraudsters can use your account to set up fake listings on eBay and rip off unsuspecting buyers. The emails typically ask you to sign in to your eBay account in the main body of the email. eBay never asks you to sign in via an email; it always directs you to the eBay site. eBay also never asks you to provide credit card details, passwords or any other personal details in emails like this. These emails sometimes include threatening messages saying that your eBay account is about to be suspended and eBay needs you to confirm your details. eBay never asks you to confirm your details in such a way. The same applies to PayPal.

- **Fake websites** Sometimes a spoof email directs you to a fake website and asks you to sign in there. Fake websites try to look like eBay or PayPal so that you are tricked into giving out your details. There are clues that betray them, for example the URL at the top of the page is not a genuine eBay URL. Use of such websites to try to gain personal details is known as pharming.

- **The eBay Toolbar** One way to be certain you are signing into a genuine eBay page is to install the eBay Toolbar. This sits at the top of your internet browser and means you can easily access the eBay site wherever you are on the net. It also has some very useful safety features.

If you are on a genuine eBay or PayPal site, an icon in the Toolbar shows green and you're safe to sign in. If you are on a site that might look like eBay but isn't, then the Toolbar shows as grey if the site is unknown or red if it is a known spoof site. If the Toolbar shows as red or grey you shouldn't sign in because your personal information will be at risk.

As an additional safety feature, if you attempt to sign in to a site the Toolbar doesn't recognise as eBay using your eBay password, the toolbar informs you of that fact. To get the Toolbar go to http://www.ebay.co.uk/ebay_toolbar.

• **What if I receive a spoof email?** If you have received a spoof and recognised it, you are perfectly safe as long as you haven't filled in any details. eBay works with law enforcement agencies all over the world to track down and prosecute the senders of spoof emails. The emails themselves contain vital information that eBay can use to trace their origin. Therefore if you receive a spoof email you should send it to eBay. Simply forward the email to spoof@ebay.co.uk and eBay does the rest. If you receive a PayPal spoof email send it to spoof@paypal.com.

• **What do I do if I fall for a spoof?** If you do submit your details to a fake site after receiving a spoof email, you have to act quickly. First, you should change your password so that the information you have accidentally provided is no longer valid. If you have submitted credit card details or bank information, then you should contact the credit card issuer or your bank immediately.

eBay is constantly updating its information about spoof emails and fake websites. You can find the full and up-to-date details at
http://pages.ebay.co.uk/education/spooftutorial/index.html

The eBay Discussion Boards are also an invaluable source of information about the latest scam emails doing the rounds. If you have received a spoof the chances are that hundreds of other people will have received one too. You can consult with other members on the boards and also warn others who have received a spoof email but might not have identified it.

My Messages

Every eBayer needs to know about My Messages and how it can help you keep your eBay account safe and secure. You'll find it on the lefthand side of My eBay. My Messages is your personal eBay inbox and every piece of correspondence from eBay that relates to your account will be in there. Things like requests to update your account details or credit card number will be there, as will your eBay bills, Second Chance Offers and Best Offers. You'll also receive emails from other eBay members or potential eBay buyers there. If an email relating to your account comes from eBay it will be in My Messages – it's as simple as that.

Some emails from eBay won't be in My Messages, but they won't relate directly to your personal information. Emails connected to transactions, such as End of Auction emails, only go to your registered email address.

So if you receive an email that asks you to submit your personal information, you have a three-point plan to ascertain whether it's genuine or not:

1 Does the email address you by your eBay ID or is it just headed 'Dear Community Member' or something similarly impersonal? If it doesn't address you directly, it's not a real eBay email.

2 Is the email in both My Messages and your registered email account? If it isn't, it's not from eBay.

3 Does the email ask you to sign in in the main body of the email or send you to a page to sign in at that doesn't show as green on the Toolbar? If either is true, it's not from eBay.

Password security

As long as your password is safe, your eBay account is secure and only for your personal use. Considering this, it is amazing how lax some people are when it comes to protecting their password. There are a few easy ways to keep your password safe and your eBay account secure.

- **Create a good password** In addition to scam or spoof emails, your account is also at risk from hacking using advanced computer programs. These keep trying to log in to your account using possible passwords until they find the right one. eBay has security systems in place to try to thwart this sort of activity, but if you have another internet account with the same password then your eBay account is at risk.

One thing you can do is to use a password that is very difficult to guess. Never use a word that is in a dictionary or obviously related to your User ID. Also avoid things related to your life such as a birth date, pet's name or hobby. Use a combination of upper- and lower-case letters and numbers to create a password that is almost uncrackable. Six characters will do, but eight or ten are better.

For instance, 'password' is a very insecure password. But if you change it so it is 'Pa55w0rD' or 'p@sSW0r6' it is significantly more secure. Be creative and your password will be safer from the hackers.

Another idea is to use total gibberish. Take a phrase or lyric you find easy to recall, such as 'There's an old mill by the stream, Nellie Dean'. Take the first letter of each word and you have 'taombtsnd'. Some of these letters can be capitalised. Some can be exchanged for numbers and others for punctuation marks or other characters and you could end up with 'T@om8+Snd'. Obviously, don't use this example but make up your own.

• **Keep your password secret** Never write your password down or give it to anyone else. The safest place for your password is in your head.

• **Change it on a regular basis** There is no need to change it daily or even weekly, but by changing your password on a regular basis you are moving the goalposts for those who want to get their hands on your account.

• **Use different passwords for eBay and PayPal** If your eBay account or PayPal account is hacked then the chances are that the hackers will try to use the password for one account on the other. After all, there's a good chance that they are the same. It's advisable to use different passwords for PayPal and eBay and for other online accounts. It may seem like a chore, but it is much more irritating to have to regain control of your accounts if they are taken over.

Safety resources

There are lots of sources of eBay safety information. So if you want to find out more, check out these additional eBay and online safety resources. Knowing the risks and managing them is the best way to avoid fraud on eBay.

> • **Safety Centre** eBay provides up-to-date safety information. It's worth taking the time to inform yourself and learn how to minimise the risks when you are trading on the site.

The Safety Centre can be accessed via a link at the base of the Homepage and at http://pages.ebay.co.uk/safetycentre/index.html.

> • **Get Safe Online** Just like on eBay, keeping yourself protected online is largely a matter of getting tooled up with the necessary information. We're all familiar with the chaos that computer viruses can create and the dangers that hackers pose. With the growth of broadband in the UK, because many people have their computers connected to the internet all day, there are new dangers and threats to be aware of.

If you are flummoxed by firewalls, need to know about virus protection or don't know what keystroke logging software is, then you should check out the Get Safe Online website at www.getsafeonline.org. This is a government initiative supported by major banks and online brands, including eBay, and is quite simply the most comprehensive guide to online safety available in Britain.

If you are running an eBay business you want to be extra careful, because it's a matter of protecting your livelihood. There's a special section dedicated to businesses and, while it might very well be a dull hour or so reading through all the information, it will be worth it.

> • **eBay Discussion Boards** For up-to-the-minute news on the latest spoof to land in a million inboxes and insight and comment from some of the brainiest and most experienced experts on eBay fraud, visit the eBay Discussion Boards. There's a lot to wade through but there's some great advice and intelligence to be found there.

• **Specialist sites and forums** For more general advice or insight into more complex issues, go to Google and start searching for the plethora of sites and forums dedicated to eBay and online fraud.

Tip: Premium-rate phoneys

Be careful of premium rate phone numbers when looking on the internet for eBay and PayPal information lines. There are numerous dodgy providers of helplines that charge premium rates. They're unofficial and expensive. Ensure you're calling a bona fide number by checking out the provider as much as you can.

16

eBay's Selling Fees

eBay's selling fees can seem complicated to newcomers. In fact they're a bit of a mystery to old timers too: they get changed frequently and with each change a further level of complexity is added. But don't let this put you off. Understanding eBay's fees is critical to being a profitable and effective eBay seller.

Different features and enhancements on eBay incur different fees. This chapter is just a quick overview and I recommend that you check out the full and official list of fees at

http://pages.ebay.co.uk/help/sell/fees.html

I've also put together a page on my own site that has the latest news and comment on eBay's fees: www.wilsondan.co.uk/ebay/fees. eBay's fees are so complicated and change so much that it would be impossible to have them in the book. Go online for all the latest and up-to-date information.

There are four types of fees on eBay:

Listing Fees These are the fees you pay to put an item on eBay. They vary depending on category, your reputation as a seller, the value of the item you're selling and the starting price you choose.

Final Value Fee This is the commission you pay when an item sells. Again, this varies depending on the value of the item that sells and the category it sold in.

Feature Fees If you want your items to stand out, then you can pay an extra fee to enhance your listing with features such as a subtitle.

Subscriptions Some services on eBay attract subs. It could be your eBay shop or using Selling Manager Pro. Whatever the service, chances are there'll be a fee.

Tip: Category-specific listing fees

If you sell technology goods such as phones, computing gear, consumer electronics and photographic supplies, or media items like CDs, DVDs and books, comics or magazines, you're eligible for a different fee structure, honed to make sales in those categories more affordable. Find it at http://pages.ebay.co.uk/help/sell/fees.html.

Final Value Fees

If an item is sold, Final Value Fees are payable. These vary across categories, but here is the basic range and an example to explain how FVFs work. The Final Value Fee is calculated depending on the final price of your item.

FINAL PRICE RANGE	FINAL VALUE FEE PERCENTAGE
£0.01–29.99	7.5% for the amount of the sale price up to £29.99
£30.00–599.99	7.5% of the initial £29.99 (£2.25) plus 4.5% of the balance of the sale price
£600.00 or more	7.5% of the initial £29.99 (£2.25) plus 4.5% of the price from £30.00 to £599.99 (£25.65) plus 1.9% of the balance of the sale price

Here's an example of how it might work for you. If your item sells for £7, the Final Value Fee is 5.25% of £7, or 37p. That's simple, but if your item sells for more than £29.99, let's say £50, the Final Value Fee calculation is a little more complex.

The amount up to £29.99 is charged at 5.25%; the rest up to £50 is calculated at 3.25%. So that's £1.57 plus 98p, a total of £2.55 on your £50 item.

These Final Value fees cover the majority of items sold on eBay but, as with Listing Fees, eBay offers different fees for sellers of technology and media items. There is also distinct pricing for motors, property and mobile phones with contracts.

How to pay your eBay fees

eBay offers several ways for you to settle your account. You are invoiced monthly and expected to pay any balance owed over £1. If you fail to pay, your account is suspended until you do. To find out the balance of your account and how much you owe, click on the Account link in My eBay. Most sellers pay their eBay fees by PayPal, but it's not the only choice.

- **Direct debit** From a seller's point of view the easiest way to pay your eBay fees is by direct debit. When you register as a seller you are given the option to sign up. All you need to do is complete the direct debit mandate online and eBay will process it. Once your direct debit is established, the amount you owe eBay is automatically deducted from your bank account on a monthly basis.

- **Credit card on file** Instead of a direct debit you can put your credit card on file for eBay to bill automatically each month. eBay accepts Visa and MasterCard and is totally secure. Some sellers prefer to pay this way as their payments do not come directly out of their bank accounts. If you put a credit card on file or establish a direct debit with eBay, you can use the site freely and run up as big a bill as you like. Otherwise eBay provides a £15 trading limit for all members. If you are going to be using eBay but are unlikely to run up more than £15 a month, you might prefer to use the pay-as-you-go options offered. Don't forget, though, that if you exceed the £15 limit your account is blocked from selling until you have paid off the balance.

- **PayPal** If you want to pay as you go, then using PayPal is quick and easy. Your payment is applied instantly to your account and you can use the money you have received from buyers to settle your bill. If you don't have money in your account you can use your credit or debit card via PayPal to settle your bill. You will find the link to pay eBay using PayPal on the Accounts section of My eBay.

- **One-time credit card payment** If you don't have a PayPal account you can make a one-time credit card payment. You can do this via My eBay in the same way as you would using PayPal.

- **Cheque** The slowest and most inconvenient way to pay is by cheque. You need to print out a payment slip and send it with the cheque in the post. It can take up to 15 working days for eBay to process your payment. You can access this option via the Accounts tab in My eBay.

Inside Information
Fees

It's a fairly obvious point to make, but nevertheless: you want to keep your eBay fees as low as possible. But that's easier than it sounds. That said, keeping a close eye on what you're paying is time and money well spent for every eBay seller.

What's the average level of fees paid by eBay sellers? It's impossible to say. But I'll stick my neck out and say that if you're paying more than 20% then you probably have room for savings.

The biggest scope for savings lies with Listing fees. You particularly want to be cutting back on incurring fees that don't result in a sale.

Tip: Fee savings

The biggest opportunity for saving on those eBay fees is with the preferential listing fees offered to Shop owners. The subs on an eBay Shop justify these reductions alone.

17

eBay's Rules for Sellers

If eBay's fees seem complicated, welcome to the world of eBay rules. There was a time when there weren't many rules at all. eBay was like the Wild West. Buyers and sellers made their own judgements and exercised their own caution. As eBay grew, consumers and sellers demanded more protection and regulation, the world's media was breathing down the company's neck and special interests demanded that that eBay 'do something' over this, that and the other, so introducing more and more rules became unavoidable. The result is the hotchpotch of policies you see on the site today.

Being familiar with eBay's rules is vital if you want to make money on eBay. If you break a rule then eBay will remove your listing from the site, which is not only a pain but it means that all the time and effort you invested in creating the listing will be wasted.

Things you can't sell on eBay

You can sell almost anything on eBay, but obviously there are certain things that eBay doesn't permit to be listed. Some items are prohibited because it is illegal to trade in them, and some are banned because eBay has taken a pragmatic stand or because the items are heavily regulated and it would be impossible for eBay to keep track.

- **Guns, knives, bootlegs, drugs and pornography**
  Firearms, illegal weapons, illegal drugs, prescription drugs and tobacco are all banned pretty much without exception, as are bootlegs and copies of recordings. You should also avoid selling anything pornographic or adult in nature (and that means no top-shelf magazines). Even items that are listed featuring nude or bare-breasted women in an adult way are likely to be ended if they are listed on eBay.co.uk.

- **Body parts, animals and plants** You can't sell human body parts or items fashioned from human body parts (apart from whole skeletons for medical research purposes as long as they have the requisite licences). There are also rules restricting the listing of animal skins, furs or pelts, birds' eggs and ivory. You aren't allowed to sell any animal that is alive (with the rare exception of some live pet foods and fish), although plants and seeds are generally permitted as long as they aren't marijuana.

- **Alcohol** You cannot sell alcoholic drinks on eBay unless you have the appropriate licence and eBay's express permission. Alcohol can be listed, however, if the bottle or container is collectable in its own right and more sought after than the contents.

- **Embargoed goods** eBay.co.uk is a subsidiary of an American company, which means that listing Cuban items is generally not allowed. There are also prohibitions on items that come from countries against which the UK has an embargo.

- **'Hate items'** There are restrictions applied to what eBay calls hate items. You can't list items that bear the Nazi swastika or the SS lightning motif. Other Second World War items are generally permissible. Items related to the Ku Klux Klan or mass murderers are also restricted.

- **How does eBay know if I am selling prohibited or restricted items?** eBay has a very effective policing system in place: all the other buyers and sellers. If a member sees an item that is not permitted for sale there is a strong chance they will report it to eBay. For some sellers it is a great way to eliminate competition, but for others it is simply a way of keeping eBay safe. The eBay community is very passionate about preserving its marketplace.

- **What does eBay do if it finds out I am selling restricted items?** eBay takes a very dim view of sellers who break the rules and attempt to sell prohibited items. If you do list an item that is prohibited or restricted and it is your first offence, eBay will probably just end the item, refund your fees and give you a warning. If you continue to break the rules you will be suspended and banned from the site.

The above information isn't comprehensive and the list of banned and regulated items on eBay changes frequently. You can find eBay's full and up-to-date list at

http://pages.ebay.co.uk/help/sell/item_allowed.html

Things you can't include in your listings

Listing policies govern what can and cannot be included in an item listing. Every seller is bound by these policies and failure to follow them can result in a warning from eBay. If you continue to violate the policies, eBay will suspend you from the site and you will no longer be able to buy or sell on it.

Most of the policies are straightforward and make perfect sense, although some are complex. This section is only a summary of the most important policies. For full details of the listing policies, which are updated occasionally, visit

http://pages.ebay.co.uk/help/policies/ia/listing_policies_for_sellers.html

- **Links policy** There is a strict policy governing the links you can include in your listing. You may not have links to other websites unless they are credits or links for payment services, photographs or further details about the item for sale. Any link that encourages buyers to leave eBay and purchase items elsewhere is not allowed. You can include links to your other eBay listings, your About Me page and your eBay Shop.

- **Choice listings, bonuses, giveaways and prizes** When you list an item on eBay you must be listing a specific item and that item alone. You cannot offer a choice between different items. For instance, if you have two identical pairs of shoes and one pair is green and the other is red, you cannot list them as a single auction and give the buyer the option to buy the red or the green pair when the listing ends. You would have to list a green pair of shoes or a red pair or both separately. You are also not allowed to offer prizes or giveaways as an enticement to buy from you. You can offer a bonus item as long as the bonus is available to all buyers alike.

- **Surcharges** It is normal practice for sellers to pass on postage and handling costs to their buyer. However, these must be reasonable and stated up front where possible. Sellers should not profit from postage costs. Escrow fees can also be passed on to the buyer as can currency conversion costs, as long as they are disclosed in advance and agreed to by the buyer.

You may not pass on the cost of taking online payments when using a service such as PayPal. If you are processing credit card payments using your own merchant service, you are permitted to charge a surcharge to cover your costs. Under eBay's rules the credit card surcharge must not exceed the costs of receiving or processing the payment and can only be passed on to buyers in the UK trading in pounds sterling.

• **Keyword spamming** You are not allowed to include irrelevant words in your Item Title so that it gets more attention from the Search facility. For instance, if you are selling a Swatch watch you are not permitted to list it as 'Swatch not Rolex' so that more people find it when searching.

• **Fee avoidance** Obviously eBay isn't keen on any feature of a listing that means that the seller is avoiding its selling fees. You are not allowed to list an item with a very low price and very high postage so that you can avoid fees but not lose money. You are also not allowed to list an item for a low price but say in the listing that the price will in fact be much higher.

• **Other rules** You are not allowed to post want ads on eBay. Any listing that includes profanity or is adult or erotic in nature will be ended. All items should be listed in an appropriate category and you are not permitted to list more than 15 identical items at any one time unless you are using the Multiple Listing format.

PART III

ADVANCED eBAY TECHNIQUES

18

Raise the Stakes

Your first selling experiences on eBay are always the hardest and most nerve-wracking as you are navigating through unfamiliar territory. But once you have successfully completed your first sale, you have mastered the basics of selling on eBay and the process becomes easier and easier.

However, when it comes to making *serious* money on eBay, one sale is not enough. Ramping up is about selling more, more often, for more money. To fully unleash the marketplace's money-making potential you need to be selling dozens, hundreds, even thousands of items a week. The biggest sellers on eBay are selling tens of thousands of items every month, often turning over thousands of pounds a day. You've sold one item: well done. Let's get down to business and have you selling much greater quantities of stock.

This part of the book examines how you can start ramping up your sales, taking steps towards building a viable business and harnessing the features and opportunities that exist to help you begin making serious money. Thousands of people have done it already, but it's not necessarily for the faint-hearted. You'll need to be open to new ideas, welcome the opportunity to learn about new things and be willing to make a few mistakes as you go along.

In this part you'll learn about opening and running an eBay Shop, maximising the content of your listings and building processes to ensure that you're as efficient as possible. You will find out about the programmes eBay provides to help you develop your sales and capacity as a seller.

It's also an opportunity to think about how you're going to use eBay. What do you want from it? eBay is infinitely flexible and how you exploit the eBay opportunity is up to you. Now is the time to start thinking about how you're going to integrate eBay into what you do.

How will you use eBay?

The opportunities eBay provides are not confined to striking out and forming your own business. You might just want a comfortable second income that could fund an extra-special holiday or help you buy a better car. How you use eBay is up to you: with eBay there are a wealth of opportunities for making money.

- **eBay as a great money-making hobby** Earn some extra cash by doing something you love. For lots of people eBay is a stimulating, money-making hobby. It could also be a great second income.

- **Building an eBay business** Start from scratch and discover the opportunity that eBay offers you. You can then branch out and discover whether you've got what it takes to be an ecommerce wizard – there is more on this later in the book.

- **eBay for existing businesses** eBay isn't just about those who want to build a business from scratch. Many people use it as an additional sales channel to breathe new life into an existing business.

Tip: Registering with the authorities

As a starting point, most sellers register with the authorities as a sole trader and as self-employed, and graduate past that to become a limited company and VAT registered as the need arises. You are required to register as self-employed within three months of starting out.

Begin ramping up

There's a lot to think about as you begin ramping up your eBay selling and the sooner you start building the foundations of your activities, the better. It's never too early to think in depth about what you're going to sell and how you're going to source it.

Case study: The scientific approach
eBay user ID: georgiegirlsgems
Website: www.georgiegirlsgems.com

Georgina Davies is unusual as an eBay seller because she has started from scratch and ramped up her business not once but twice and expects to do so again in the future. In Autumn 2005 she was successfully selling in the equestrian supplies category and she had an offer to buy the business she had established.

She took the chance and used it as an opportunity to think about what she was going to do next with eBay. 'I had several ideas for future projects,' she told me. 'But I decided to rest awhile and travel around the world. So, we sold our house, stored our belongings, lodged the cats with a friend (who I met through eBay!) and set off overseas for the trip of a lifetime.'

She returned with a clear idea of what she wanted to do: 'My other hobby was making jewellery, so the next move was obvious. I like to stick to what I know, as I think this helps me understand my customers well.' She didn't launch straight in to her new venture but rather took the time to research and plan and she advises other sellers to do the same. 'Researching and preparing first will really help you get off to a flying start. Plan, plan, plan and plan some more. Set some goals before you start.'

Her advice for sellers who are embarking on eBay is simple: 'Do lots of test purchases. Which experiences made you go "Wow" and why? What problems did you have? How can you make sure that your business delivers consistent customer delight? It's exceptionally competitive in all categories on eBay and "OK" doesn't cut it any more. You may get away with it once, but the customer who thought you were "OK" is far less likely to return to you. Without a good level of returning customers you will find business growth far harder.'

She also advises against simplifying buyers' motivations. 'Price is very rarely the only motivator. Please don't think that all your customer wants is "cheapest".' She reckons you can make more of an impact and more sales with good customer service. 'I truly believe that the lack of customer focus and drive is very much the weakness of many eBay businesses.'

For Georgie, eBay lets her live the life she wants without the stress of a corporate career. 'As an individual, eBay offers me exceptional flexibility and a quality of life I had not experienced up to now. To succeed in style, rather than just scrape along, you need to work very hard, but the upside is you can plan your workload and sort out your work/life balance permanently. In fact I don't even regard it as work.'

She has already started from scratch twice and she plans to do it again: 'I am very good at setting up systems and businesses and moving them on from start-ups to solid small businesses. I intend to keep spotting niches and filling them, building up a website or printed catalogue and then selling the business on.'

Find your market

The easiest way to succeed on eBay is to find a niche. If you can identify something that lots of people want to buy but no one else is selling on the site, you've cracked it. Needless to say, that isn't as easy as it sounds. With hundreds and thousands of sellers out there the chances are that someone else is already doing what you're planning. But don't let that discourage you.

Perhaps you can surf a current trend or even predict one. If you can get your hands on a product that is going to be the next big thing, you're on to a winner. I know a number of people who simply bought up lots of Harry Potter Lego and waited until it was scarce and unavailable in the shops. That Christmas it was the must-have gift, and they were quids in. But more often than not this is a one-off and it's difficult to make a living this way. Nevertheless, by keeping your eyes open you soon get a feel for what's going to sell well on eBay.

If you can't find a niche, don't worry. You can offer goods cheaper than other people and do it with greater panache. Buyers on eBay value the extra mile that sellers go to make their purchases pleasant and trouble free. Describe your items in a better way. Take better pictures. Make yours the items people want to buy and compete with the sellers out there already. If you can stand out from the crowd and make people notice you, customers will buy from you.

The best advice is to sell something you are knowledgeable about and comfortable with. Utilise experience you already have to attract buyers. If you like a challenge, don't be afraid to experiment and do something a bit different. There are a lot of people already on eBay who sell original craftwork and paintings. If you have a hobby or skill, consider whether you can produce things that other people want.

Sort out supply

You need to ensure that you have a ready source of inventory if you want to succeed. You can't sell stuff you don't have. How to get stuff to sell in sufficient quantities at a price where you can still make a profit is a very real challenge that every seller faces.

You want a supply of items that meets your capacity as a seller; that is, a quantity of inventory that will keep you going and make money. Build a relationship with a supplier who can provide you with a regular supply of goods. Lots of sellers have multiple suppliers so that if one source falls through they are not left in the lurch.

One source of supply you might consider is eBay itself. Many wholesale sellers list pallets and lots that they don't have the capacity to sell themselves. If you can take the time to break the lots down and sell them on, you might be on to a winner. Buying some of these lots from the Wholesale category can also be a great way of starting on eBay.

Buy your stock at a price that ensures you have a good profit margin. It's an obvious point, but one that many people don't consider. You can sell 100 things for a tenner, but if you are only making a quid on each, you are going to need to sell a fair few to make a living. Of course it's not impossible, but it's better either to find something with a bigger margin or sell more expensive things with the same margin.

Don't forget to factor in your time to your costs. Selling can be time consuming. It's going to be a bit galling looking over your sales for the month and realising that you would have been better off behind the checkout at your local supermarket earning the minimum wage.

Inside Information
Where do I get stock?

> It's the one question that you never get a straight answer to. Sellers who have a reliable and well-priced source of goods would be mad to tell anyone else and you'd have to get the thumbscrews and rack out before they'd crack. It's a problem you have to solve alone. Don't worry, there's more on the subject later in the book.

Tip: Paying your dues

Her Majesty's Revenue and Customs (HMRC) are quite clear on the fact: if you're buying things in to sell, you're a business and you need to be registered as such and making your contributions to the government's coffers. Find out more at

www.workingforyourself.co.uk/etraders/helpline.htm

Know your enemies

Keep an eye on what other sellers are doing, especially if they are competitors. Not only will you be able to emulate what they are doing well, you can learn from their mistakes. Most eBay sellers even have secondary accounts so that they can buy items from competitors without them knowing. This way you have a full picture of how a competitor trades and you can strive to do better. (You are allowed to have as many eBay accounts as you like, so it's perfectly permissible to do a bit of spying.)

eBay buyers are very price conscious and by undercutting your competitors even by a little you will attract sales. Don't forget to be competitive on postage costs too. If you can offer cheaper shipping costs, you are at an advantage.

Never forget your customers

Your customers are the key to your success: never take them for granted. You can get everything else right, but if you neglect the people who are buying your stuff you will fail. Many PowerSellers (see later in the book) say that the most valuable customers are repeat customers. You should strive to offer every customer a seamless and easy transaction.

In many ways good customer service is just about being prompt, polite and responsive. Buyers love a swift turnaround on their purchases and often provide glowing feedback if they receive their item in super-quick time. Consider including a note with your despatches. It can be pre-printed and simply signed, but it does make every buyer feel looked after.

Buyers also love flexibility and personal service, so try to be open to their requests. It may only take a minute or two, but you'll reap the rewards when they come back to you to buy again.

Case study: The mumtrepreneur
eBay user ID: Book-bags

Clare is a mum who started selling on eBay as part of a competition run by the *Guardian* newspaper in 2005. Five contestants were given £1500 to start an eBay business and turn a profit in a few months. She didn't win the competition, but she is still selling on eBay and looking to expand her enterprise further.

Being handy with the sewing machine, Clare launched her business selling personalised PE bags, laundry bags and bunting for kids. If you want a lovely drawstring bag with your child's name on it, Clare can knock it up in no time at all. Her merchandise has proved very popular with parents who don't have the skill to make bags themselves or who want something a bit different for the little ones to take to school.

Early on Clare branched out into other items that might appeal to parents and children. She buys in fair-trade children's clothes and for a while sold books, but found that her sales fell away when eBay made changes to the books categories.

'When I first started I thought I had to "pile it high, sell it cheap", so I was selling lots but with a small profit margin,' Clare told me. 'But recently I put the price of all my bags up £2 and there was no change in the quantity of orders coming in. I could have been earning more for the previous few months. Bummer!'

Clare makes her bags to order because she never knows what sort of personalisation will be requested next. Despite the uncertainty of her work she manages to fit it in easily to her daily life. 'I do it when the kids are at school, or in bed, or watching television. If I'm very busy with a lot of orders, my husband will take the kids out for the day at the weekend. It fits in really easily.'

For Clare, selling online is about constantly improving and trying new things. 'You need excellent photos,' she says, 'and I'm certainly in the process of raising my game with this aspect even now. And you need to sell new things to keep things fresh.'

Clare is even thinking about opening her own website but has hit a few obstacles. 'I've bought the domain name bagsforkids.co.uk but am not finding it easy to set the shopping cart up. I'd expected it to be as easy as building a shop on eBay and it's not!'

19

Develop Your Selling Skills

You already know how to create a straightforward auction listing, you know about managing your sales and dealing with buyers, and you're aware how to despatch items and ensure you have happy customers. Once you have mastered these selling basics you'll want to explore the other selling opportunities that eBay offers. This isn't just about considering different selling formats; you also need to work out how best to exploit international trading, selling for charity and developing your eBay selling with an About Me page.

Fixed-price selling

You don't have to sell your items by using the auction format. For many, if not all, items, getting buyers to bid against each other is usually the best way to find the fair market value. Lots of buyers like the amusement and drama of bidding and enjoy the search for a bargain. Some people, on the other hand, have neither the time nor the inclination to place bids and wait days for an auction to end: there is no certainty about the price and no guarantee they will win the item. When they see an item they want at an acceptable price, they simply want to buy it now like they would at other online shopping sites. Sometimes they are willing to pay a bit more for the convenience of an instant purchase.

As a seller there are advantages to using a fixed-price option. You have the opportunity to choose a price you are more than happy to accept for an item you are selling. It also means that you don't have to wait until your auction has ended: if somebody likes your item and buys it, you can get payment faster and turn the sale around more quickly.

eBay calls this option 'Buy It Now' and as a seller you have two ways of using it. You can either add it to an auction or you can ditch the auction altogether and stage a pure fixed-price Buy It Now listing. Depending on the sort of listing you want, you need to make your choice at different stages of the Sell Your Item form.

To add Buy It Now to an auction item you need to choose to sell your item at online auction at the first stage of the Sell Your Item form. You then need to specify the Buy It Now price on the 'Enter Pictures and Item Details' stage of the form. The principles of selling the item are the same. All you need to do is add a higher Buy It Now price. Choosing the price is up to you. Obviously you have a starting price in mind for the item that is the lowest amount you are willing to let the item go for, so your Buy It Now price should be a realistic amount you would be very happy to sell the item for.

If someone bids on your item when you have Buy It Now included, the option immediately disappears so that people can only bid on the item as an auction from then on. Adding a Buy It Now option to an auction listing only costs 6p and for the right items in the right situation it can be well worth it.

To use the pure Buy It Now option for a listing, you need to express your preference on the first page of the Sell Your Item form. Choose the 'Sell at a Fixed Price' option. You can then list your item as you would normally, choosing a duration and price in the usual way. eBay's fees are determined in the same way as they would be for an auction listing.

Don't forget that you need more than 10 feedbacks or a direct debit established with eBay before you can use Buy It Now. If you aren't eligible to use pure Buy It Now or to add it to an auction listing, you won't be offered the option to choose it.

Multiple item selling

If you have several of the same items you want to sell, you have a number of options available. You can list multiple items in a Buy It Now format, which means that buyers can buy as many as they like at a fixed price you choose. The listing stays on the site until all the items have been sold or your listing expires.

You can also sell lots on eBay in the same way you might at an old-fashioned auction. To list multiple items, you need to enter the details on the main page of the Sell Your Item form.

Multiple item selling best suits what can be described as 'commodity' items; that is, items that are not one of a kind and have an easily determinable value. Things like books, DVDs, CDs and computer games all fall into this category. But be aware that selling multiples is a slightly different science to selling individual items.

It's not usually a case of listing an unlimited amount of items and selling them all with ease, unless you're very well priced. Often, it's a case of the opposite and giving an impression of relative scarcity. So don't list too many in one go and be realistic about how many you'll shift. It's also fair to say that a multiple item listing is not likely to garner the same sort of excitement as an auction. You'll get the hang of it after you've tried it a few times.

The fees on multiple items are not calculated by the value of individual items but rather the collective value of the items you sell: 10 items at £4.99 attract the same fees as if you were selling an item with a starting price of £49.99. The listing fee is capped at £3. It's also definitely worth combining multiple fixed-price item sales with auction items. You'll attract buyers to your multiple listings and also you'll gain a better understanding of what price the market will bear.

International selling

Roughly 15 million Britons visit eBay each month and eBay's total global membership exceeds 300 million. Your eBay fees are the same whether you limit them to the UK or open them up to the whole world, so it makes sense to make your items available to the widest possible market.

Selling internationally is something that you need to incorporate into your selling mindset as you build your eBay business. Some sales come to you from overseas without your having to canvass for them, but to maximise the sales you make you need to add specific information to your listings and your shop if you have one.

The key is to make it as easy for your international buyers to buy from you as it is for domestic buyers by giving them the information they need to take the plunge. The simple fact is that selling internationally can mean a bit more work and hassle, but if you get it right international sales could easily become a significant chunk of your business.

One thing you need by the bucketload is patience. There will be times when you feel like you are dealing with an idiot who is deliberately trying to make your life hell. Many international sellers I've spoken to say that that sometimes it's just impossible to explain to some buyers why postage to Venezuela is much more than posting to the UK.

You also need to be firm. If you have made arrangements for payment to be possible by the means you prefer, and an international buyer wants you to take payment by a method you don't accept, feel free to let them know. If someone buys something from you and claims to be the nephew of the former chief aide to the finance minister of Nigeria and wants you to ship a mobile phone or a laptop to them on the promise of untold future wealth in gratitude, don't do it.

Six steps to international selling success

• **Postage** Save yourself time and hassle by researching postage in advance. If you can determine postage costs for the UK, then you can use the internet to determine them for just about anywhere in the world. You should wise up to the different deals for international carriage, not just from the Royal Mail but also from other carriers. Certainly for heavy or bulky items, the chances are that other services will be cheaper.

• **Customs and exports** Sales within the European Union are blessedly easy: you might as well be sending items to Shoeburyness as to Strasbourg. For sales outside the EU, however, you need to fill in the appropriate green customs slip, so you'd be wise to get a bunch of these from the Post Office and complete them at home in your own time. This form declares the value of the item you have despatched and whether the item is a gift or not.

Many buyers ask you to tick the gift box so that they can avoid import duties. It is illegal to declare an item as a gift if it isn't. It's a good idea to say that you won't mark items as a gift on your About Me page or a custom page in your shop.

Make sure that you can actually export the items you sell to the country in question. There are all manner of arcane rules and restrictions that you may need to be aware of. For instance, there are rules that restrict the import of electrical items to Canada.

• **Language** If you have language skills that might attract international buyers, you should make a note of it in your item listing. A friendly word or greeting in a buyer's language may well be the clincher for an international sale.

Language can sometimes be an issue, but many eBayers are happy to conduct a transaction in English even if it isn't their first language. If you don't have a common language between you, then free online translation services such as Babelfish can be helpful, but they aren't always accurate because they translate words literally.

• **Item titles** If your items might have special appeal to residents in a particular country, then it could be worthwhile including the relevant keywords in that language. This way when potential buyers search eBay you'll be in the results returned. You can research what keywords are the most relevant in other markets by using the Pulse feature on other eBay sites such as eBay.de.

• **Payments** PayPal is the grease to the international trade wheel. It is simply the easiest international payment method and you can take payments from just about anywhere in a variety of currencies in the same way as you accept payment from UK buyers. If you do want to take other payment methods, make sure they have the same protections and safety measures to ensure that you don't find yourself out of pocket.

• **Managing expectations** Avoid confusion early on when trading across borders. It is best to overcommunicate in advance and make sure that there is no room for misunderstanding rather than assuming prior knowledge. Don't forget that as a seller you'll be the more experienced party in the transaction. Let international buyers know that postage costs and delivery time will doubtless be greater than within the UK and keep them informed if you know there are problems. People are very understanding if they are aware of what's going on.

20

Take On Turbo Lister

Of all the activities an eBay seller has to do, one of the more irritating is listing items. As an ambitious seller it can seem like you can't get the listings up on the site as fast as buyers are snapping them up. The Sell Your Item form is rather cumbersome when it comes to listing groups of items one after another, especially when many details in your listings, such as location and payment and postage, are likely to be either the same or very similar for every listing you create.

Turbo Lister helps you list more items, more quickly. Turbo Lister is very easy to use, so there is no reason you shouldn't start using it as soon as you want to begin selling more than two or three items at the same time. It is a very convenient way of organising your selling and is suitable even for low-level sellers. But it's when you are ramping up the number of listings that you are putting on the site that Turbo Lister really comes into its own. If you're used to the Sell Your Item form, trading up to Turbo Lister is like exchanging your Morris Minor for a Boeing 747. It's faster, it's got way more capacity and your sales might actually take off.

Go and download Turbo Lister now. It's free and it will revolutionise your selling. You can load it onto your computer from http://pages.ebay.co.uk/turbo_lister. It is compatible with PC systems and doesn't require too much disk space. It is advisable to download the full version even though this might take a while over a 56k connection. It is not compatible with Macs, however.

What exactly is Turbo Lister?

Turbo Lister is a tool that allows you to list multiple items from your computer. There's no need to be online and you can manage your listings in one place. And it's not just a listings tool. You can also store your listings templates in Turbo Lister and bulk edit and amend whole batches of items in one go.

If you have text that you use in all of your listings, you can save this in Turbo Lister so that it automatically appears in each listing. Payments and postage information can be automatically saved and included in each listing to save you time too.

Turbo Lister basically offers you flexibility. If you want to list a collection of items on a Saturday night, you don't need to slave over eBay when you would rather go to the pub. You can create your listings in any spare moment you have during the week and save them on your computer until you want to send them to eBay.

How to use Turbo Lister

When you download Turbo Lister and install it on your machine, you need to set up your ID and import your contact details from eBay. You only need to do this once. If you sell using multiple IDs it's easy to add as many as you like to Turbo Lister and keep your item batches separate.

Turbo Lister is updated roughly once a month, so make sure you update it periodically: most of the problems you may encounter with Turbo Lister are a result of not updating the program. Get into the habit of making sure that you have the latest version. You'll find the update button under the 'Options' tab.

Once you're up and running, you can make a start by creating a new item. You'll see the button in the top left of the Turbo Lister screen.

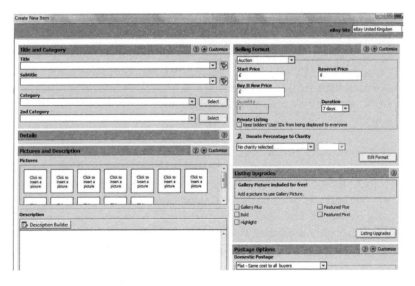

Every item you create will have its own page in Turbo Lister like the one opposite. Unlike on the Sell Your Item page, you don't have to move back and forth from page to page. Every option you need is immediately available and if you want to rationalise the page and get rid of certain functions that you don't use (say you only accept PayPal, you don't need to see all the other options), you can.

On the lefthand side is the field where you write your title, add your item specifics, attach pictures and tinker with your item description. Like on the Sell Your Item form, you can edit your item description using the Design View or the HTML editor. In fact, everything you can do on the Sell Your Item form you can do in Turbo Lister. On the righthand side you can enter your price, duration, auction format and your payment and postage details.

At the bottom of the page you can see the buttons to preview your item, send the item to eBay and save the information as a template. This last option is particularly useful if you're selling lots of similar items. Simply create one listing and copy it as many times as you need. You can then just edit the aspects of each listing that are different, thus saving lots of time. You can change the appearance of the page using the 'Customise' button.

Once you have created your individual listings, you can store them in Turbo Lister until you want to upload them to eBay. When you want to send them live or schedule them, simply click 'Add to Upload' and they will be sent to the site. You can schedule items in Turbo Lister as you would normally do in Sell Your Item.

Make the most of Turbo Lister

There are lots of natty features in Turbo Lister that you might find useful. It's rather like a mobile phone. You don't have to use all the functions but you might be surprised at all the things it can do if you have a sniff about.

- **Editing in the 'grid'** On the main page of Turbo Lister you'll see a digest of all the items you have created. It's from here that you can keep track of your inventory and make changes as you like. By selecting the items you want to edit, you have the option to make bulk changes to your entire inventory. If you want to standardise the returns policy on all your listings, for instance, it won't take you a moment.

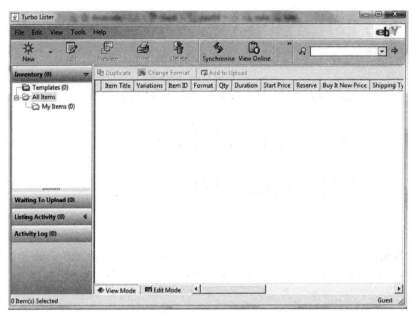

• **Search** There's a handy search option in Turbo Lister. This is particularly useful if you have a selection of thousands of items and need to find a particular listing quickly.

• **Import and export active or ended items** If you have items that have run their course on eBay and you want to keep the details to use again in future listings, you can easily export the details to Turbo Lister for recycling.

• **Import and export with CSV** If you like to keep the details of your listings in a spreadsheet (such as Excel) you can easily plug Turbo Lister into your own system. By using CSV you can import and export your listing details quickly.

21

Upgrade to Selling Manager or Selling Manager Pro

When you started off on eBay as a seller, you managed and monitored your listings via the selling tab in My eBay. There you could see how your sales were progressing and also perform tasks like leaving feedback at the click of a button. But as you've been discovering as you increase your sales, you need different and more powerful tools that recognise the changing scale of your activities and sales.

eBay offers two customisable options to sellers who are making more than a handful of sales. You should think about them as beefed-up equivalents of My eBay honed to the needs of sophisticated users. They both reside in My eBay and when you upgrade, they simply replace the Sell tab. The tools are called Selling Manager and Selling Manager Pro and each has different options and services that are of use depending on your experience. Upgrading is definitely going to save you time and effort as you expand your sales.

Bear in mind that both Selling Manager and Selling Manager Pro are management tools rather than listings tools. If you are looking for a service that helps you list more quickly and easily, then these won't really help you. Take a look at Turbo Lister instead.

Selling Manager

The less sophisticated of the two tools is Selling Manager. It's free to subscribe to and offers some great time-saving features. There really isn't a reason not to get started with Selling Manager because it's free and useful. It's also very much like My eBay, so you shouldn't find it too tricky to get used to.

Selling Manager offers you all the functions that My eBay provides: you won't lose anything by upgrading. As before, you can use it to manage all your current, past and pending listings and in addition you can enjoy some extra features:

- **Buyer emails** Every seller has to deal with a lot of emails. Whether it's informing buyers that they've won, chasing payments or telling customers that their item has been despatched, it's not unusual to be sending two or three emails per transaction, if not more. Multiply that by the number of items you sell and you're sending hundreds if not thousands of emails a week. So anything you can do to be more efficient is good news. With Selling Manager you can automatically generate emails with pre-populated details about the items that have been sold. eBay provides you with templates, but you can produce your own to ensure that you get your message across.

- **Bulk relisting** Relisting unsold items one by one can be a time-consuming and dull experience. It's also highly inefficient. In Selling Manager you can relist in bulk: you simply tick the items you want to relist, click one button and away you go.

- **Print labels and invoices** Selling Manager is hooked up with PayPal. You can use it to print out invoices for your buyers or address labels for your parcels. Once you've got this set up, you may find it a great way to claim back some minutes every day. The templates from eBay also look smart and professional.

- **Store feedback comments** As a seller you probably find yourself leaving the same feedback comments again and again. It may only take a moment to do one, but when you look over the course of a month you might be leaving hundreds of feedback comments and that all adds up. In Selling Manager you can store up to 10 customised feedback messages that you can then use as appropriate.

Selling Manager Pro

Selling Manager Pro has all the functions of Selling Manager plus some very neat extras. Selling Manager Pro is a paid-for extra and costs £4.99 a month. Some people baulk at this additional cost, but it's best to think of it in terms of the time you save. Even if you can claim back an hour a week by upgrading, it's a bargain.

- **Bulk emails** In Selling Manager you can write and create your own standard emails to send out to buyers. In Selling Manager Pro you can send out these emails in bulk. So, if you need to send 10 emails telling 10 buyers that their item has been despatched, you can select them from your list of sold items by ticking a box and send them all an email en masse. This can save you a whole lot of time.

- **Automated emails** Not only can you create reusable templates but you can choose to automate when they're sent, so you can despatch personalised emails to buyers automatically when they pay, for instance. It's a great way of coming across as a very diligent seller when in fact you might not be anywhere near a computer.

- **Automated feedback** Leaving feedback is one of these jobs that you just have to do day in day out and it can be repetitive and dull. With Selling Manager Pro you can automate feedback to be left when a buyer performs a particular action. For instance, you can automate your feedback to be left the moment someone pays with PayPal, or you can program it to leave feedback only after the buyer has left you a positive remark.

- **Reports** Selling Manager Pro can be a source of some interesting and useful numbers and reports that help you understand your activities. You can use it to calculate profit and loss as well examine your conversion rates (how many items sell when you list them) and average selling prices.

- **Inventory management** If you're selling lots of identical items, it's worth checking out the inventory management tools. If you've got 100 widgets and you sell 100 on eBay, when you try and sell widget 101, Selling Manager Pro lets you know that you're out of stock.

- **Manage inventory templates** You might frequently be selling the same items and using similar or identical listings. In Selling Manager Pro you can download listings from the Sell Your Item form or Turbo Lister and update them as required.

Other tools

If you've found that neither Selling Manager or Selling Manager Pro is what you're looking for, it could be worth turning outside of eBay for options. There are lots of commercially available programs produced for different types of sellers and their specialist needs. However, few offer the broad benefits and ease of use that you can enjoy with Selling Manager or Selling Manager Pro and none integrates as seamlessly with My eBay.

For more advanced sellers the best and most widely used is the suite of tools available from ChannelAdvisor (www.channel advisor.co.uk). The company offers help and support to all sizes of online retailers as well as brand-name organisations such as Schuh and Hewlett-Packard.

ChannelAdvisor doesn't just assist with management tools, it offers services to make listing more efficient, as well as offering strategic consultancy. If you think that the eBay tools are holding you back, it's well worth checking out ChannelAdvisor or looking for other services.

Case study: The part-time business seller
eBay user ID: the-cd-collector

Michelle's passion for music and selling on eBay is obvious from the moment you meet her. 'I've always dreamt of having my own music store, from a very early age. I've always been a collector of music, going back to the days when vinyl and cassettes were the "in" thing and in those days there was no such thing as a compact disc!'

She started on eBay in 2004 when she heard about the site from a friend and that Christmas she decided eBay was an ideal place for her to do all her present buying. She found it easy and fun and 'hugely addictive'. So it's hardly surprising that in February 2005 she began selling on eBay too. She didn't find it difficult to get started: 'I had already bought things on eBay so I was familiar with how the site works. To me, it was quite straightforward once I had read all of the help pages and done the research on the postal costs.'

Despite holding down a full-time job, Michelle is now a PowerSeller running her own eBay Shop. 'I would recommend getting an eBay Shop: it is a lot easier to keep track of stock and listings, plus it is cheaper too.'

Michelle operates from home but has found it easy to put her business on a sound, legal footing. 'I knew if I was buying to sell, no matter how big or small, that I was a business and that I needed to register as self-employed with the Inland Revenue, even though I am already paying tax in my full-time job. I also have an accountant as well as it saves me a lot of time... and money!'

Michelle's advice to new sellers is: 'Stay determined. What you get out of it is dependent on what you are willing to put into it. I am intending on going full time on eBay as well as running my own website, which is currently being made as we speak.'

What other sellers can learn from Michelle is how a can-do attitude and a positive outlook are vital weapons in an eBay seller's arsenal.

22

Maximise Your Listings

The chapter on selling your first item looked at how you can create a basic listing that engages a buyer and encourages them to bid on your item. But when you're trying to make dozens of sales and build your turnover and profitability, you have to work harder at crafting your listings. This won't be as big a chore as it was when you were an eBay newbie, because your experience and knowledge will be greater. Nevertheless, 'making do' isn't an option any more. You need to look slick, professional and competent in order to stand out from the army of other sellers.

eBay is a competitive marketplace and the Darwinian principle of 'survival of the fittest' really does apply when it comes to buyers selecting sellers from whom to buy. eBay offers you many ways to differentiate yourself from the hordes. Obviously, price is one key area (some people like to buy the cheapest item available regardless of anything else) and feedback is important too. But there are other ways in which you can compete and your greatest opportunity to differentiate yourself from the competition is by crafting superior listings.

In fact, if your listings are compelling enough you can even compete effectively with sellers who are selling the same items for less than you are, because your listings will be more attractive and will thus generate greater trust.

Think about it in terms of displaying items for sale in the offline world. At a car boot sale it's perfectly acceptable to lay a sheet on the floor and put the items you're selling out on that. On the high street you generally see something more sophisticated, and even those displays vary from a basic line-up of products (like you'd see in a local shoe shop) to the extravagant works of art you see in somewhere like Selfridges.

Displaying your items correctly, finding as many customers as possible and engaging them sufficiently to persuade them to get their wallets out is the name of the game. It's also about saying as much as you can about yourself by implicitly reassuring buyers that you're the best seller to buy from. This chapter is about crafting the perfect listing and maximising its effect and impact, as well as making sure that you get the best return on your listing fee investment.

The title is vital

When you are building the perfect eBay listing, the most important aspect is the Item Title. This is the number one tool every seller has to attract buyers in the marketplace, and yet many sellers spend little time and effort honing it. Titles are something almost everyone is failing to maximise.

It's how buyers find you

Why is the Item Title so important? It's how buyers find what you are selling. It really is as simple as that. It's the single most vital piece of marketing every eBay seller has. Everything follows from the Item Title. You can have perfect pictures, a compelling item description, correct categorisation, rock-bottom postage and a superb price that buyers will love. You can have all this and so much more, but if people can't find and view the listing you have lovingly crafted, then you have, frankly, wasted your time and listing fee.

You can even pay eBay extra fees for glitzy features like Bold and Highlight and it won't make a difference. When it comes to getting the buyers in, you need to make sure that your Item Title is working as hard as it possibly can for you and your sales. To do that you need to understand how eBay works and how your buyers think.

What is an Item Title?

On the most basic level an Item Title is the name of the listing you are building. But actually it's much more than that. When you are building your listings it's easy to fall into the trap that catches the vast majority of sellers. They have a very clear view of what an Item Title is and that's what they enter. Their titles work for them and that's enough. Often a seller says to me 'It describes what I'm selling' or 'It's how I would search for what I'm selling'.

The problem is that an Item Title isn't about describing an item at all and it doesn't matter for a second what the seller searches for (because a seller is selling their own products, not

1992 ROLLS ROYCE SILVER SPUR II AUTO CREAM J713 BARCLAY
MULLINER PARK WARD CENTENARY MODEL(57 out of !00)

buying them). An Item Title is not a headline and it's not a way of cataloguing something. It's actually how you match your item to a buyer who's looking for it. Simple, huh?

Dead simple. But is attracting buyers your primary motive when you write your title? Or do you just type in something that works for you, or maybe the first words that come in to your head? I think every seller on eBay can improve their Item Titles, and they can do it by discarding their own views and embracing those of the people who want to buy something.

Only 80 characters

Your Item Title is limited to 80 characters, which isn't a great deal.

It's exactly this long with the spaces and punctuation.

You need to be brutal and scientific to get the most out of it. Many people think that the subtitle and the item description are also searchable on eBay (and they are), but the default is Item Title only and the vast majority of people on eBay don't change that default. You need to base your thinking on the assumption that people are only going to search for the Item Title.

You also need to think about the 'browsers': the people who don't search eBay using keywords. They browse through the category structure, starting with the long list on the lefthand side. They start with 'Home and Garden' and then narrow down their search until they find your antique lamp, without ever putting 'antique lamp' into the search engine. Roughly 25% of eBay buyers browse, so you also need to make sure that your Item Titles make at least a semblance of sense to people who find them in the relevant categories.

But my Item Titles work already!

I'm sure they do. I bet people find your items and I bet that the people who find them think that the Item Titles you use are great. But what about the people who are looking for what you're selling and haven't found you? You haven't constructed an Item Title that works for them. If you want to succeed on eBay you're going to have to hook those people too.

You can attract new buyers simply by making small changes. Here's a great example. There's a seller I know who sells women's fashion. She was doing very well using Item Titles that described exactly what she was selling. She was including sizes, details of designers and great information about the fabrics and quality of her clothes that was accurate and useful and she was selling plenty. In fact, she didn't think there was anything wrong at all: she was happy with the amount of stock she was shifting. But the trade she was doing was a fraction of the potential sales available: her Item Titles weren't doing the job for a great many of the people who were searching for her product on eBay.

Once she'd done a bit of research she found that some of the most commonly used search terms relating to what she was selling were not included in her Item Titles. When she did include those terms, in the first week alone her sales were up 30%. After a few months she has dramatically expanded her operations and taken on two staff – business is booming.

Are you missing out on extra sales because you aren't maximising your Item Titles and are unaware of what people are searching for? Are there actually hundreds of extra buyers out there who can't find you because you're set in your ways?

Gaming Best Match

The system that eBay uses to display search results to buyers is called 'Best Match'. It's reasonably complex and eBay isn't entirely clear on exactly how the system works. But we do know a few things for sure. First, your feedback DSRs are important and if they start to slip, you'll soon find that your prominence in search will be diminished. The only solution there is to work on upping those DSRs by dramatically improving the service you provide. As ever, underpromise and overdeliver to wow buyers with an amazing service that's better than expected: it's the best tonic for flagging DSRs.

The other factor that affects Best Match is past sales on particular listings. This is where the importance of eBay's new 30-day multiple fixed-price listings come in. If a listing makes a sale, eBay considers it to be more important and will present it more frequently to buyers in search. This makes it vital to get sales on items early on so that, for the rest of the duration of the listing, it enjoys greater buoyancy.

Some ideas:

Just be the best The best listings will always win. Forget about Best Match and simply think (again) about amazing titles, perfect pictures and engaging descriptions. Being best is the best way to beat Best Match.

Promote new listings In your Shop, using cross-promotion and via other marketing channels such as email, always promote new listings. Make an early sale and reap the benefit for 30 days.

Relist successful listings If one of your listings is very successful, make sure you relist it if you can so it can continue to perform strongly.

Free P&P eBay loves sellers who offer Free P&P and promotes relevant listings on the site. Make use of this additional profile and make sales to boost your Best Match performance.

Keep experimenting We don't have a definitive notion of exactly how Best Match works, so experiment with timings and improving your listings, and see if your changes have a positive impact on how you appear in search. You may be pleasantly surprised.

How to improve your Item Titles

What are people searching for?
The key to constructing a winning Item Title is making sure that it aligns, as closely as possible, to what the people who want to buy your item are searching for. But how do you know what they are searching for? There are a number of resources available to all sellers and most are free.

Obviously, the first thing you want to do is figure out what's working: which words in your Item Titles are already bringing the bidders in. You can find this out anecdotally or using the reports that eBay makes available. First up, ask your customers how they found your item by asking what keywords they used. You can also ask people what keywords they would use to find your products as a sort of informal market research. Don't forget that you, as a specialist, might use very different words to describe your products in comparison to the layperson.

Potential buyers might also be searching for your items but thinking about them in a very different way to you, the seller.

When it comes to a mobile phone, for instance, make and model might not necessarily be uppermost in a buyer's mind. For instance, some people will be simply looking for a phone they can use with a particular service provider, or a phone with a good camera, and some other buyers might be swayed by colour. By doing some research you can work out how best to optimise your Item Titles to appeal to the broadest possible audience.

Traffic reports

Some of the eBay tools help you find out exactly what keywords people are using to get to your listings. If you have an eBay Shop, one of the best benefits is the free traffic report. In many ways these reports are worth the shop subscription alone, because you should easily be able to get your money's worth by optimising your sales. This is just one of several really useful reports you can use to improve your sales. If you don't have a shop you can still subscribe to the reports function for £3 a month. (eBay Shops are covered in more detail later in the book.)

The report you are looking for is the 'Top keywords that drove traffic to your Store', because it shows exactly which keywords people used to get to your Shop and your listings. In the first instance this information tells you what's working already and what you shouldn't be ditching from your Item Titles.

It also tells you what *isn't* working. If you have a keyword in your Item Titles that isn't driving traffic or isn't driving much traffic, then you might want to consider dropping it in favour of a more useful one. Many sellers like to include their shop name or user ID in their Item Titles, for instance; while it might bring in a few customers it's not likely to be a significant driver. You can use the traffic report to validate your own hunches and your informal customer research, but if in doubt, trust the numbers. You may not agree that a certain search term is the right one, and your customers might have given you different ideas, but if the data says that something works, trust the data.

You can access the traffic reports from My eBay. On the left-hand side you'll see the link 'Manage my Shop'. Click on that and on the Shops Management page, again on the lefthand side, you'll see a link to 'Traffic Reports'. Click on that and sign in to access the reports.

eBay Pulse and the Marketplace Research tool

Once you know which of your keywords are working already, it's time to look outside your listings and examine the whole eBay marketplace. What are the most popular and relevant search terms? These will help you judge whether there are critical terms that you need to be including to increase your traffic and sales.

One of the most useful tools is free: eBay Pulse. There are links to Pulse on the eBay.co.uk homepage and the site map or you can go to http://pulse.ebay.co.uk.

Pulse tells you what the top ten search keywords are by category. On the Pulse page you can see the top ten search terms for the whole site. If you want to see the top ten results in more detail, you need to pick your category from the drop-down menu at the top left of the page. If you are interested in 'Books, Comics and Magazines', for example, choose that and you will be shown the top ten for that category. Pulse lets you drill down to the lowest level of a category and shows you that, for instance, the most searched-for term in Books, Comics and Magazines > Non-fiction > Computing and IT is C++ (which is a type of computer language). You can research the top ten search terms for every category on the site.

Although Pulse is very accessible and offers a great starting point for your research, it's quite basic. To finely tune your Item Titles you need a research tool with greater detail and more func-

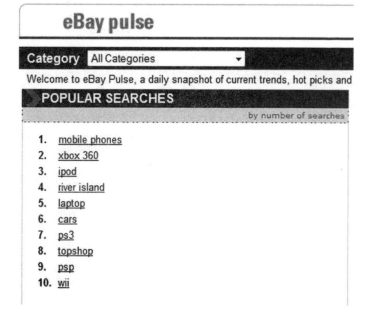

eBay pulse

Category All Categories

Welcome to eBay Pulse, a daily snapshot of current trends, hot picks and

POPULAR SEARCHES

by number of searches

1. mobile phones
2. xbox 360
3. ipod
4. river island
5. laptop
6. cars
7. ps3
8. topshop
9. psp
10. wii

tions. This is where eBay Research from Terapeak comes in: www.terapeak.com.

This tool allows you to examine up to 90 days of information relating to completed items in a number of different ways. It can give you information about average selling prices, the number of items that have been sold and whether they perform better as Auction or Buy it Now. It's an amazing amount of information that can be exploited to your advantage. The tool also helps you interpret the data by allowing you easily to manipulate it into graphs and charts.

For the purpose of your Item Title the vital information you can get from eBay Research relates to popular keywords on eBay in general and also those specifically related to your sales. It tells you what keywords people are using to find items in your categories in much greater detail than Pulse does. It also provides information about the prices related to those keywords. This helps you if you have to choose between two terms because there isn't space for both: opting for the one that is getting higher prices is probably the smarter bet.

The eBay Research tool isn't free and pricing depends on how much detail you want and for how long you want it. The monthly full bells-and-whistles version will cost you £12.99, which could well be worth it. But in the first instance, do try the two-day introduction for £1.99.

Popular internet search terms

Another interesting tool you might want to look at is provided by Yahoo!, which owns the web advertising service Overture. It has a tool called the Keyword Assistant, located at

http://searchmarketing.yahoo.com/en_GB/rc/srch/oyr.php

The Keyword Assistant tells you what the most popular search terms are on the internet in general, according to the results from the Yahoo! search engine. It lets you know, for instance, that the keywords "doctor who" are searched for more than twice as often as "dr who". Check on your own keywords and see what you find out.

Title tips

- **Variations on a title** I had a look in the Curtains section of the Home and Garden category on eBay just now. It's not a regular haunt, but it proves my point. If you want to search for a curtain that is 90 inches by 90 inches, I have found numerous variations from sellers: 90"x90", 90x90, 90" x 90", 90 x 90", 90 by 90, 90 wide by 90 long.

Which is best? Well, probably the first. When it comes to attracting searchers it's a case of belts and braces. On the most basic level it's matching a keyword search to your Item Title, and the first one has the most info. It also has no spaces, which are wasteful.

• **Ditch the punctuation** Resist the temptation to use up room with punctuation: it's not really relevant to search engines and it just uses up precious space in an Item Title that could be better used. Ditch those inverted commas, apostrophes, brackets and commas, however hard it is. Brackets and commas are the worst waste of space, and usually a space will suffice.

• **Plurals** The eBay search engine is sophisticated enough to understand that 'curtain' and 'curtains' are very closely related and will return the same results for both. But if in doubt, add the 's' and mop up searchers for both 'curtains' and 'curtain'.

• **The lowest common denominator usually works** You know those big metal covers that well-dressed waiters pull back with a flourish in films and posh restaurants to reveal a meal? They're accurately described as cloches, but actually not a lot of people know that. If you're close to what you sell, you may well want to step outside your expertise and think like a punter when creating your Item Title.

• **Business buyers often like specifics** Savvy business buyers and specialists are out there too, so don't forget them entirely. It doesn't necessarily take up too many spaces to be specific and lots of people who are searching do know what they're looking for, so don't forget the model number or the like. In particular, if there is a product code or name, as many technology items have, do put them in if you have customers who are likely to use them. But remember to complement these with accessible terms for the people who don't have the insider knowledge.

• **Not nice, or beautiful or delightful** Discard meaningless, descriptive terms and replace them with genuine search keywords. Words like pretty, nice, old, beautiful and delightful are not useful keywords. You should be opting for keywords such as retro, shabby chic, Victorian or classic, or going for brands, colours or types. People very rarely search for a 'nice new television' or a 'sexy skirt'.

• **You say potato...** If you are offering your items to international buyers, don't forget that what a Brit calls a mobile an American calls a cell and a German calls a handy. There are doubtless international keywords you can add to boost your exports.

Inside Information
How buyers on eBay have changed

How often do you stop and think about who your buyers are? Every single one of those items you send out is going to a real person. But who? As a good seller you should be thinking about your buyers every day. The most successful eBay businesspeople centre their activities and focus their energies on knowing their customers better than their competitors do and thus give themselves an edge. It's a good thing to do.

My own perspective on eBay buyers relates to how they have changed over the years. Way back when, eBay buyers were typically quite sophisticated internet users, early adopters of technology and savvy judges of the risks. Over time this has ceased to be the case. The internet has gone mass market and eBay buyers are now ordinary folk who might not necessarily be completely familiar with the web or ecommerce. They are still taking baby steps and learning all the time. But they do have money to spend.

The thing to remember is that they are very likely to be unsure, wary or looking for reassurance. As a seller if you can make this army of new buyers (who number in their millions) trust you, then you're on to a winner. So don't assume that your buyers are as proficient as you when it comes to the net or eBay: they might not be. Assume that they are a little bit scared, be patient and help them along, and you'll reap the rewards.

A word about keyword spamming
Keyword spamming is when you add a keyword to your Item Title that is popular with searchers but not relevant to the item you are selling. On eBay keyword spamming could be as easy as adding a

totally irrelevant term (for instance if you're selling Adidas trainers, adding Nike) or saying that something is like or not like something (stating 'Adidas not Nike' or 'Adidas like Nike', for example.)

When it comes to keyword spamming, don't do it. Not only is it against eBay rules and you risk being sanctioned, but it also doesn't really work. After all, if people are looking for one thing and they are presented with another, it's not a great experience. Keyword spamming also says something about you as a seller and is one of those things that dodgy sellers do, so it could actually cost you sales.

Your Item Titles checklist

- Find out what's working: talk to your customers.

- Find out what's not working: use the research tools.

- Remove needless words and punctuation to create more space.

- Optimise your titles and experiment with new keywords.

- Review your Item Titles over time and optimise them again if necessary.

Make your images work for you

It definitely depends on what you're selling, but in general terms if one picture is good, two are better and five pictures are better still. If you're selling a car, for instance, another high-value item or something unique and unusual, it's essential to get a full impression and view of what's on offer. You want to make a profitable sale, so it's worth taking the time to boost your description with brilliant pictures. Of course, for a bog-standard CD or DVD or any other commodity item, just one picture will suffice. But that doesn't mean that you couldn't be making that one image do more work for you.

What is a good photo?
A good photo is one that persuades a buyer to place a bid and choose you as a seller. It's crisp, clear and unambiguous. If you're using multiple pictures you want to give a complete 3D impression

of your wares. With a car, for instance, you want pictures that show every angle, including the interior and maybe inside the boot, and perhaps even a snap of the milometer.

Take a good, cold look at the listings you have now and be hard in your analysis. Are they really as good as they could be? Are you making do with some sub-standard images? Are there any improvements that you can make? Be honest. If you think some of your pictures are a bit dodgy, the chances are that some of your buyers do too and you might be losing sales as a result.

Invest in a good camera and learn how to use it. Every poor craftsperson blames their tools, but you can make a tangible improvement to the quality of your images by investing in a better camera. Needless to say, it's perfectly possible to create poor images with top-of-the-range equipment, but the quality of your camera can make a real difference. And if you actually learn how to make the most of the camera's many functions and features, that's even better. Some of the features on a good digital camera are mind-blowing – utilise them and give your eBay sales a boost.

- **Photo-editing software** Good images can be spoilt by too much background, distractions or peripheral space. It's also astonishing how many images on eBay you see at 90 or 180 degrees away from the right way up. Your computer may well have a photo-editing program installed: lots of machines come free with software that will do the trick. Otherwise, get something from the web for free (Picasa) or buy something tailor-made such as Photoshop. Good pictures help you sell more. It's the accumulated small changes and improvements to images that add up to make a big difference.

- **Hosting your own pictures** There is some irony in the fact that eBay's own picture-hosting service is one of the factors that decreases the quality of images being used on the site. It's a highly convenient and effective service, but because you are charged for the extras and enhancements and are effectively thereby penalised for best practice, some sellers (and by extension their buyers) are settling for second best. By hosting your own pictures and then dropping them in to your listings (in the free HTML field in Turbo Lister or Sell Your Item) you can include as many images as you like free of charge. You can also position the images where you want them in your listing and display them at whatever size you like.

For help with hosting photos, search the net or check out www.flickr.com and www.photobucket.com (both of which have free options). For HTML advice get your hands on a manual or check out Webmonkey's advice at www.webmonkey.com/webmonkey/frontdoor/beginners.html

• **Picture manager** As you know, your first photo on eBay is free. But if you want eBay to host more images, you have to pay extra. This all adds up if you're listing lots of items. If you're not interested in hosting your own pics but you are paying for extras, it's worth checking out Picture Manager. For a subscription starting at £4.99 a month you can host and display more photos and probably save money too.

What about a video?

You don't have to stick to static images. As you are ramping up your sales you might even want to consider including videos in your listings. People often ask me whether it's permissible to include a video. It is, and it's surprising that more sellers don't do it. Videos are an absolutely superb way of showing off your products and they are seen so rarely on eBay that they still have a real impact on buyers.

Recently, I saw a listing selling remote control cars and the seller had included an exciting video of tricks and stunts. It was captivating. If you might be in a position to benefit from videos, the option is really worth looking at.

eBay doesn't actually offer you the opportunity to host videos so you have to find a hosting service yourself, but this shouldn't pose too much of a problem. There's a whole range of companies you can use and most are free.

• **Possible video hosts** If you make a video you'll need to store it somewhere so the video can be inserted into your list-ings. Services such as YouTube (youtube.com), vimeo (vimeo.com) and Revver (revver.com) are well known and offer a good service, for free. The real benefit of using a site like YouTube is that you can put the videos on the site and even link back to your eBay listings, making your videos an advert for your sales. Another option is vzaar (vzaar.com), a

UK-based enterprise founded by former eBay staff. It plugs into eBay's API, meaning that your vzaar-hosted videos can be directly inserted into your eBay listings without too much fuss. There are free and paid-for options depending on how many videos you want to use.

• **Making a video** Making a moving digital image is pretty easy. Many phones and digital cameras have video capabilities nowadays, so if you don't mind a slightly scratchy film quality that will do the trick very nicely. To be fair, the better the camera, the better the video, so some of your results could be very good indeed. For top-notch videos a digital video camera is what you need. Although they are still quite pricey, they enable you to create videos with a wow factor. Most photo-editing programs also have video-editing capabilities, so you can use these to polish your videos.

Optimise your item descriptions

The other critical aspect of your listing that can be tweaked to improve your selling success is the item description. Unlike with the title, where the secret is cramming in as much as you potentially can, optimising your description is about taking things out. Being as descriptive and helpful as you absolutely can be in as short and succinct a way as possible is the key. How your page is structured is also important: leading your buyer through the item in a reassuring and helpful way is best.

• **Picture first** eBay's off-the-peg item layout puts the pictures at the bottom of the page, under the written description. To get the best out of your listing, put your picture at the top and middle followed by an easily digestable summary. There's nothing worse than finding an item you think you might want to buy and then having to scroll down and down until you're given a glimpse of it. Don't make your buyer do the work. Get your picture right at the top where they can see it.

• **Keep it short** You're not Tolstoy, so do try to keep the written aspect of your description as compact as possible. Acres of text are a real turn-off for buyers, so provide the necessary information, but use columns and bullet points to make sure your buyers can get the info they require quickly.

• **Ditch the blurb** Some sellers really put off their buyers by including long, commanding and forbidding rules in their listings: 'I won't do this' or 'You have to do this' and 'I don't accept that'. In many cases this makes the seller look somewhat misanthropic and unpleasant. Where possible, cut out the extraneous details or confine them to a page other than your View Item page.

• **Returns** As eBay has become increasingly professionalised and ecommerce in general has grown more sophisticated, peace of mind for buyers has become more important. Buyers really do like the reassurance of a returns policy and the opportunity to exchange items. Experience shows that while few buyers actually do return items, they like to know they can.

Inside Information
Invest in HTML

I hope you're already learning lots of new things as you ramp up your sales. Two of the key qualities you need to succeed on eBay are willingness to learn and the flexibility to face up to change (on which more later).

HTML - HyperText Markup Language - may look like a slightly pointless and rather dull thing to find out about, but you'd be wrong. A basic understanding of how the language works is something that will serve you well. I'm not suggesting complete fluency, but rather a few key phrases, rather like when you go on holiday. It's nice to be able to say please and thank-you and hello and goodbye in the native tongue, even if anything else leaves you lost.

It's also worth learning the HTML tags for hosting an image and creating a hyperlink. Get your hands on a cheap manual or check out some of the HTML sites that have details of all the tags you will ever need. I cannot promise that you will have a fun-filled time getting to grips with HTML, but it will certainly be time well spent.

Case study: GMDC Global

John Pemberton manages GMDC Global Ltd, a company that sells on eBay using three different shops: give_me_designer_clothes, designer-clothes-2u and premium_designer_clothes. Not only is a fourth eBay shop in the pipeline, John also sells on Amazon and is working on his own webshop: www.designerclothes2u.com. He sells suits, jackets, coats, trousers, shoes and accessories from over 500 world-famous designer brands, including Dr Martens.

John is typical of the new breed of eBay seller. He identified the eBay opportunity and proactively decided to build a business rather than stumbling into ecommerce accidentally like so many eBayers do. Early on he realised that selling online is massively different from running a High Street shop. 'Online you have to present the item and convince a customer it is right for them without them touching or trying it on for size,' says John. 'One thing I offer that many shops don't is detailed measurements and in-depth information about an item.'

John has been operating his business for four years. He broke even at the end of year one and has since been profitable. He has consistently grown and developed his sales and describes his business as the number 1 menswear seller on eBay UK. However, it wasn't always easy. 'Running and growing a business is a challenge,' John told me, 'and it takes resilience. As time goes on, profits grow, and the nature of obstacles changes.'

John is sticking with eBay because it's a well-established marketplace and he still sees room for growth there, but he is also looking elsewhere. Amazon was his first stop: 'Amazon is a wonderful marketplace, innovative and technically well constructed. As a buyer I find it uncomplicated, clutter-free and easy to buy on.' His move to Amazon is about finding new customers. He wants to attract new customers and sales in addition to eBay, not as a replacement. Amazon is also harder to use from a seller's point of view, John says.

What's the secret of successfully starting an ecommerce business? John is clear: 'For me it's a simple thing – success is being able to sell lots of product for a net profit in the least time possible, while achieving a high customer satisfaction rating.' He makes it sound so straightforward.

23

Build Your eBay Profile

When you are selling items on eBay you are not just selling your products: you are also selling yourself as a good person to trade with. You need to inspire trust in buyers, so you should use every opportunity available to you – and you won't be spoilt for choice. eBay isn't just about commerce, the community activity that the trading relies on is vital too. Obviously that can just mean feedback and the ratings that people give to each other after a transaction, but there are other ways for you to build your reputation.

Here are the tools you can use:

- **About Me** A personalised page where you can tell the world about you and what you sell.

- **Reviews and guides** You opportunity to express your views and demonstrate your expertise. Reviews allow you to give a short précis of your views on a certain DVD or CD. Guides allow you to demonstrate your expertise or knowledge on just about any topic.

- **eBay My World** My World aggregates all the information you've compiled into a profile that other members can see and read.

Tip: Food for the search engines

One of the real benefits of building your profile on eBay is the boost it gives you in search engines. Written content such as blog entries and reviews and guides will be picked up by search engines and hopefully enable you to attract buyers who aren't even on eBay.

About Me

One tool that many sellers overlook is the About Me page. Building an About Me page is an essential part of ramping up.

- **What to include on an About Me page** A member's About Me page does exactly what it says on the packet: it's your chance to tell the rest of the eBay community all about yourself. At the most basic level you can use your About Me page to talk about your passions, interests, activities on eBay and general information about who you are. But as you start selling you can use it as a valuable part of your reputation as a seller.

- **Build trust with your About Me page** As you decide what you want to include on your About Me page, don't forget the purpose you are building it for: to get an edge on your competitors and come across as a person a buyer wants to trust and buy from. This of course doesn't mean you need to be stuffy or formal: you simply need to present details that cast you in a good light.

Be real and don't pretend to be something you aren't. If you do you'll just seem like a fake and no one will trust you. Coming across as a real person will benefit you more than trying to sound like a business or a corporation.

Many sellers like to include funny stories, pictures and details about themselves. But be careful not to give too much away. There are people who might want to misuse personal information, so protect your privacy.

How to build an About Me page

To create an About Me page, write the text in a Word document before you even log on. You can find the link to create an About Me page on the site map and in My eBay.

The easiest way to build the page is to use one of the ready-made templates that eBay provides free of charge. If you use one of the templates you can simply choose a layout you like and copy and paste your pre-prepared text into the fields provided. You don't need to be familiar with HTML: you can style the text to the way you select using the edit functions.

If you want to include pictures you can, but you need to host the images on your own web space and paste the image location or URL into the page. You can also include links to your favourite websites. If you know HTML and would prefer to start from scratch and make a truly individual About Me page, that is perfectly possible.

Inside Information:
Your eBay personality matters

In the daily scramble to ramp up your sales and get your fledgling business onto a solid grounding, the idea of spending valuable time building profiles, writing and blogging might seem a long way down the 'to do' list. And of course, it's vital to offer your existing customers good service, get those despatches out the door and make sure you're listing everything you can on the site.

But once that's done, turn your hand to building a useful and engaging About Me page and a vibrant eBay My World presence. There are three good business reasons to invest time in building your eBay personality.

It's about being competitive and differentiating yourself from your competitors. On eBay price isn't the only deciding factor when buyers make that purchasing decision. They will also assess your listings, feedback and your eBay profile. Investing in an About Me page and a My World profile helps you stand out from the crowd and is another chance to talk to your buyers. Don't forget: lots of sellers don't use these features, so even just a basic attempt means you're streets ahead.

eBay rests on a foundation of trust and, despite all the protections in place, buyers are often still wary about dealing with a stranger online or have an irrational fear of losing their money. A seller who has invested in the social side of the site is very unlikely to be a fraudster. Take an eBay blog as an example. As a buyer you might see a seller blogging about their daily routine, new lines or a trip they've made to an exciting place to buy stock. In turn, the blog posts have lots of lovely comments from other members. It's just reassuring.

The third major benefit relates to search engines. When it comes to getting top ranking with the likes of Google, the written word counts and it's a simple case of more is more. Having as much text as possible (preferably updated frequently) makes you sexy to the search engine bots.

Those are the business benefits. But I want to highlight another benefit that might not necessarily affect the bottom line: it's simply good clean fun.

Reviews and guides

One great way of building your reputation on eBay is to establish yourself as an expert. You can do this by producing reviews and guides. This part of the site is a place for members to review and rate products and also share their wisdom and write a guide. Find out what others are writing about at http://reviews.ebay.co.uk.

Writing a review

A review can be about almost anything. Check out the Reviews and Guides sections for inspiration. The most popular products to review are DVDs and CDs, but there are many options, including household goods.

To get the most out of your labours, choose popular products or those that don't have a review already. One sentence isn't enough: try to write something that's genuinely useful for other members and you probably can't do that in fewer than 100 words. If you can review items that are particularly relevant to your sales, so much the better: start by reviewing your top-selling lines.

There's no need to write dozens of reviews in one go to build your profile – it's better to start creating a portfolio over time. Consider writing one review a week so that you accumulate a collection and then do one a month. Don't forget to check the effectiveness of your reviews by tracking them with your Traffic Reports in your eBay Shop.

Writing a guide

A guide is longer than a review and you can write one on just about any topic that is useful to other members. Write an authoritative guide that shows you know what you're on about. Check out what other people are writing for inspiration, but it's good advice to start with something you're genuinely passionate about. Your passion and enthusiasm will come out in your words and attract readers and positive ratings.

eBay My World

My World is where eBay gathers all your written content together as a single profile. You can organise it as you like, design it and add an image and biog that reflect what you sell. It's your opportunity to build a brand on eBay that is congruent with your listings and shop, if you have one. You can access My World via the Community tab on the navigation bar. If you are already blogging and have written reviews and guides, they will be presented here with details of what you're selling and your feedback too.

You can also build custom pages in eBay My World. It's a great opportunity to gather together all your important information for buyers. You can then link to your My World from your listings.

Tip: Google juice

> To give your My World pages extra 'Google juice', don't forget to use the features that help you link to other sellers and list your interests. Ensure that they are relevant to your business and try to get reciprocal links from other sellers you know.

• **Selling policies** Your My World pages are a great place to lay out how you do business. Obviously you want to include some of this information in your item listings, but it doesn't do any harm to make information common to all your listings available on My World too.

• **Postage terms** If you prefer to send your items using insured methods such as recorded or registered delivery, you can note that here for all your buyers to see.

• **Refunds and returns** Many sellers note the circumstances under which they will accept a return and offer a refund. The benefit of putting this in My World is that you don't need to clog up your listings with too much detail. You can simply have a link in your listing that says 'Click here for my refunds and returns policy'.

- **Keep it up to date** It shouldn't take you too long to decide what to include in My World, but once the information is live on the site, make sure you update it every now and again to ensure that it is current and helping you to win over buyers.

Tip: Search for yourself!

Check out how you're performing on the search engines by searching for yourself. Before long you should see that your eBay profile pages are among the best performing. This shouldn't be a surprise: they have been developed by eBay to be as attractive as possible to search engine spiders.

Marketing on the eBay Community Forums

The secret of marketing is to find an audience that might be interested in your goods and telling them about what you're selling. It's obvious, really. A fruit and veg seller in the middle of the wilderness wouldn't sell much produce. A similar shop on a bustling high street would do.

eBay itself is bustling with browsers and customers perusing the goods for sale, but eBay buyers also gather in other areas of the site. Most notably, hundreds of thousands of buyers and sellers visit the Discussion Boards every month. They're not there to trade, they're there to socialise, chat and exchange advice and gossip. You're not allowed to market directly to other eBayers on the Discussion Boards, but don't let that discourage you. Think of the pubs and cafés around all those London markets. No trading actually occurs there, but business does get done, if you know what I mean.

So take a leap and introduce yourself to other eBayers in eBay's social areas, which you can find by clicking Community in the navigation bar.

Some dos and don'ts:

- **Do introduce yourself** and talk about your business and what you sell.

- **Don't advertise**. It won't be appreciated and your post might be removed by the board moderators.

- **Do help other users** with their problems if you think you might have some useful advice.

- **Don't be argumentative, rude or offensive**: remember that your comments will reflect on your selling.

- **Don't give away too much**. Personal details such as your address, children's names or other sensitive information are best left unshared.

Tip: StumbleUpon

Have you heard of StumbleUpon? This is a service (owned by eBay) that allows you to share sites you like with other web users. You download a special toolbar that sits in your browser window and whenever you are on a site or page you like, you click a button, describe it and explain what it is. That page is then provided to other StumbleUpon users who share your interests or are looking for something new. When you have your eBay profile pages up and running, don't forget to 'stumble' them to attract visitors and hopefully some buyers.

eBay's AdCommerce

If you're familiar with Google AdWords, you'll get eBay AdCommerce too. It's a pay-per-click system that allows eBay sellers to promote their items and Shop in eBay search results. It's less dependent on your DSRs and if you meet minimum conditions you can bid for keywords and get added exposure to buyers. Like those ads on Google, you get top billing above 'natural' reports.

Is it worth it? Reviews from eBay sellers are decidedly unenthusiastic. It's another distraction for very busy sellers: it's something new to learn and administer, it takes time and brainspace and there are already huge demands on both if you're running an eBay business. I'd avoid AdCommerce until you're happy that you're already doing the most you can without shelling out extra.

Find out more here: http://pages.ebay.co.uk/adcommerce/

24

Open an eBay Shop

If you are serious about making money on eBay either as a lucrative hobby or as a business, an eBay shop will be an essential part of your offering. An eBay shop is an off-the-peg, instant ecommerce presence that you can personalise and use to reflect your own sales and eBay persona. Opening a shop not only provides you with lots of useful tools and features to help you sell even more successfully, but sends a message to your buyers that you are an advanced seller. Typically a shop owner sells 25% more than a seller without a shop.

According to eBay, 75% of eBay sellers who have a shop say that it has helped them increase sales. It seems fair to assume that the other 25% haven't built their shop correctly or have failed to utilise the shop functions correctly. A well-constructed shop is sure to give you a boost in your sales.

The good news is that you don't need to be a computer whizz or know HTML to build a shop. When you open one you are able to customise it from a selection of options and you're guided through the process by the eBay Shop Builder. You can personalise your shop with a logo and colour scheme and also organise how your items are displayed in a matter of minutes.

The benefits of an eBay shop

An eBay shop is your own ecommerce website. It sits on the eBay site and people can easily navigate to it via Search and Browse, but it can also act as though it's a standalone entity. The shop comes complete with your own URL (web address) that you can use as you wish on business cards or other promotional material to direct buyers straight to your shop.

You have control over the shop design and how you organise your items. This means that whether you are selling dozens of things or thousands, you can build your own category structure just like on the eBay site to help buyers navigate your wares quickly and easily. You can also advertise special offers or great deals using the promotional options. An eBay shop can be a dynamic selling environment that you can tweak to your liking.

Visit the eBay Shops homepage at http://stores.ebay.co.uk and check out shops that have been opened by other sellers. When a seller has a shop they also have a small red door logo by their User ID, which you can click on to visit their shop.

Why do you need a shop?

Put simply, buyers like them. An eBay shop is a familiar environment where buyers can not only easily browse what you're selling but also find out more about you as a seller. A well-ordered and well-maintained shop is a great way of increasing the confidence of buyers.

eBay knows this and shops are promoted to buyers all over the site in the hope of tempting people to buy. A shop is also useful because if someone buys, say, a camera from you, by visiting your shop they can be in no doubt that you also offer complementary accessories such as memory cards or tripods. There are opportunities for you to cross-promote and merchandise your full variety of goods.

The features and tools available in a shop also give you the opportunity to reach out to your past buyers and tell them about your current sales. You can create mailing lists, advertising emails and flyers. The visibility that a shop gives you in search engines also means that you can attract people to your shop even if they aren't on eBay.

How to set up shop

First, examine what other sellers are doing and how they are using their shops. You'll doubtless get some excellent ideas from them and will gain a good grasp of the functionality on offer. It can also be worth checking out the eBay Shops Discussion Board for the latest news and gossip before you get started: it's always an engaging source of information. You can access it using the Community tab on the navigation bar.

There are five constituent parts you need to consider in relation to an eBay Shop and it's best if you prepare them in advance.

You need to provide a shop name, choose a design, describe your shop and what you're selling, and also build your categories. In addition, although this won't be visible on your shop front, you have to enter keywords especially for the search engine spiders. Opening your shop is an investment, so don't do it on the fly. Choose a quiet afternoon or evening to follow the process properly and with care. You can come back and amend and update the details any time you like, but make sure that 'sort out my shop' isn't another recurring item on your to-do list that never gets done.

Choose a name

You already have an eBay User ID and you can use that for your shop name if you like, but it pays to be more adventurous to ensure that you reap the full rewards. Much like item titles, with a bit of thought you can really squeeze extra value from your shop name. It's obvious from shop names you see on eBay that most sellers aren't aware of the huge dividend a perfect choice could bring them: don't make the same mistake.

The temptation is to name your shop something cute or personal – 'Dan's Den', for instance – but this might not be the best way to attract buyers. The name of your shop is critical to its appearance in search engines. Good visibility means that you can also attract buyers from outside eBay to your shop. Search engines pay great attention to the shop name, so you benefit from choosing one that will be picked up by internet searchers. People aren't going to search for 'Dan's Den', but 'Bargain Books and DVDs' will be found by people searching for bargain books and DVDs.

Try using good keywords that are descriptive, are searched for often and are relevant to what you are selling and you'll attract more browsers. Take a look on Google for proof. If you search for 'eBay Shop UK toys', you'll see that the shops that appear at the top of the list have the word 'toys' in the shop name. Try it with any other goods and you'll see that the shop name is critical. Making sure that you get it right will boost your sales.

You should also check that you aren't using someone's registered business name. You can double-check this on the Companies House website, www.companieshouse.gov.uk.

Choose a design

You can easily choose a colour scheme and layout using eBay's free templates and designs. This won't take long and it gives you an opportunity to personalise your shop. You can also add your own logo to the shop. eBay has made a selection available, but it is best to create your own for that really personal touch.

Building your shop is an excellent opportunity to review the branding and design of all your listings. To get the nuclear benefits that a shop can give you, a coherent design and brand across your shop, shop items, auction listings, About Me page and emails are essential. Use consistent colours and fonts across all your eBay pages and get a logo designed, if you don't have one already. The aim is to ensure that your buyers know they are shopping with you and notice if they leave your pages.

Getting a logo designed is not tricky: lots of eBay sellers offer design services (do a search!). It really adds an edge and a look of professionalism to your eBay listings and shop. The logo should also reflect your chosen colour scheme, suit your online persona and perhaps give other people a clue about what you sell. You can use the logo on your business cards and letterheads.

Customised shop designs

For any fledgling seller, the off-the-peg designs you can knock up yourself using eBay's templates and design wizard will be more than adequate for your needs. Actually, even some big sellers tell me they don't reckon they need anything more than one of the free, basic layouts provided. But your eBay Shop is completely customisable and many bigger sellers want something that looks more professional and exciting. If you have HTML and design skills you can do it yourself, or there are companies out there who will do the design and coding for you.

Here are some things to bear in mind:

- **Pros:** Designing and developing your own eBay Shop means that you get exactly what you want. It can look very professional and you can really imprint your brand and personality on it. You can choose to organise your goods your way and display them in a manner that benefits your best-selling lines more effectively, and you can minimise eBay's own branding and logo.

- **Cons:** Diverting too far from the norm will mean that your shop is different to the majority of layouts that buyers are used to. This may confuse customers and mean they go elsewhere. It will also take you longer to maintain and update your shop if it's your own work. Getting someone in to design a personalised shop can be costly: will it necessarily deliver corresponding returns?

If you're interested, check out some of the services that can help you, such as Frooition (www.frooition.com) and Just Template It (www.justtemplateit.com).

Tip: Fools rush in...

Whatever you do, don't rush in. Make sure that your shop is working for you before you call in the professionals to tart it up.

Describe your shop

You also need to write a shop description and create your custom categories. Again, these are important for making your shop attractive to search engines. Search engines pay attention to words or phrases that are repeated on a page, so make sure that your categories and description reflect what you sell as well as your shop name. Here's an example of a shop description:

My name is Dan and welcome to my shop. I take pride in selling lovely old books that I have collected over the years and also DVDs. Thanks for stopping by!

That might be friendly and personal, but this would be much better:

Buy books and DVDs. Paperback books, Hardback books, Fiction, Non-Fiction, First Editions, New and Secondhand, DVDs, Thrillers, Comedy, Drama.

Obviously your description will be relevant to what you are selling, but be aware that specialist terms that people are familiar with are ideal. You should include brand names and alternative terms too, whenever possible.

Case study: The eBay shop expert
eBay user ID: Mountcomp

Chris started selling on eBay because he needed an income quickly: he'd been made redundant and just taken on a mortgage. He's now a successful full-time seller who wouldn't dream of going back into the workplace. In fact, things have been so successful, Chris doesn't think he could physically sell any more than he already does. 'I've reached the limit on the amount of product I can stock, list, ship and manage as a sole trader,' he says. 'In fact last January I could barely cope with shipping due to the volume of sales.'

For Chris one of the secrets of his success has been making the most of his eBay shop. He told me, 'Shops are all about image, your image, your business's image. They're your opportunity to present your items to buyers in the format to give the buying experience that you want. A shop will help you sell more, more often to more buyers.'

He doesn't think that setting up a shop should take you long. 'Set aside a couple of hours and let eBay make it easy for you.' But he cautions against getting too carried away. 'Avoid the fancy shop schemes and use either "Classic Top" or "Classic Left" – they look a lot better once you add logos,' he reckons. 'Have an idea what colours you want to use before you start; work from the colours in your company logo or the colours you choose for your auctions.'

And once you're up and running he has more suggestions: 'Use categories and give them meaningful names. It's possible to gain high natural placement on Google with eBay listings simply from good listing titles as long as you repeat the relevant keywords.

'Use email marketing combined with a call to action. For example, list a limited number of items on Buy It Now with Best Offer and in your email marketing let buyers know what Best Offer you'll accept. Your stock will walk off the shelves if stock is limited for this offer!

'Use Traffic Reporting to find out what buyers are searching your eBay shop for, and then use the keywords in your item titles.'

To Chris, a shop is about 'being able to control and guide buyers' behaviour and the actions you want them to perform'. Take a look at his shop at http://stores.ebay.co.uk/Mount-Road-Computers.

Design your shop categories

When you design your category structure you should have two aims in mind: cramming in as many keywords as possible and making it easy for buyers to find what they want. It's your opportunity to craft a navigation system honed to suit your sales and your buyers, so you want relevant, descriptive terms that reflect what people search for. You also want to remember what search engines will be looking for.

Here are some examples of potential categories:

Fiction	Books: Fiction
Non-Fiction	Books: Non-fiction
First Editions	Books: First Editions
DVDs	Books: Antique
Others	DVDs: Thrillers
	DVDs: Comedy
	DVDs: Drama
	Other books and DVDs

The righthand category list is much better because it repeats the keywords relevant to what you are selling. If you combine a good title, description and category list in your shop a search engine will be in no doubt about what you sell and the shop will stand a far better chance of being found via a search engine by a potential buyer.

You can further boost the relevance of your keywords by using any of the online resources, such as Overture, that catalogue how often certain search terms are used on the internet. You can find the links to these resources in the section earlier in this book called 'The title is vital'.

Chris, eBay User ID Mountcomp, is enthusiastic about the impact good shop categories can have. 'I *know* this works,' he says, 'which is why I have categories and subcategories such as Dell Laptop Accessories, Dell Laptop Power Supplies, Dell Docking Stations and Dell Accessories, and then auction titles such as "Dell D/Port Dock Replicator Inspiron 8600 Precision M60".

'I might not always be top on Google, but for detailed searches that count I'm often on the front page and even higher on the front page of Google.co.uk. The reason is simple: the words "Dell", "laptop", "docking station" and then the laptop model are repeated in the shop description, category, subcategory, auction title and auction description, so Google think they're highly relevant.'

Enter keywords

The final stage requires you to enter keywords for each of your shop pages and categories. The keywords you enter when you are setting up shop are of great importance to search engines, but their power is only completely unleashed if you have chosen an effective title, optimised your categories and crafted a really good description. You can find the fields to enter your keywords under the heading 'Keywords' in the lefthand navigation pane of your shop management console.

All you have to do is enter the keywords that are relevant to your shop. eBay will help you make the right choices and then conceal them in the code of your shop, where search engines can find them and use them to catalogue and index your shop correctly.

Tip: Learn from the masters

Using eBay Pulse you can identify the biggest shops in your category. Seek out sellers who list things like you and check out what they're doing. Don't copy them directly, it's important that you build your own distinct brand, but do use other sellers as an inspirational resource.

Get the most from your shop

You want to keep your shelves well stocked using the cheaper Shop Inventory Format for listings. But you also need to make sure that you make it easy for buyers to find your listings and your shop.

• **Shop header** Add your shop header to all your listings. This is a graphic that sits on your listings directing people straight to your shop. The header has your shop logo and name in it and you can also include a selection of your shop categories so buyers can get straight to the items they want.

The shop header is a vital way of building your brand and putting your shop sales right in front of browsers and buyers.

Take a look at how other sellers are using it and think about how you can design it to maximise sales.

• **Cross-promotion options** You can cross-promote your shop sales in all your listings. At the bottom of many listings you see boxes displaying other items that seller has for sale. As a shop seller you have lots of options related to which items are cross-promoted and how they are displayed and prioritised.

Depending on what you want to sell you can opt to display the most expensive items, the cheapest or those without bids. You can set your cross-promotion preferences and your shops header in My eBay via the link 'Seller, Manage Shop'.

• **Maintain your shop** Try to keep your shop up to date and fresh. You want to make it as dynamic and welcoming an environment as possible. You can do this by using the various features available to help you promote your sales.

• **Promotional boxes** You can create promotional boxes for your shop that you can position on your homepage to draw attention to your special sales. You have total flexibility in titling the promotional box and you can link directly to one of your items or perhaps one of your shop categories. You can also use these boxes to give buyers the chance to view your shop items in a preferred order. On the eBay site many buyers are attracted by search and browse listings set to a Gallery view, with items ending soonest shown first. You could use a promotional box to do the same.

• **Custom pages** One way of really personalising your shop is to create pages of your own. You have great flexibility in what you can do and a quick browse on the site will show the variety of ways shop owners use this kind of customisation. It's a great means of setting out all your policies and telling buyers why you are a great seller. And there's also a business benefit to creating these pages: they get picked up by search engines.

• **Markdown Manager** Everyone loves the buzz of the sales and the thrill of finding a bargain. But to get your buyers salivating, they need to know how much they're saving. The Markdown Manager is a tool available to shop sellers that shows buyers how much the item they are looking at has been discounted. As a seller you can choose when items are discounted and by how much, even determining it in advance. Don't worry: you're completely in control and can change and edit your reductions at any time.

Mailing lists and email marketing

You can invite browsers and buyers to join your mailing list. Email marketing is a powerful way of reaching out to other eBayers and encouraging repeat sales. You are not permitted to send out unsolicited emails to all and sundry, but if someone opts in to your mailing list, your shop enables you to send them emails advertising your wares.

You can encourage people to join your mailing list by advertising it in your listings, shop header and all the emails you send out when people buy items. You can organise people who opt in by adding them to particular lists depending on what they have bought from you in the past.

Once you have a list of members, you are ready to reach out to them with email marketing. You can use eBay's special email marketing tool to build a tailored email in a matter of moments. You are free to craft your own introductory text and email title and then automatically add items and gallery pictures of items you have for sale. You can also use HTML to help you create a very personal email. Don't forget to preview your email first to check that it's what you want.

People get tired of receiving too many emails, so when you reach out to your list make sure that you have something to say and something good to sell. Emails sent in this way take about four hours to be delivered, so take a moment to think about the best time to send your mail. To build and send a marketing email, click 'Email Marketing' in your shops management console.

Shops reporting

Of all the functions you get with an eBay shop, one of the most important is the shop's traffic and sales reporting features. From what I've heard from the shop owners I've met, it's also one of the most overlooked.

The traffic reports tell you how many visitors you've had to your items and shop. You can find out which of your pages are the most visited, which of your listings is getting the most hits and which keywords buyers are using to find your listings, which means you won't leave the most important ones out.

Traffic reporting is a great way of understanding what's working and what's not. For instance, if that seven-day auction format listing that you start at 8pm on a Tuesday is getting three times more visits than the ten-day one started on a Thursday at noon, you might want to ditch the Thursday listing or start it at 8pm instead.

Sales reports contain your full sales data, including buyer information, sales prices and how much you paid eBay in fees. You can export the report into a spreadsheet program and it can form the basis of your accounting system. You need to download these reports regularly, because your records are only stored for four months at a time on the eBay site.

On the Manage My Shop page, you can access sales and traffic reports from the links on the lefthand side.

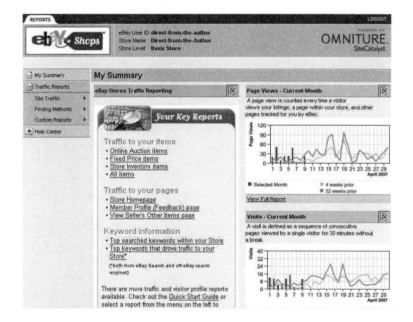

Featured and anchor shops

A Basic Shop represents excellent value at £14.99 per month. If you want to take your shop selling to the next level, you might want to upgrade your shop. For £49.99 a month you can have a Featured

Shop, which offers some enhancements and also much greater prominence on eBay. For £349.99 you can have an Anchor Shop, which gives you placement on the Shops homepage and means that your shop has the greatest possible visibility.

People often ask me how eBay can justify an Anchor Shop costing seven times as much as a Featured Shop. Does it drive seven times more sales? Probably not, is the answer. But I think they're asking the wrong question. Far better to ask whether it drives more than £300 more in sales each month. If it does, it's worth thinking about getting.

These advanced options are for serious sellers and won't be suitable for everyone. As with Listing Enhancements, you can't buy sales on eBay and if you haven't got the basics right such options are a pointless waste of money. However, for some advanced sellers they can be a very sound investment.

Inside Information
Shops and search engines

If you've ever tried to build your own website and have it ranked and findable in any of the search engines, you'll know that it isn't easy to get your site at the top of the list. This is because of how search engines index and rank websites and the various factors that they take into consideration. Obviously, a website needs to have the relevant keywords on it for a searcher to find it, but the order in which the results are displayed is determined by a number of factors. One of the most significant is how important the search engine thinks the website is.

A website such as eBay is considered very important by a search engine such as Google because lots of people link to it and because there are lots of links from eBay out into the internet. For the 'spiders' that search engines send out to explore the internet and gather information, eBay comes up a lot so that makes it important.

These spiders also find the eBay site attractive because it has been optimised to be easily readable and digestible for them. The page titles, headings and text are designed to give eBay the greatest possible profile in search results pages.

So when you open an eBay shop you have an automatic advantage because you can use the profile that eBay has built up to help you get your shop to the top of the search engines. You can basically piggyback on eBay to attract buyers who are searching the whole web and not just eBay.

Obviously, there are things that you can do to further enhance the chances of your shop being prominent. Using popular keywords and repeating them in your shop content will make spiders like it. Your shop name is vital too, so choose it carefully.

I've spoken to sellers who cite the search engine benefits of an eBay shop as its primary value. You can buy visibility on search engines, as many eBay sellers do, but it is time consuming and expensive and there is no guarantee of browsers turning into buyers. With a shop you can get internet visibility cheaply and easily.

Tip: Passing trade

Your eBay Shop is a destination for shoppers and buyers who find you on the net via search engines. Your visitors won't just be finding you via eBay. Make sure that your shop is approachable and usable to people who pop by unexpectedly.

eBay shop checklist

• **Choose a good shop name** Make it descriptive and relevant to what you are selling.

• **Write a shop description** List the sort of things you're selling – and don't forget that the right text is vital for good rankings in search engines.

• **Choose a colour scheme** Decorate your shop to suit your type of sales and eBay brand.

• **Design a logo** Unleash the designer within and create a logo that is right for you rather than using the ones off the shelf.

• **Optimise your categories** Remember the search engines and use the categories in your shop to help buyers find what they want.

• **Fill the shelves** Stock your shop using the cheaper Shops Inventory Format and make your full selection of items available to buyers.

• **Switch on the shop header** Get buyers into your shop through advertising by including the shop header in all your listings.

- **Cross-promote to attract buyers** Promote eye-catching and complementary items in your listings to bring in buyers.

- **Measure and analyse** Use the Traffic Reports tool to find out what's working in your shop and what's not.

- **Create a mailing list** Reach out to your loyal customers with special offers to encourage repeat custom.

25

Become a PowerSeller

If you successfully ramp up your sales, with any luck you'll be selling £750 worth of goods every month. That's a magic number on eBay: you become eligible to be a PowerSeller.

While you've been buying and selling on eBay you might have seen a PowerSeller logo beside some sellers' User IDs. A PowerSeller is someone who has been recognised by eBay for their high level of sales. Naturally, eBay wants to retain high-volume sellers and the PowerSeller programme is a sort of loyalty scheme that encourages them to keep on trading.

PowerSellers must meet certain criteria to achieve that status and if you start selling seriously on eBay you should definitely think about becoming one. Not only will PowerSeller status provide you with a certain kudos within the eBay Community, you'll also enjoy some benefits and perks.

What is a PowerSeller?

A PowerSeller is a seller who meets a set of minimum criteria laid down by eBay. First, they must maintain a certain level of sales: to qualify you must sell a minimum of £750 worth of goods a month.

But just having one good month isn't enough. A PowerSeller must maintain their sales for three consecutive months in order to qualify. They must also make up those sales from more than four listings a month: selling a £1000 car each month for three months won't work.

But PowerSelling isn't just about selling lots of stuff. It's about being a good eBay citizen and having excellent feedback. PowerSellers must have a minimum feedback of 100, maintain a 98% positive rating and also be professional, diligent and trustworthy. Breaking eBay's rules or getting a bunch of negative feedbacks is the fast track to losing PowerSeller status. PowerSellers must keep their eBay account in good standing and pay their fees, as well as be sure to contact buyers within three days of the end of a listing. And beware: eBay doesn't make exceptions for PowerSellers. Being a PowerSeller is something of an honour and it doesn't buy any exemptions.

There are five different levels of PowerSeller: Bronze, Silver, Gold, Platinum and Titanium. You can also become a PowerSeller by selling a minimum number of units a month. Here are the levels and qualification criteria:

	Bronze	Silver	Gold	Platinum	Titanium
Monthly sales	£750	£1500	£6000	£15,000	£95,000
No. of items sold	100	300	1000	2500	5000

Different PowerSeller levels offer different benefits and there is great competition to move up the ranks and join the increasingly more exclusive groups. There is only a handful of Titanium PowerSellers in Britain.

Being a PowerSeller isn't a lifelong club: to maintain their status PowerSellers must keep selling the minimum amount each month and maintain a good feedback level too. If they fail to meet the criteria they will be given a warning before being removed from the PowerSeller programme.

How do you become a PowerSeller?

If you meet the criteria you will automatically qualify; you don't need to apply. eBay contacts potential new PowerSellers every month with details of how they can take advantage of the service. You can check whether you are eligible by visiting the PowerSeller pages, which can be accessed from the Site Map.

What are the benefits of being a PowerSeller?

The higher the PowerSeller level, the greater the benefits. All levels are permitted to use the PowerSeller logo in their listings and also utilise it in any promotional material they produce. For instance, many PowerSellers take pride in including the logo on their business cards and letterheads. A lot say that the logo is the best perk of the programme: it shows buyers that the seller is professional and bound by special rules. This inspires buyers to bid with confidence.

All PowerSeller levels are eligible for invitations to PowerSeller events (such as meetings with eBay staff and masterclasses in eBay selling from experts) and have access to a dedicated PowerSeller Discussion Board to meet and talk with others about eBay selling. Every PowerSeller also has access to priority customer support via email and can expect a response in super-quick time. PowerSellers can also receive advice and troubleshooting on how to develop their business.

Silver-level PowerSellers and above have access to customer support on the telephone. During business hours they can reach a member of the Customer Support team dedicated to PowerSellers' needs. This is ideal for high-volume sellers who have a complex query that might be difficult to resolve via email. PowerSellers can also enjoy preferential rates from PayPal: the higher the level, the lower the fees.

Gold-level and above PowerSellers also get access to a Personal Account Manager. An Account Manager is a trained member of eBay's Customer Support team whom you can contact directly by phone or email. Having a regular point of contact who can get to know you and your business is a major benefit and they will be able to give you the most appropriate and relevant support and advice. Best of all, an Account Manager isn't just there to solve problems. They can also help you build your business.

You can schedule a call and get their take on how you're doing and any suggestions they have. It's great to have another pair of eyes analysing your sales and thinking about how you can sell more. Your Account Manager will also be able to keep you up to date with recent changes and how they affect you.

Inside Information:
The PowerSeller logo

One of the most visible benefits of the PowerSeller programme is the logo that appears by your User ID everywhere on the site. Surprisingly, it's one of the most controversial aspects of the programme and is often the topic of vitriolic debate on the eBay Discussion Boards. Some buyers (a vocal minority) have a negative view of PowerSellers, believing them to be less credible and trustworthy than ordinary community members. For this group the logo serves as a warning 'not to buy'.

For PowerSellers this represents a dilemma. You can switch the PowerSeller logo off so it isn't visible if you like, and some do. But isn't the logo an attraction for some buyers? Personally, I think so. I find it reassuring to know I'm doing business with an experienced trader, especially if I'm spending a few quid.

What do other sellers say? The jury's still out. Some swear by the logo, others think it's a liability. A small number think all this is hot air and it makes no odds. So it's up to you, but it's worth knowing that not everyone sees the PowerSeller logo as a badge of honour.

PowerSeller discounts

The most significant benefits of the PowerSeller programme are Final Value Fee discounts. In basic terms, the more you sell the greater your Final Value Fee discount. The discount can be as much as 40% off the fees that non-PowerSellers pay, so they're truly worth having. It's a real departure for eBay. Traditionally, everyone on the site paid the same. There were no discounts for big sellers and no preferential treatment.

But it's not just a case of discounts for selling more: eligibility is also determined by offering good service, as I explain below. It's a clever eBay way of ensuring that buyers come back for more, and in return big sellers can get a whack off their fees.

The level of discount a PowerSeller is eligible for is determined by the PowerSeller level achieved. Titanium sellers get more off than Silver sellers. This is intended to encourage sellers to aspire to sell more and rise up the ranks.

POWERSELLER BENEFITS BY LEVEL

	Account Manager	Phone support	Priority email support	Final Value Fee discounts
Bronze	✗	✔	✔	20%
Silver	✗	✔	✔	25%
Gold	✔	✔	✔	30%
Platinum	✔	✔	✔	35%
Titanium	✔	✔	✔	40%

Detailed Seller Ratings and PowerSeller benefits

The PowerSeller benefits you receive depend on your having Detailed Seller Ratings that denote what eBay calls 'good service'. In basic terms this means that the scores you have received in the past 30 days must be above 4.6. If you stray below this magic number you'll lose your PowerSeller Final Value Fee discount, so it's worth keeping a close eye on your DSRs.

How are you doing? What needs to be improved? For Power-Seller purposes the score is calculated over the preceding 30 days, so it is possible to make good on low scores by raising your game. Improve your listings and ensure that your descriptions are full and accurate. Make sure that you've got your templates and automated emails in order to score highly on communication, and review your costs and processes to ensure that your carriage costs are reasonable and your delivery swift.

This might seem like a chore, especially if your business model is based on being a pile-it-high, churn-it-out seller, but it's not a bad thing. It can be a good opportunity to review your sales and improve your profitability. Don't forget that it's not just the discounts that are affected by your DSRs: your visibility in Search and Browse is connected too.

Tip: Business registration

Every PowerSeller needs to be registered as a business seller to qualify for the PowerSeller benefits.

PowerSellers and the rules

If anything, as a PowerSeller you are under more pressure to abide by eBay's rules. If one PowerSeller does break them you will find that other PowerSellers, keen to protect the value of the PowerSeller programme, report them to eBay. Buyers too expect more from a PowerSeller, which renders them open to greater scrutiny and more attention than other sellers.

PowerSellers don't get any special treatment from eBay. As a PowerSeller you'll be warned and sanctioned like any other member. It really pays to be aware of the rules and follow them. After all, if you do break them you have a lot more to lose than most members.

Inside Information
PowerSellers

PowerSellers are an important part of the eBay Community. Not only do they make up a significant proportion of listings on the site, in many ways they set the tone for how other members trade. Of course, there are PowerSellers who push the rules to breaking point and give the others a bad name, but generally they are good people making an honest living on eBay.

Nevertheless, it isn't an exclusive club. If you are serious about selling on eBay, reaching the minimum level of £750 a month shouldn't be difficult. But if you want to make a living you need to shift a great deal more stock than that!

Over the years I have met dozens of PowerSellers and most of them are people who took a punt and have succeeded. You don't need a business degree or even a GCSE to be a PowerSeller: you just need to sell things. I've met former cab drivers who have chucked that job in to sell event tickets. There's one guy who does very well selling vintage sewing machines to America. There's a lovely woman near Bristol who sells equestrian items to fund her expensive dressage habit.

While it isn't easy to become a PowerSeller, anyone can do it. All you need is to research your market, have something to sell and put the hours in. Before long you'll be an expert in postal rates and packing material, but you'll also be your own master. That's the attraction for so many PowerSellers: eBay has given them the opportunity to strike out on their own and do something they never dreamed they could.

26

eBay for Charity

The eBay for Charity programme was launched on eBay.co.uk in 2005 to support the BBC's Children in Need's Great Big Bid event. Members of the eBay community supported the charity by buying and selling items and they raised hundreds and thousands of pounds. You can use eBay for Charity to raise money not just for Children in Need but for pretty much any bona fide charity in the UK. Not only is it a great way of tapping into the generosity of eBay buyers, but it's an easy way of raising money for that good cause close to your heart.

You can check out the 'eBay for charity' homepage at http://pages/ebay/co/uk/community/charity/index.html

How does it work?

Basically, you sell your items and donate all of the proceeds or a percentage of the final selling price to a charity. This means that if you have some trinket or bauble that you don't want any more, you can in essence donate it to a charity of your choice.

eBay has teamed up with a UK-registered charity called MissionFish, which administers the process and guarantees the donations. MissionFish also takes care of applying for Gift Aid, meaning that if you are a UK taxpayer an extra 28p in each £1 goes to the charity courtesy of the Chancellor of the Exchequer.

eBay displays the listings in a special Charity section of the site and also gives every charity listing a ribbon icon so they stand out in Search and Browse results. You'll discover that many generous souls on eBay actively seek out charity listings and bid on them if they want to buy something. You'll probably find that your charity listings sell for more than they might usually, because they are for a good cause.

Two ways of selling for charity

There are two ways of getting involved in eBay for Charity. You can sell items yourself and nominate a charity to receive the proceeds. This is called community selling. If you have close ties with a charity or want to raise money for a specific cause, you can be a direct seller. This means that you can essentially become the charity's official eBay selling agent.

Community selling

Community selling is by far the easiest way of disposing of a few items for charity. You just select a charity and sell your item on its behalf, donating the money to the charity once the item has sold. You can list anything you like within eBay's rules, but the usual listing practices apply and you still need to take the time to construct a great listing.

Remember, you don't have to donate 100% of the item's sale price to the charity you have chosen. You can donate any percentage you like from 10% to 100%. So if you'd like to sell something of real value but can't afford to give all the proceeds away, you can pledge 20% and still make a difference.

For community selling there is a minimum £2 donation, or 10% of your item's final selling price, so that even if your item goes for less than a fiver you have to donate that much. MissionFish takes a 40p minimum donation from that to cover its costs, but don't forget that it also sorts out the Gift Aid for you.

It's very simple to set up your charity sale. First, you need to register with MissionFish and provide a credit card so that your donation can be guaranteed. This won't take more than a few minutes. Then in the Sell Your Item form or Turbo Lister, choose a charity that you want to benefit and the percentage you want to donate if the item sells.

Direct selling

If you want to make a number of sales for a particular cause, then direct selling is for you. It's also the best way for charities to sell things themselves: you'll see big-name charities like Oxfam doing just that already.

Here's an example of how it might work. If you are associated with a charity that gets gifts of items or perhaps has a charity shop or drop-off point, you can register an ID for direct selling on eBay and sell those items. Obviously not everything will be appropriate for sale, but some items donated may be just the ticket and you can sell those. Rare, collectable or big-ticket items may well fetch a good deal more on eBay than they might at a jumble sale.

To get started as a direct seller you need to register with MissionFish. For direct sellers there are no minimum donations or processing fees.

You can find out more about community and direct selling at http://pages.ebay.co.uk/community/charity/sellerinfo.html

How do charities get involved?

If you are involved with a charity, you can register with eBay for Charity so that people can sell on your behalf as well as setting up as a direct seller yourself. It could be a fun and innovative take on the old jumble sale theme. You could encourage people to sell as community sellers on eBay to raise money. And let's face it, more people use eBay than can fit into even the largest village hall. Charities can find out all about the scheme at http://pages.ebay.co.uk/community/charity/charityinfo.html

Inside Information
eBay for Charity

> *Even if you are a money-grabbing, hard-nosed capitalist who is only on eBay for the profit, you should think about selling some of your listings using eBay for Charity.*
>
> *Not only will it be good for your soul, but it's all good marketing. eBay markets charity listings extensively on the site and many people take a few moments to browse through them. It's a good way of getting in front of eBayers who might not necessarily know that they want what you're selling.*
>
> *I've spoken to a number of PowerSellers who reckon that eBay for Charity is a sound investment because it is a good way to draw members to their other sales. If you cross-promote your items correctly, you'll easily be able to attract buyers to your non-charity sales. And you'll also feel a warm surge of deep satisfaction.*

PART IV

BUILD AN eBAY BUSINESS

27

Start a Business

There are two certainties in life: death and taxes. eBay may be a virtual marketplace, but the money you earn is not. eBay exists in the real world and you have all the same responsibilities as you would if you were running any other sort of business. You have to deal with suppliers, officials and government bodies, just as businesspeople the world over have to as they try to earn a crust.

Nevertheless, these responsibilities shouldn't be onerous. In many ways making the jump from having a hobby to running a business is a great opportunity to raise your game and truly investigate the possibilities and potential of your eBay business idea. If you've got to do the extra work to comply with the law, why not make sure you're really profiting?

Just because your eBay business has emerged from a hobby or you work from home, it doesn't mean that you can run it haphazardly. You need to keep records, analyse your sales and numbers and make sure you operate within the law. You require commitment, perseverance and a willingness to open up your mind and learn about new things. It's best to understand the landscape of running a business before you take the plunge.

When do you need to start worrying about officialdom?

Her Majesty's Revenue and Customs has recently started targeting what it terms as 'etraders' with a new website: www.workingfor yourself.co.uk/etraders. HMRC is keen for online sellers to come forward and get registered, and has let it be known that it is also collecting information proactively. It has a special 'spider' that's crawling the web collecting details about sellers who look like they should be paying tax. The implication is that if you don't come forward voluntarily you should expect a knock on the door.

The guidance from the site is pretty clear: 'If you sell the odd, unwanted gift or some personal possessions, you might not qualify as a trader. But if you buy items with the intention of selling them on as quickly and as profitably as you can, then you are a trader and likely to be self-employed.' So if you've been buying in stock, you should get on the case and go legit.

This part of the book outlines the most-trodden path for eBay sellers going legit. For most sellers it's a case of starting out as self-employed, operating as a sole trader and taking it from there.

Inside Information
Facing up to change

Since 1999 I've closely followed the trends that eBay has created and surfed. In particular, I've always been fascinated by how sellers use the site and make money. Way back at the beginning, everyone selling on eBay was doing it as a hobby or a sideline. eBay's categories and functionality were pitched at collectors and it was impossible to imagine anyone managing to sell more than 50 items a week. It was just too labour intensive. Nothing was automated. You had to email your buyers individually and manually copy and paste their email addresses. There was no PayPal, just cheques and sometimes cash.

Managing auctions (because there were just auctions before 2001) once they'd ended was a primitive affair: I used to have a ream of print-outs with different pages for what had sold, what had been paid for and what I needed to despatch. There was no Selling Manager and My eBay held only scant details.

Fast forward a few years and businesses started to use the site to sell more and more items. Improvements to sales management software, the introduction of a proper Checkout system and PayPal meant that it was possible to sell hundreds, even thousands of items. And over the years seeing a business selling on eBay has become commonplace and quite normal.

Since 2005, I've noticed that most sellers have a sort of lifecycle. Business sellers tend to expand their sales to a certain point and then stop growing, typically maintaining sales but not increasing them. They 'plateau'. The reason behind the slowing growth is typically one of a few things.

One reason is capacity. The sellers physically can't do any more than they are. They are reluctant to take on staff, usually because of the hassle and annoyance of National Insurance or health and safety rules, so they just continue as a one-man band. Often these sellers are a bit set in their ways and they could find more capacity by reviewing their working practices and becoming more efficient.

Very often a seller's growth slows because they claim that the market into which they are selling is saturated, too competitive or diminished. Often when I start talking to these sellers I realise that it's none of the above. It's more a case of the market having changed in some way and the seller having failed to change with it.

It might be that the seller ought to review their listings, tweak their titles or improve their images. In more drastic cases the seller might need to examine a new sector, diversify into selling other products alongside current lines or look at selling something new altogether.

It could also be the time to start looking beyond eBay and apply the same selling skills to setting up shop in other online venues or establishing an independent ecommerce outlet.

When everything's going swimmingly, remember that bad times might be just around the corner. Start thinking about what you might need to change to keep on top of the competition.

That's what the rest of this book is about: change. Once you've conquered eBay by doing one thing, it won't be long before you have to begin doing something differently. Ask any seller who's making a good go of eBay and they'll tell you that they're constantly reviewing what they're doing, transforming how they do it and running an operation that's different to how it was a year ago. Change is inevitable on eBay. If dealing with it isn't your idea of fun, you're in the wrong business.

Register as self-employed

You need to register as self-employed within three months of beginning to operate as such. If you don't, you might be liable to a penalty. So, when you place that first order for goods you're going to sell on when you're ramping up your eBay sales, it might be a good time to fill in the forms. You can do it online at www.hmrc.gov.uk/startingup/register.htm.

It's essential to ensure that you're making the Class 2 National Insurance contributions that are required from a self-employed person. When you're self-employed you're also required to pay class 4 National Insurance and income tax on your profits. You pay these through your self-assessment tax form each year.

Self-assessment is easily completed online as long as you are registered with the HMRC website. Make sure you have requested your password and activated your account well in advance of the deadlines to avoid a panic or fine. You can register online at www.hmrc.gov.uk/individuals/iwtfile-a-self-assessment-tax-return-online.shtml.

When you're self-employed you are also liable to pay VAT if you exceed the threshold (turnover of £70,000 at the time of writing), but unless you're turning over tens of thousands of pounds don't worry. I'd heartily advise getting professional input from an accountant or business expert even if you're not hitting the VAT limit. There's a lot to absorb as you set up a business and a mentor or guide will be invaluable and save you a lot of needless fretting.

Ask the experts

In addition to the tax authorities themselves, you'd be astonished by the huge amount of business advice and expertise that is available if you seek it out. Much of it is free and I've heard of some eBayers getting free accounting for two years, personalised mentoring and support funded by Europe, as well as ongoing business advice from experts. This shouldn't be surprising, because governments of every political persuasion love small businesses and want to see more of them succeeding.

If you have never run your own business before it can all seem rather daunting. Should you be a sole trader, create a partnership, form a limited company, become VAT registered? The decisions you make depend on your individual circumstances and your aspirations; while you'll be able to get all sorts of advice, the decisions are ultimately up to you.

• A good start is Business Link, an organisation offering advice to businesses with local branches all over the country. Go to www.businesslink.gov.uk.

• Check out the National Federation of Enterprise Agencies' website at www.nfea.com. This site specialises in information for small businesses and business start-ups. If you want to ask its advisers a specific question for free it has a handy service at www.smallbusinessadvice.org.uk/sbas.asp.

• The Institute of Business Advisers is an independent and respected organisation of individuals that can advise you on specific issues related to your business. You can find its website at www.iba.org.uk.

Partnerships and limited companies

You might not want to operate as a sole trader if your circumstances warrant another approach. For instance, if there are two of you in the business you might want to create a formal deed of partnership. In a partnership each partner pays income tax as well as Class 2 and 4 National Insurance contributions like a sole trader. The business is required to pay VAT when it hits the threshold.

You might also want to consider forming a limited company. You can buy an existing company via an agent or form one yourself with Companies House (www.companieshouse.gov.uk). Limited companies face legal requirements and must display company details on their premises and stationery. A limited company also has to file certain documents and the tax obligations are different from those affecting sole traders and partnerships. Forming a company is a step best taken with the guidance of a solicitor or accountant, who can advise you on what is best for you.

Tip: eBay Business Centre
You can also find a good deal of information and help in eBay's Business Centre: http://pages.ebay.co.uk/businesscentre.

Business plans and accounts

There is no escape from paperwork when you run your eBay sales as a business. The first bit of paperwork you need to turn your hand to is some sort of business plan. The scale of the plan will depend on what you are using it for. If it's to be presented to the bank manager for the purposes of getting finance, then it needs to be detailed enough to satisfy the bank's lending requirements. But if it's just for you to use in forecasting expenditure, sales and income, it won't need to be so robust.

At its most basic, your plan will detail the costs of setting up your business and keeping it going, forecast your sales and also project running costs. You also want to spend some time thinking about a marketing plan and the future development of your business. You can find examples of different business plans online and you can also get all sorts of guidance from the various bodies mentioned earlier. If you'll be presenting the plan to the bank, these organisations will be able to give you information on what financiers require.

Above all, your plan must be realistic and achievable and there is no point in overforecasting your expected sales or profits. Make sure that you factor in all your eBay fees and all the extras like postage and packaging material. Scouring skips and bins for discarded cardboard and unwanted bubblewrap may be fine for a hobby seller, but a business needs to professionalise its service.

The other paperwork and records you need to keep are accounts. That means detailing the money you receive for your sales and what you spend. How you do that is up to you, but the best stop for information on what the taxman wants is the tax office again. Your records can be as simple as an accounts book or you can keep a computer spreadsheet detailing your sales. What you want to avoid at the end of your first year is a shoebox full of receipts and only a vague notion of what you have sold. Keep good records from day one and that will save you loads of aggravation in the long run.

This could be a good opportunity to take a course in bookkeeping to make sure that you're doing it all correctly, or perhaps invest in some accounting software to keep track of the numbers. But whatever you do, keep on top of the paperwork and don't leave it until the end of the year. In fact, part of your operations plan should include regular slots of time to update your records.

Many business sellers say that engaging an accountant from the outset is money well spent, but that's no substitute for keeping records as you go along: what you want to do is present your accountant with sound records at the end of the year and then let them weave their tax-efficient magic. Of course, an accountant can also be a very good source of general business advice.

Tip: VAT

VAT must be included in the buying price and quoted postage and can't be added after the sale.

Inside Information
Tax doesn't have to be taxing

It may seem like a crazy suggestion, but the best people to talk to about tax are the tax people themselves. This will seem even more bonkers: they're also actually very nice. Whenever I say this people look at me in disbelief, but if you think about it, why wouldn't they be?

They want us to pay our taxes and however much we all don't want to, we know we have to. That's that. It's far easier for the authorities to be open and approachable and cooperative from the start and help people pay their taxes than for them to come chasing after us in the long run. As you are starting your eBay business, get yourself along to your local tax office and find out for yourself: they have lots of handy information and resources to help you get started.

While I'm at it, I'll debunk another myth: eBay hasn't given everyone's sales information to the tax authorities. It's been reported in the press that eBay has opened its books for HMRC's free perusal. Not so. Obviously, eBay has legal responsibilities to the tax authorities, but the Revenue would need to apply for information on a case-by-case basis. Don't forget, though, that eBay is a very transparent environment and if anyone wants to take at a look at your sales and guess how much you are making, they could do it with a simple browse through your feedback.

28

Laws for Online Sellers

When you trade as a business you need to be aware of the laws that govern your type of business. Some regulations are general and relevant to all types of sellers, but some are particular to online selling. The business resources mentioned earlier will be able to give you more information, but here are the basics:

- **Trade Descriptions Act 1968** The Trade Descriptions Act is familiar to most people and it governs anything that is sold in the UK. In essence, you mustn't apply false information to anything you sell or supply, or offer to supply. As any successful seller will tell you, you won't last long if you mislead buyers about an item you're selling, so complying with this law is just common sense.

- **Sales of Goods Act 1979** This Act says that as a seller you must ensure that the items you are selling are as you say they are, of a satisfactory quality and fit for their purposes. For any eBay seller, being open and honest in your description will be second nature already, so complying with this won't be a challenge if you're serious about making a success of your sales.

- **Consumer Protection (Distance Selling) Regulations 2000** Commonly referred to as the Distance Selling Regulations or DSR, these apply to sales, such as on eBay, where no face-to-face contact occurs between the trading partners involved. If you are a business seller on eBay you have to make sure that your buyers have a seven-working-day cooling-off period, during which they can cancel the contract. Under the DSR you must also provide information about yourself and the items you are selling.

- **Electronic Commerce (EC Directive) Regulations 2000** This is another law that applies to online sales only. In addition to the requirements of the DSR, a business seller must detail their postal address and email address. If you belong to any trade organisation or an authorisation scheme relevant to your internet sales, you must also disclose the details. If as a seller you are VAT registered and your online sales are subject to VAT, you must publish your VAT number on eBay. These details could be in your listings or on your About Me page.

How eBay business registration can help

If you are already running a business or start trading on eBay as a business, you can register as a business with eBay. There are two particular benefits to this. First, eBay will display that you are a business seller in all your listings and help you comply with the relevant laws. Secondly, eBay will communicate with you as a business and let you know about relevant site changes and information that directly affects you.

When you register as a business seller your personal details will be verified by post, which means that when you are described by eBay as a business seller (as you will be on every listing) buyers can have extra confidence in your trustworthiness. You can also ensure that you comply with the relevant laws that require you to provide your contact and business details. You can enter all your details into eBay and they will be automatically included in your listings.

You can register as a business seller on eBay via the Business Centre at http://pages.ebay.co.uk/businesscentre.

Tip: PowerSellers
It is compulsory for PowerSellers to be registered as business users on the site.

29

Build the Back End

Tools such as Turbo Lister, Selling Manager and Selling Manager Pro will save you bags of time. But it's by improving the way you work and creating a robust and efficient back end that you discover the most scope and opportunity to improve your efficiency and ramp up sales more quickly, particularly as a business seller.

You need to unleash your inner Henry Ford and examine the tasks that you do every day to understand what's taking up your time, what can be done more swiftly and what can be done away with altogether.

However you look at it, your time is your most valuable resource. You don't want to waste it. On one level it might be galling to work out the 'hourly rate' you're earning from your eBay sales and discover that it's pitifully small, but that can be a useful wake-up call, reminding you that your productivity isn't what it could be. To boost your earnings per hour, you need to be more efficient. And if you want to develop your business and eBay activities, you need time to invest in them. Or you might just want to spend more time with family and friends.

That's what improving your efficiency means: doing more in less time. Only *you* can take ownership of your time. Some of the tips listed below will work for you, some of them won't apply, but there is something here for everyone. I haven't yet met an eBay seller (and I've met thousands) who can't benefit from at least one of these suggestions.

To give you an idea of what you might gain, consider the car parts seller who reorganised his whole warehouse around his eBay sales. He developed a system of stations based on the stages of an eBay sale: one station for photography, one for listing, one for packing, one for despatching and so on. He employed a number of people, so being as efficient as possible really was about saving money. He examined his new system and discovered that he was about 20% more efficient. That's like getting another day in the working week for free. Henry Ford would be proud.

Batch up tasks

Think about it. Taking ten photos doesn't take ten times as long as taking one. Not when you take into account the time you spend getting the camera out, preparing an uncluttered space to form the background, firing up the image software and realising that your batteries have run out. Batch up similar tasks such as writing descriptions, packaging, taking photos, replying to emails and crafting listings and do them all in one go.

Apply a production line mentality and tackle each task in turn. When you research your categories, for instance, it's easier to do them all in one go while you're in the relevant part of the eBay site. With Turbo Lister or using the scheduling function, it makes no odds when you create the listing or in what order you gather together the various components of a listing. Print out your despatch notes once a day and 'pick and pack' once a day too. You could even consider packaging items in advance, rather than 'on demand' when they've sold.

Optimise your workspace

First up, if you possibly can, have a workspace dedicated to your eBay selling. It can be anywhere from a whole room to the corner of a table, just as long as it's got everything you need easily to hand. It drives me mad to have to dash to the kitchen to get the tape or the scissors, the cupboard under the stairs for a padded bag, the desk for a print-out and the bottom of the wardrobe for the item itself. Those kind of shenanigans are a monumental waste of time.

I went to see a seller once and she was in the throes of getting her despatches ready for the day. She was complaining that she never had enough time to list more items, she could just about keep up with the ones she was doing and eBay needed to be easier and quicker to use. As she was ranting, I must have looked rather like a tennis umpire: she was flitting from one end of the room to the other, from her desk to the printer, grabbing despatch print-outs one at a time. She wasn't amused when I suggested she might save a bit of time if she moved the printer next to her computer.

Analyse the tasks that you need to do and how they can be done most efficiently – form your working space around that process as best you can. Aim to create an eBay production line.

Let your listings do the work

If you're getting lots of emails during sales, find yourself chasing buyers for payment, responding to queries about combined shipping or dealing with non-payers, you need to optimise your View Item pages. Make sure that your listings are doing as much of your work as possible.

Are there changes you can make to ensure that people don't have to come to you for an answer? If there are, make the change once and eliminate the need to do it time and time again. Don't forget the FAQ facility that you can insert into the Ask Seller a Question process.

Bulk up and automate

Are you really getting the most out of the tools that eBay offers to make you more efficient? The automated email systems in Selling Manager and Selling Manager Pro can be an absolute godsend. Automated feedback is a boon too. But it could be that you can save time by using the function that allows you to bulk print your invoices, or changing one single aspect across all of your listings with the bulk edit tool.

It really is worth familiarising yourself with these various programs to see what you're not using or checking what's been added since you last looked. eBay is often improving and developing the tools with little fanfare or explanation.

Consider whether other services might also be useful. Many companies offer handy eBay tools (alas, often with a charge) that might be just what you need. Ask fellow sellers or have a look on Google.

Post haste

If there's one thing that eBay sellers sink more time into than anything else, it's posting and despatching their items. From weighing and assessing the cost of postage, to queues at the post office or dealing with the fallout from a Royal Mail snafu, it all takes time.

Here are some aspects to think about:

- You can print out postage labels without going anywhere near a Post Office. Check this out at www.royalmail.com.

- Fill in your paperwork at home. Get a stash of forms from the Post Office and complete them before you leave.

- If you're sending out lots of parcels, look at getting the Royal Mail to come by and collect them. It may not be as expensive as you think and if you're sending out a serious number of parcels (a yearly spend at the Post Office of £15,000 or more) they won't charge you at all for this service. Again, costs and how to set up an account can be found at www.royalmail.com.

- Talk to the staff at your Post Office. If you're spending a lot of time there, see if they can help you. When are their quiet, queue-free times? I've even heard of some accommodating branches that open early or late to deal with valuable, regular eBay customers.

Have the right tool

Is your kit fit for purpose? Simple improvements to your gear and equipment could free up time. A faster, more reliable printer might be a very sound investment. Fed up with struggling with brown tape? Buy a tape gun!

Always ensure you have the right packaging to hand. Recycling packaging is all very well for one-off items, but if you're selling lots of items, customising packaging can be a waste of time. Having plenty of packing materials to hand won't save the planet but it will save you time.

Consider your computer too. Broadband is essential, is now available just about everywhere in the UK and is getting cheaper. Also check that your computer is running as fast as it can. Don't forget that there are often preferential allowances available to businesses when upgrading computer equipment courtesy of the Chancellor of the Exchequer.

Embed record keeping in your processes

No one likes doing the paperwork, but it has to be done neverthe-less. Make sure a problem isn't looming over you by understanding what records you need to keep and doing them as you go along.

The most efficient sellers I've seen at work have paperwork seamlessly embedded in their daily routines. It's certainly better than staying up all night with a shoebox full of receipts and the self-assessment tax deadline fast approaching.

It's less bovver without a hover

How much time do you spend 'just checking' your listings? How many times a day do you find yourself 'having a quick look' at your emails? How much of this is strictly necessary?

There are very few emails that can't wait a few hours or that require a response within the hour. Of course a swift reply is good practice, but it doesn't have to be immediate. You certainly don't need to remain hunched over your inbox waiting for emails to arrive. Dealing with emails at dedicated times each day, in one go, makes much more sense.

In the same vein, hovering over My eBay obsessing over your latest Buy It Nows and bids is not time well spent. Limit your checking to certain times each day and try sating your (admirable) curiosity with your reports. Understanding which of your keywords is driving the most traffic and sales is more valuable than knowing that at 18.41 you got a new watcher on item X.

Plan and set deadlines

Making plans, setting deadlines and creating lists of what you need to do and by when are invaluable ways of making sure you are achieving what you want to achieve. Without a boss keeping an eye on you, it can sometimes be difficult to motivate yourself to get down to the daily tasks or look forward to the longer term and maintain your business. An informal list of objectives or a short quarterly plan, in addition to your immediate to-do list, is good practice.

Kick the bad habits

Always leaving your daily packaging too late? Every trip to the Post Office a last-minute panic dash before it shuts? Constantly running out of padded bags? Always doing your listings late at night? Every eBay seller has a bad habit that they could eliminate and become more efficient. You know what yours is. Kick it.

Trade safely as a business

Just because you're now a business, it doesn't mean that you can forget about safety. As a business you are potentially at greater risk from the fraudsters, so you mustn't let your guard down.

All the same threats remain as for personal sellers and you need to make sure you're protected. Obviously there's the eBay Safety centre as a source of information, but do check out Get Safe Online, which has a dedicated section for businesses. It's your indispensable guide to what you need to know:

www.getsafeonline.org

30

Make the Most of eBay's Advanced Features

The rewards and satisfaction you get from a successful eBay business can be considerable. Your freedom as a seller is huge, your costs (compared to running a shop, say) should hopefully be low, and if you've applied the rigour of Henry Ford and closely examined how you work, you should be efficient and 'time rich'. How you spend your time is up to you. You can spend it on leisure and your family or plough it back in to selling even more. But whatever you choose, reinvest some of it in planning and developing your business.

Sometimes when you're neck deep in padded bags and tied up with brown tape, the last thing on your mind is examining your business and planning for the future – but it is essential. If a problem is brewing you want to know about it rather than waiting for it to explode suddenly and waking up one morning to discover your livelihood is at stake. You don't want to have to solve your problem in a panic at the same time as trying to get those urgent despatches out of the door.

Try to ringfence some time each week to examine your records and numbers. Approach them scientifically. Set yourself targets and understand how and why you reach them, exceed them or miss them. Understanding your business is not a luxury: it's the smartest way of knowing where your business is going.

Take the time to explore some of eBay's advanced, and sometimes preferential, services available to businesses.

PayPal for businesses

If you're operating at volume, or as a business, PayPal has a great number of tools and tweaks that can save you time and money. You can find them under the 'Merchant Tools' tab in your PayPal account.

The most important service that PayPal offers to volume sellers is discounted fees. If you're accepting more than £1500 a month in payments you can get a reduction in fees. But you don't get this automatically, you have to apply. You can do this on the PayPal site. You can also easily incorporate PayPal into your own website and accept payments via email without buyers having to register on eBay.

PayPal also has an API (application program interface) that you can use to produce your own payments back end and plug directly into your accounting software. It's not as comprehensive as eBay's API (see overleaf), but you can use it download your transactions, search your payments and automate refunds.

Research and marketplace intelligence

The eBay Shops chapter gives information about shop sales and traffic reporting. This is your first stop when looking at the success of your own sales and the listings that are performing best.

However, if you are serious about selling on eBay, trying to spot emerging trends and further opportunities for sales is vital.

One indispensable aid that any dedicated eBay business seller should explore is the eBay Research tool provided by Terapeak (www.terapeak.com), which allows you to examine the marketplace in its entirety. That means having available an enormous amount of information that should be pretty representative of general retail trends. However, don't forget to look beyond eBay if you can. Keeping an eye on retail on the high street could be a good way of spotting the next big thing.

You can examine up to 90 days of information about items that have been bought or sold on eBay. This data enables you to look at average sale prices and also the start prices of items. You could use this information to see what the correct pricing strategy is for your items or check if your pricing is competitive or not. You can also explore the top keyword searches on eBay by category to understand in a more detailed way than Pulse provides what people are searching for on the site.

The information can be displayed as you wish and one of the most engaging ways of examining it is to use charts, which can easily be created by the tool.

The eBay API

If you have a bit of technical know-how, you should consider experimenting with eBay's API (application program interface). It allows anyone to mine eBay's databases and provides sellers with the option of building their own bespoke back-end management tools and services that are complementary to eBay's own.

An API is simply a means for one website to communicate and interact with another using a defined set of terms called API calls. In an eBay context this means that you can use the API to perform eBay tasks (such as selling, leaving feedback, managing your sales) without visiting the eBay site. Not all functions are covered by the available API, but eBay has a very comprehensive system that enables developers to create almost any application imaginable.

To test out your ideas, eBay also provides www.sandbox.ebay.com, which is a mirror of the main website where you can play around, test your application and get it right. If you want to know more about the API you can visit:

http://developer.ebay.com

Become a trading assistant

You know how to sell on eBay and that in itself is a valuable skill. You can put it to good use by setting up as a trading assistant or a trading post.

A trading assistant is someone who sells on behalf of other people for a fee and a trading post is the premises from which they operate. You qualify as a trading assistant if you've sold at least four items in the last 30 days, have a feedback score of 50 or higher and 97% or more of your feedback is positive. Your eBay account must also be in good standing.

Over the past few years I've heard a lot of encouraging stories from people who have turned their hand to selling for others. For some it has been a lucrative sideline and it's definitely best to think of it as an addition to an existing eBay selling business rather than a whole new avenue. In the US there have been some successful businesses established around selling for others, but in the UK many of these firms have failed to make a mark. So when you set out as a Trading Assistant, be cautious and don't stake your shirt on the enterprise.

Some things to think about:

- **What can you sell?** When you're a Trading Assistant you have to be more picky about what you list on eBay. If an item doesn't sell, you will have wasted your time and not made any money. So do your research and make sure that the things you're listing are things that buyers want to snap up at a decent price. You also need to be aware of the costs you will incur and make sure they are factored into the price. Ideally, you want to be selling high-value items.

- **What will you charge?** You're selling on someone else's behalf. What will you be charging the person who owns the item? The most common formula is to plump for a percentage and a minimum fee. Something along the lines of 25% of the selling price and a minimum of £15, say. You'll need to work out what suits you. You might also offer a batch price if you're selling a load of stuff for one person.

- **What are your terms and conditions?** Make sure you have watertight T&Cs that form an agreement between you and the owner of the goods. There is considerable room for disagreement, so ensure that the relationship is above board. Try to avoid problems before they happen. Does the owner understand, for instance, that if an item doesn't reach the price they'd like (but has been bought fair and square) they can't back out after the auction? It's your feedback on the line, so you can't be too careful.

- **Manage expectations** Does an owner have unrealistic expectations of the price that their item might achieve? Do they understand what they'll be paying you or how long the eBay process takes? Be clear, communicate often and manage the owner's expectations.

Find out how to become a trading assistant at
http://pages.ebay.co.uk/tradingassistants/hire-trading-assistant.html

eBay business checklist

- **Research the market** Make sure that you know the environment in which you're selling. Explore trends on and off eBay to make sure that there is a market for you to sell into.

- **Talk to the experts** There's no substitute for knowledge. There's tons of advice out there for you, so seek it out.

- **Compete successfully** Make sure that you can turn a shilling by planning out your business. Forecast your likely level of sales, and ensure that your margins are good and your pricing is realistic.

- **Know the eBay rules** It will be a dull few hours, but get to know all the listings rules on eBay so that you don't fall foul of them.

- **Organise your operations** Make sure that your listing, managing, packing and despatch processes are as efficient as possible.

- **Keep good records** A shoebox full of receipts isn't sufficient. Understand what records you need and set aside a regular time to keep your books straight.

- **Know the law** Special rules govern sales by businesses and you should make sure that your eBay sales comply.

- **Register as a business seller on eBay** Inspire confidence and let your buyers know that you are bona fide by registering as a business on eBay.

- **Measure, analyse and understand** Make sure that you know what's working with your sales and drop what isn't. Use the numbers to become a more successful seller.

PART V

TAKE ON AMAZON, BUILD A WEBSITE AND PROFIT FROM SEARCH ENGINES

31

Branch Out

What did your granny always say? 'Don't put all your eggs in one basket!' Your granny probably said it before the internet even existed, but it is sound advice for any business relying on eBay for its income.

To put it bluntly, if you have a thriving business that's depending on eBay alone, your income is at risk. There are dozens of things that could go wrong. And without eBay, you'd be sunk. That's why it's sensible to have alternative means of making a living. The question to ask yourself is: 'Could I survive without eBay?'

eBay could change its listing or final value fees and make you uncompetitive or even ban the items you're selling (as has happened variously to sellers of 'virtual items' and pre-sale listings). eBay tends to change fees once a year and even professional, prepared sellers can find this disruptive. Bad press coverage could affect you: an eBay-related scandal or a simple dip in consumer confidence could cause a wobble. eBay might suspend your account, rightly or wrongly, and cancel your listings. It's not easy to get an account reinstated and all the while you're trying, you ain't earning. Counting on eBay on its own could be dangerous.

A huge opportunity

But looking to sell beyond eBay isn't a case of doom and gloom. In fact, it's about making *more* money. The ecommerce opportunity in Britain alone is extraordinary and when you look beyond the UK it's truly staggering. By limiting your online selling to eBay, you're missing out on a huge chunk of the action.

It's fair to say that shopping online is now very much the norm. Think back to the bad old days: people would happily buy books, CDs and airline tickets online, but other things were less often purchased and the scene was dominated by eBay, Amazon and the like. Nowadays, folk are willing to buy literally anything. It's intriguing to note that one of the fastest-growing sectors in ecommerce is Clothing and Accessories. The highest spending demographic group is women. The over-60s are increasingly gaining confidence and buying more online or, equally important, using the internet as a research tool for offline purchases.

The IMRG (a leading British ecommerce monitoring body) forecasts that ecommerce will continue to grow every year between now and 2012 regardless of the global economic difficulties. It's not the share of commerce that will increasingly go online, it's the total expenditure in real terms. This is great news for anyone who wants to get their bite of the ecommerce cherry. The future is rosy.

But one thing is obvious: if you don't broaden your horizons, diversify your sales from eBay and embrace new opportunities, you'll be limiting your customer base. eBay's share of ecommerce has been dwindling for several years as consumers become more confident and adventurous. If you want to grow your sales you'll need to start thinking about Amazon, other marketplaces and setting up your own website.

It might seem daunting or feel scary as you consider moving beyond the relative safety of the eBay bosom, but just remember the rewards and the possibilities. If you get it right, you'll be running a valuable online retail business rather than just an eBay business. To quote the Romans rather than your granny: 'Fortune favours the brave.'

Google has rewritten the rules

The biggest enabler of ecommerce and the most significant player on the scene is Google. Back at the end of the 1990s it was all the rage to open an eshop and sell your wares online. But search engines weren't what they are now. It was more difficult to find buyers and people hadn't embraced online purchasing with as much enthusiasm as they have now. In fact, it was in large part due to this inefficiency that eBay prospered. Buyers and sellers started to congregate on eBay because everyone knew that was where ecommerce happened: search engines weren't even part of the consideration. eBay also did a good job of reassuring buyers who might have otherwise been nervous.

Now that the internet has been Googlised, buyers are increasingly using the search engine as their shopping starting point. People trust Google to give them good, relevant results and help them find what they want. eBay and other sites and services know how valuable Google traffic is and they invest a great deal in optimising their sites in the hope of mopping up as many customers as possible. So opening your own website, using other marketplaces or plugging into comparison shopping sites in addition to selling on eBay is a way of having your cake and eating it too.

Online payments have also changed

The other sea-change that we've seen in recent years has been the attitude people have to paying online. Paying online is no longer the gamble it once was: people are more confident of using their credit and debit cards and the result is a bigger online buying public. PayPal is in part responsible for this transformation. Some 15 million people in Britain have a PayPal account, so that's a lot of people who can happily pay you as soon as you set up your own website or take your trade to other marketplaces and websites. Remember back to the year 2000: people were wary about paying online. Today it is a commonplace, normal, everyday occurrence.

You're doing it already

The point is, when it comes to setting up your own trading site anywhere online, you're already doing 90% of what you need to run an online business already by selling successfully via eBay. You're already sourcing the supplies, making your despatches, doing the accounts, giving customers the right kind of service and taking payments. All these skills can be transferred to other sites or even to your own site with relative ease. Of course, there will be plenty to learn and you'll have to have your wits about you, but in essence it's just about eBaying without eBay.

This part of the book is about taking what you know already and applying your experience to new situations. I look at plugging into other marketplaces and sites where buyers are searching for goods and I examine how you can create your own site and profit from it.

Inside Information
It's about a successful mix

While I've been researching this part of the book I've spoken to lots of eBay sellers who have taken some of their selling off eBay, either to their own website or to other marketplaces. I've also spoken to a number of industry commentators and internet pundits. Everyone's agreed: more and more eBay sellers think that having their own website is the way to go.

It is, however, intriguing to note the different motives these sellers have. For some, the impetus is disgruntlement with eBay driven by their concerns about fee changes, site developments and the like. For others it's about finding ways to increase turnover and profit.

I'm wary of people who are driven by antipathy for eBay. I don't think they fully understand just how difficult it is to run a market-place as big as eBay or quite how hard they would have to work to emulate what eBay provides. They certainly don't appreciate how much money they would have to spend to get the traffic that they can so easily plug into on eBay.

I think that if you're serious about maximising your business, eBay is always going to be part of the mix. I'm not saying it will be the core of your business or provide the majority of your sales, but it's got to be in your portfolio. You'll find additional custom elsewhere and if you get your website working hard it could very easily be a real profit source, but I don't think that saying farewell to eBay is going to do you much good.

The trickledown benefits, the credibility, eBay's magnificent marketing machine and the fact that some buyers want to stay with what they like and what they know mean that the site is always going to have its value in your ecommerce mix. Don't let your heart overrule your head, however satisfying you think it will feel.

32

Explore New Marketplaces

One part of diversifying your sales away from eBay is exploring the plethora of other websites on which you can sell. That's actually easier said than done. eBay's stranglehold on the market and domination of the person-to-person selling scene is very strong indeed. Since eBay came to the UK in 1999, it has effectively been number one, with the rest of the field lagging a long, long way behind.

Trevor Ginn, an eBay consultant, talks a lot about the online marketplace landscape on his blog (www.trevorginn.com) and he points out that data from Hitwise shows over 97% of the traffic in the internet auction marketplace going to eBay. His own experiments selling the same items on different sites are recorded on his blog. The lacklustre prices and traffic he received persuaded him that people expecting to make good money on other marketplaces should proceed with caution. So why bother, you might wonder? The answer depends on what you're selling.

James Scott of ChannelAdvisor points out that not all items are suitable for the eBay channel and other marketplaces can be more liberal in terms of what they allow, so you might be able to eke out some more sales. After all, a sale is a sale. Other marketplaces are often cheaper and can provide different selling features that are possibly better suited to your items.

So which marketplaces are worth looking at? Amazon is definitely the most prominent and widely used, but don't be mistaken in thinking that it's just for books and CDs. The company has diversified into all sorts of areas and you can now sell a wide range of new goods – and lots of people do. As for the other marketplaces, none is making a very big splash.

It's also interesting that more and more people are turning to smaller, specialist sites honed to a particular sector as possible avenues for selling. It seems to me that unless Google or Microsoft makes a significant move into online selling, it's probably unlikely that a very big 'general' marketplace will emerge. But smaller niche sites, which have become more possible with the Web 2.0 boom of online communities and improved search engines, are a growth area. It's often been a complaint that eBay's one-size-fits-all service doesn't in fact fit anyone perfectly and that a specialist, focused website is often easier to use.

One example that leaps out is Abebooks (www.abebooks.co.uk). It's a site for secondhand and rare books and claims to have 80 million books available. It's very popular with academics and students and my own buying experience on it (buying a book from America) was excellent. eBay didn't even have the tome I wanted to buy.

In the world of crafts and homemade goods, innovative start-up etsy.com is causing a ripple of excitement. This US-based site is developed with crafty types in mind, and has some really interesting products and a simple but attractive layout. If you're selling in this area it's worth checking it out and experimenting.

What has Google got in store?

The question that's exercising ecommerce pundits and eBay sellers alike is 'What are Google's plans?' It's a good question. To many critics of eBay it seems like only Google has the size, traction and resources to mount a challenge to the eBay hegemony. Some disgruntled eBay sellers have even started an online petition begging Google to come to their rescue and establish a rival site.

Of course, Google has made some moves suggesting an entry into the market is likely. Google Base (www.google.co.uk/base) is a service that allows sellers to upload details of their inventory so that it can be effectively ordered and catalogued. It's been out there for a good while now and it's failed to make a splash (in fact many people are bewildered by it and don't know what it's for) and it is currently still in beta format. Froogle, too, is a service from Google that helps buyers find things they want to buy. Again it's still in beta and isn't really an ecommerce engine yet.

James Scott of ChannelAdvisor advises his clients to keep a close eye on Google. He agrees with Trevor that there isn't much life out there beyond eBay and certainly there is no great hunger for a rival 'giant site', but suspects that Google is the one to watch.

The most interesting move from Google has been the launch of Google Checkout. It has been billed in the press as a 'PayPal killer' and is being watched carefully because it takes Google right into eBay's space. When you have a payment mechanism and system, you can attach that to an inventory and soon you have something that's rather like eBay. Google denies that this is the case, obviously. It has also been innovative in terms of pricing and offers scale discounts to sellers, even offsetting any money spent on Google Adwords advertising against the fees you pay with Google Checkout. For more information about Google Checkout, visit http://checkout.google.co.uk.

So, to answer the question: we just don't know what Google's plans are and until we do, any speculation that it's going to be good or bad for eBay sellers is hypothetical. This chapter deals with what exists at time of writing and the opportunities of which you can take advantage.

Case study: A multichannel seller
eBay user ID: drstevew
Website: www.retrowarez.com

Steve runs a limited company with family and friends that sells tens of thousands of DVDs and computer games every month. A look at his eBay shop reveals an extraordinary array of stock (about 5000 items at time of writing) and a monumental feedback score. He also runs a website, sells stock wholesale to other eBay sellers and uses Amazon. Looking at Steve's portfolio of outlets it's difficult not to be impressed by the scale of his operations, but it started with only a handful of stock.

'I was made redundant from my job as a management consultant,' says Steve. 'I knew where there was a DVD wholesaler so I bought 7 DVDs. I'd already sold some of my stuff on eBay so it was easy to make the move.' He built up the business over time, ascribing his success to superb customer service and huge dollops of 'patience, persistence and communication'.

He thinks part of his attraction lies in 'offering a wide and eclectic range of DVDs and games. eBay was built on variety and being able to buy stuff that isn't readily available in the shops.' But while he is keen to continue selling on eBay for as long as it's 'financially viable', he's already branching out.

Steve says that starting a website was an 'obvious thing to do' when he went full-time with eBay. It has also been beneficial for the company's reputation, especially with suppliers, because it makes the business look more important. Being competent at website design and programming, he found the site easy to build and maintain, claiming that his only problem has been with unreliable hosting companies.

Steve points out that one of the major benefits of having his own website is the absence of listing fees; a quick look at the site reveals a greater selection of products than he sells on eBay. But it's also clear that Steve has enjoyed crafting his own site. The website is intuitively laid out and very user friendly. The checkout feature is easy to navigate and it's simple to find what you're looking for. Steve hasn't done much marketing, but his site is performing well. 'The results of magazine marketing were not as good as they could have been, considering the outlay,' he says. 'It's mainly word-of-mouth marketing and the signature line on emails.'

Steve also sells on Amazon and claims it's 'easier to deal with than eBay and less hassle overall. No html, no messing about, just stick the barcode in and away you go.' But there is a downside: Amazon is a very price-sensitive marketplace. Listings are sorted by cheapest first, meaning that buyers are automatically drawn to the lowest-priced items. Good for buyers, but not necessarily for sellers.

Amazon Marketplace

That anyone can sell items on Amazon is not a widely known fact. But you can and it's by common agreement rather easy. Of course, Amazon isn't as flexible as eBay in the sense that customers go to Amazon for new, 'commodity' items, but there is more to the site than books. It now sells domestic goods, electrical items, DVDs and computer games, although it certainly isn't home to as broad a sweep of goods as eBay is. Apart from selection, there are also some keen differences to when you're selling on eBay.

> • **You're selling alongside Amazon** eBay doesn't sell any goods on the site: it just runs the marketplace. That's not true on Amazon. Amazon is a retailer in its own right: it sources stock, holds stock, runs warehouses and despatches goods. When you're selling on Amazon, you're competing with one of the biggest retailers in the world on its home turf. But

anecdotally it seems that Amazon approaches this situation with decency, knowing that it can't squeeze out the small guys. In fact, before Christmas 2006 Amazon itself ran out of a particular brand of camera. Rather than not offering the camera to customers, it widely promoted a Marketplace seller who still had stock to fill the gap.

• **There's less opportunity to personalise** One of the reasons Amazon is so easy to use is that you incorporate its pre-prepared descriptions into your listings. For example, when you sell a DVD you simply put the EAN (barcode) number into the site and Amazon has all the details there for you. Handy, but it makes it very hard for you to stand out from the crowd and differentiate yourself from other sellers of the same item.

• **It's a price-sensitive market** It's the difficulty differentiating yourself from other sellers that makes price so important on Amazon: being cheaper is one of the few ways you can stand out. The way in which Amazon displays products favours cheaper items. The site also determines the postage costs, so you can't be more competitive there either.

Selling on Amazon

Getting started on Amazon as a merchant can be time-consuming and tricky. Amazon screens and vets every seller and you'll be required not only to verify your details but prove that you are the kind of seller the company wants on the site. This can take weeks or even months. There will be forms to fill out and from what I've heard it's a tricky process. But, in the end, if you want to sell on Amazon this is something you'll have to live with. On the other hand, it means that there is less competition from other sellers.

When you start selling, you can choose which category your item will appear in (there's a choice of about 10) and you need to find the Amazon-provided description using a barcode number or keywords. Once you've found the catalogue information, you specify your price.

Items don't expire on Amazon, so your item can remain available for as long as you like. When your stuff does sell, payment is taken by Amazon via its in-house system called Amazon payments. It deposits your takings directly into your bank account.

Amazon is very clear on your responsibilities as a seller and prescribes the postage costs and how you should mark and address the envelope, as well as giving clear guidance and instructions on dealing with particular issues. You can view that guidance at www.amazon.co.uk/gp/help/customer/display.html?nodeId=3149411

There is a feedback system on Amazon, but it's different from eBay's in several ways. First, there's no facility for you to rate buyers but they can rate you on your performance using a scale of 1–5. It's also not as important and integral to the trading system as it is on eBay.

The fees on Amazon are also structured differently to eBay's. There are no listing fees and there are discounts and benefits for larger-scale sellers. As an individual you pay £0.86 per item on completion plus a commission of 17.25% of the sales price (11.5% for Electronics & Photo items). If you subscribe to Amazon's Pro Merchant service you pay a monthly subscription of £28.75 plus 17.25% of the final price (8.05% for Electronics & Photo items).

More about selling on Amazon

Pro Merchant services Amazon offers preferential treatment, better fees and professional terms to merchant sellers and if you're serious about selling on Amazon you'll want to sign up for the Pro Merchant service. Here's the link:

www.amazon.co.uk/gp/help/customer/
display.html?nodeId=3149141

Postage is pre-determined Amazon decides what the appropriate postage cost is for merchandise on the site based on the company's broad experience of postage and despatching items. You don't have a say in the matter.

Location details You must have a UK address and a UK bank account to be eligible to sell on Amazon.co.uk.

Fulfilment by Amazon Obviously, Amazon has warehousing, staff and processes to store and despatch items bought on Amazon quickly and officially. Its reputation as a fast shipper is excellent. But did you know that if you're selling on Amazon the company can take care of all that side of things for you, if you like? Basically, you send your merchandise to an Amazon warehouse, where it is stored until it is purchased. Then, when someone buys it, Amazon picks, packs and despatches it on your behalf, for a fee. It's a great service. Find out more here:

www.amazon.co.uk/gp/help/customer/display.html?ie=UTF8
&nodeId=200292880

Amazon payments Buyers pay you via Amazon and you receive your money once Amazon has taken its cut. Payments are processed on a rolling 14-day cycle.

Amazon insights

Selling on Amazon is dramatically different from selling on eBay. Here are a few things that sellers who have migrated some of their sales to 'the river' have said to me:

Less sophisticated tools While Amazon is geared up for merchant sellers, the day-to-day management that a seller has to do on Amazon is much less than on eBay. The company takes much more of the strain. This is of course reflected in the fees taken and also the lack of control a seller enjoys, but it's also seen in the tools available to sellers. Many people say Amazon's selling tools are less sophisticated than the ones eBay makes available.

Completely different relationship People and sellers still talk of the relationship between seller and eBay as a community-based, warm partnership (although many sellers don't feel this is the case in reality). With Amazon, it's quite simply a business relationship. eBay sellers say that they like the stark honesty of the relationship without the schmaltz.

Sales are steady Amazon sellers report that they can pretty much bank on their sales from that channel. Amazon obviously markets hard and promotes certain lines, but if you're not selling the hottest, in-vogue items then you can probably predict week to week what you sell.

Strong seasonal surge Amazon sellers have told me that the surge of custom in the run-up to Christmas is huge and more dramatic than on eBay.

Inside Information
Surf the Amazon

eBay remains the big daddy of ecommerce. It's still the number one destination for online shoppers in the UK, attracting the most traffic and sales. But even the most seasoned eBay watcher has to question how long this can last.

Since 2006, Amazon has been growing fast. This growth has been largely fuelled by the company's successful integration of third-party sellers. It didn't begin as a person-to-person marketplace like eBay, but it has taken a leaf out of eBay's book and successfully brought business sellers within the Amazon fold. It's been a huge boon for Amazon and now you're just as likely to be buying from a merchant as from Amazon itself.

This is good news for consumers, who benefit from the competition and a greater selection of goods for sale. It's also good news for ecommerce professionals: it's a whole new and totally different outlet for sellers, attracting buyers who might not use eBay.

If you can, sell on Amazon. You'd need your head examined, as far as I'm concerned, if you could and didn't. The time to start is as soon as you feel you've cracked eBay and while you're hungry for growth.

Amazon and eBay will doubtless both continue to survive and compete as twin titans of ecommerce. To be able to enjoy success in both is a remarkable opportunity. But if truth be told, your operations for both are likely to be almost identical. When it comes to succeeding you'll need the same skills, efficiency, stock and gumption, whether it's eBay or Amazon.

Other marketplaces

There are hundreds of other sites trying to get a piece of eBay's action. As we saw before, none is particularly buzzing, but more and more sellers are experimenting with the competition. They're open for business and if you want to expand your activities you'd be wise at least to size them up and perhaps have a punt.

There are essentially two reasons selling on other marketplaces is potentially beneficial. eBay does have some arcane and prohibitive rules that can be constricting to some sellers. Some of the smaller sites are more liberal and permissive, so if you have found yourself falling foul of the eBay police you might like the freedom.

The other benefit is the lower fees that other sites may charge. While eBay is in such a strong position, it can be aggressive in the way it monetises every transaction and additional feature. The pretenders know they have to be more flexible and attractive, so they are at pains to point out that they are cheaper.

The sites worthy of your consideration are:

- **eBid.net** eBid has been in operation for a number of years and appears to be gradually growing in size. It does a good job of appealing to eBay sellers' disgruntlement and seem to enjoy making cheeky side-swipes at eBay on its discussion boards. The major attraction of eBid is its competitive charges: there are no listing fees or shop subscriptions. eBid pays the bills with the final value commissions of 2% it charges. You can also upgrade your account and not pay any 'per item' fees at all if you pay a subscription.

- **Aroxo** If you're selling anything with a battery or a plug (so electronic stuff, basically), Aroxo is a UK-based marketplace that is gaining traction, publicity and plaudits. If you sell this sort of thing it's well worth experimenting with. I can see it doing very well and stealing some of eBay's action.

- **Bonanzle.com** eBay sellers on the other side of the Atlantic who became disenchanted with the mothership have embraced a new service called Bonanzle. It's just landed on this side of the pond and it seems likely that it will attract business. Definitely one to watch.

- **CQOut** Very much an eBay-a-like, CQOut.com is an auction site that looks and feels like the original but lacks the vibrancy and bustle. Very low fees may tempt you to take the plunge, but don't expect too much.

Case study: Branching out
eBay user ID: gadgets_and_gifts_uk
Tazbar ID: gadgets-and-gifts-uk
Website: www.gadgetsandgiftsuk.com

Nici began on eBay, as many sellers do, selling secondhand clothes and unwanted stuff. She was nervous at first, but says that she soon got the hang of it. 'eBay is relatively easy to use,' she says. 'That is probably where eBay wins and other auction sites are falling behind.'

Nici has been testing out other marketplaces recently after a bad experience with eBay and is encouraged by the early results.

It's been a giddy ride, because not long ago Nici was a complete novice. She 'had no previous experience of online selling, in fact the only experience I had of the internet was as a research tool and I knew absolutely nothing about eBay'. She gave up a demanding job as the sponsorship and promotions manager of a radio station to spend more time with her children after difficulties organising childcare.

Her current business is selling gifts and goodies for hen parties. 'After trying many different lines, I found gifts suited me best. We have some lines which provide a 300% markup, and some that we break even on, and like any business we use some lines as loss leaders.'

She advises sellers starting out to concentrate on 'research, research and more research. You have to invest time and money into any business. Probably the most important thing I have learned is that cheap isn't always best.' But despite her prudent approach Nici has not found selling on eBay trouble free and has been forced to review her strategy.

'A manufacturer of a product decided that they didn't want me to sell a similar product on eBay and issued VeRO notices against me for patent infringements and closed my eBay business down overnight.' The issue was resolved but afterwards she 'wondered why on earth I was considering spending £10–20,000 a year with a company who could pull the plug overnight'.

'I've started selling on other marketplaces – or rather I try to. Sales aren't great. But Rome wasn't built in a day. Other online auction sites are messy and difficult compared to eBay. My next move will be to crack the Amazon market.'

Nici has also had a custom-built website constructed and she's encouraged by the first results, describing it as 'very successful'. 'I had used off-the-shelf web packages before, but didn't have the knowledge to make a real success of them. A fellow PowerSeller convinced me that a custom-built site was the way to go, and I had nothing to lose, so I went for it. The custom site was built in a couple of weeks and all I have to do is upload products, which is so simple it takes minutes.'

33

Comparison Shopping and Classifieds Sites

Comparison shopping

Comparison shopping sites are web destinations that aggregate information from other internet-based shops and online sellers and present it to buyers in an intuitive and easily approachable way. So, if you want an electric toothbrush and you go to a comparison shopping site you will be presented with information from a variety of vendors about similar products. The idea is that you can then easily view and compare different sellers and as a consumer make the best choice.

It's a popular and successful model that is appealing to buyers because it's the online equivalent of 'shopping around', but without the hassle of schlepping down the high street, popping in and out of every relevant shop before returning to the first one you went to because it really was the best deal. Consumer champions such as Martin Lewis of www.moneysavingexpert.com often promote the use of comparison shopping sites as the best way to bag the best bargains.

Comparison shopping sites don't actually sell anything: the transaction itself takes place on the vendor's website. Comparison sites make their money by charging sellers for the traffic they send to the sellers' sites. It's done on a cost-per-click model, so sellers only pay for the people who click through to their website. In some ways, comparison shopping sites are a throwback to an age when search engines weren't so good and it was easier to go to a specific site to do your shopping, but they are still popular and effective.

Because of the popularity of comparison shopping, the big sites provide an opportunity for sellers that's potentially more lucrative than other eBay-like marketplaces. But because of how the process operates for sellers, they aren't suitable for all.

Getting your inventory on comparison shopping sites is pretty straightforward. You provide up-to-date information about your products, and when your items are clicked and a customer comes to your site from a comparison shopping site, you pay a fee. The cost-per-click model has its challenges. It means that you pay even if the person who visits doesn't buy anything.

Comparison shopping sites are also pretty cagey about what they charge. This is because there isn't a level playing field where everyone is charged the same. They operate on a more traditional, commercial model, meaning that if you are a big player with deep pockets you can doubtless negotiate a very good deal. As a small-time seller, you might not find that the door opens quite so easily. If you decide that you're interested in tapping into comparison shopping traffic, you're probably best to contact a site directly to get information on terms. One benefit of this more traditional approach is that when you're up and running you'll probably be allocated an account manager who you'll be liaising with as you develop your sales.

Kelkoo

Kelkoo (www.kelkoo.co.uk) is owned by Yahoo! and claims to attract 10 million unique visitors every month, making it one of the most visited shopping sites on the web after eBay and Amazon. It's also the biggest comparison shopping site in Britain.

According to its site, 'Kelkoo only charges you when a user clicks through to your site after choosing one of your offered listings. Each category has a different minimum cost. Your offers and shop will appear more prominently depending on popularity, relevancy and the price you pay.'

The close links with Yahoo! power most of Kelkoo's traffic. Yahoo! is still a major player on the internet, getting millions of visitors a month. It gives Kelkoo prominence and when people shop on Yahoo! they're usually using Kelkoo. From a seller's perspective this can be attractive, because it's a way of plugging in to the traffic of another of the net's giants.

In terms of getting your products on to Kelkoo, you have two options. You can choose a free Product Feed Upload, where Kelkoo helps sellers produce a file in a special format that can be uploaded every night. Or for a fee you use the Kelkoo Spider to scan your site and list your products automatically.

You can find more information about how to join Kelkoo at www.kelkoo.co.uk/b/a/co_4292_128501-online-merchants-and-stores-partner-with-kelkoo.html

Shopping.com

Shopping.com is one of the big players in the comparison shopping market and it's owned by eBay.

eBay bought Shopping.com in 2005 because it wanted to broaden its portfolio of ecommerce sites. It was also attracted to the huge number of member reviews and the wealth of product information the site held.

Shopping.com is the only major comparison shopping site to publish its fees on the site, but even the published fees are displayed as a range. To give you an idea, the cost per click varies from category to category: from 5p in travel to 50p in electronics. The full fees list is at:

https://ukmerchant.shopping.com/enroll/app;jsessionid=64E95271 A9847C2E9DCC852423C7952F?service=page/RateCard

According to the site: 'When merchants sign up with Shopping.com, they send us a list of the products that they sell. We then promote these products on our comparison shopping site. You can manage spending on a category basis, rather than juggling long lists of keywords. Our automated reports and free ROI Tracker help you track your cost of sales to maximise your profits.'

PriceRunner

PriceRunner (www.pricerunner.co.uk) is an independent comparison shopping engine (in the sense that it's not owned by any of the big internet players). Its parent company is called Valueclick. It started in Sweden in 1999 and has expanded to the UK, other European countries and the US.

The website is coy about what it will cost to get your products on to PriceRunner, but it does provide an email address that you can use to obtain more information. PriceRunner accepts feeds from sellers like the other companies, and it also automatically scans the web for prices and product information. It claims to have teams of 'PriceRunners' who compare prices offline too.

To find out more about PriceRunner, try www.pricerunner.co.uk/userguide.html

Classifieds

For a business it might seem counter-intuitive to suggest that you have a go and see what you can get out of online classifieds, but it's nevertheless a good idea. Traditional classifieds that used to be found in newspapers are typically favoured by consumers selling one-off items. The classified format has been transferred online very successfully, but not by newspapers. It has been famously pioneered by the kooky web phenomenon that is craigslist (www.craigslist.com).

Craig Newmark started the site in San Francisco and it has spread around the world very successfully. Despite overtures from many of the big players, and despite being valued at billions of dollars, craigslist remains independent. The service is largely free to advertisers (there are some fees in jobs and property sections) and is likely to remain so.

It's a model that has been successfully taken on by a whole host of imitators. The best-known version in Britain is probably Gumtree (www.gumtree.com), which is owned by eBay, but there are dozens of others.

Promoting your sales and your website is about getting the traffic wherever you can find it and channelling it to where it can create sales. Classified sites are buzzing with visitors and traffic, so see what you get out of them. Certainly consider advertising individual items or lines and make sure that you get links back to your site.

34

Build Your Own Website

Let's begin with a word of caution. Your website is going to take time to find a life of its own. So before you start, prepare yourself to be patient and make sure that you can keep your eBay sales ticking over. Building the site itself will take some time (depending on how you choose to create it), and it will then require time to start indexing and performing well in search engines. Your marketing is unlikely to kick in overnight and even when the site is attracting buyers, generating sales, making you money and everything is tickety-boo, the site will still need maintenance, love and attention. A website is always a work in progress.

Don't let that put you off. Lots of sellers are already doing it very successfully and they don't necessarily have any experience of running a website. In fact, if it's of any consolation, I meet very few sellers who regret setting up a website. Most of them regret not having done it sooner.

This section of the book lays out some of the things you need to think about when you're setting up a website of your own. But there's a wealth of extra information available, so if you want to find out more, Google is probably a good place to start your search.

Conceptualise your website

- **Step 1: What do you like?** Take some time to get out on to the web and identify sites you like. Think specifically about sites you like to buy from and make a note of why. It could be the navigation (how you are guided around the site), the way pages are laid out, or how you are led through the checkout to complete the purchase. What you like counts for a lot. First, when it comes to your own site, you are more likely to be proud and confident of something you like and that means you're more likely to make a success of it. Secondly, if you like something then the chances are that other people will like it too. In the absence of the huge research budgets that companies such as eBay have, you have to trust your instincts and experiences when it comes to building a winning website.

• **Step 2: What do you need?** At some point in the process of building your own site, you have to construct a brief or requirements document. This will explain to you, or to whoever builds the site, exactly what the site is intended to do and look like. A very good start, early on, is to determine exactly what the site needs. You obviously want a homepage of some sort, but what will it do? Display items? Talk about your company? How will shoppers know what you've got for sale? Should you have a search function? Do you need a checkout function on the site? How will people contact you? Will there be different pages for different products? Make your list and decide what aspects are 'must haves' and 'nice to haves'.

• **Step 3: Look and feel** Whole libraries full of books have been written about the theory and practice of web design and what works and what doesn't. If you ask five web designers what a good website looks like, you'll get at least ten contrasting answers.

Go for a website look and feel that you like and that's reflective of your business and what you sell. Again, look at other sites to confirm what you like.

There are a few factors worth bearing in mind though:

• **Not too much clutter** While stark, white minimalism isn't required, do avoid the opposite. Chintzy, cluttered sites with busy backgrounds and no obvious structure are difficult to use. When there's too much going on, people won't be able to get down to shopping. You should also be mindful of the visually impaired too, who find lurid websites difficult.

• **Use images** Pictures are a must. Whether they are of products, you, your premises or anything else relevant, they bring your business and website to life. It's not difficult these days to produce a really engaging, image-rich site and with the growing use of broadband you don't need to worry so much about slow download times when people visit your pages.

• **Clear calls to action** Make sure that people know what to do and where to go to buy and pay. To make certain things stand out, make them big. To make them stand out even more, make them big and red.

Choose a web address

When it comes to setting up shop with a website, giving it a good URL or web address is essential. Your first instincts will probably be to name it after you or your business or to give it a quirky, maybe funny, cute or punning name. That's what we're used to: it's how shops have been named for years. High streets are full of shops called 'Wilson & Sons' or 'Wilson's Laundrette' or have pen shops called 'His Nibs' or fish-and-chip shops called 'The Codfather'.

But when you set up shop online and you want to attract as many searchers as possible, being practical and straightforward works best. Match your URL to what people are searching for by using these tools:

• https://adwords.google.com/select/KeywordToolExternal

• http://inventory.overture.com/d/searchinventory/suggestion

They tell you what the most popular keywords are and also make suggestions for other words you might consider. You want to match your web address to what people are searching for. Bobthebrickie.com isn't as good as brightonbuilders.com.

Build your website

You have three options when it comes to building your website. The path you choose depends on your technical know-how and the sort of website you want. If you have the skills, you can build your own site. This option offers you the opportunity to create exactly what you want. If you don't have the skills but want a site that's personalised and bespoke to your needs, consider hiring someone to do it: there are countless individuals and companies that offer this service and you shouldn't find it hard to locate someone to do the job. The third possibility is buying an off-the-shelf shop that you can customise. Even this option requires you to have some technical expertise as you host and set the shop up.

Do it yourself

If you have the skills and expertise to build a website, then that's the obvious choice for you. It's fair to say that when you create a site as complicated as an ecommerce shop, you won't be building the whole thing from scratch. You'll probably be building a 'mash-up' and combining different bits of functionality to construct your site. You can embed a search functionality from Google, a checkout from PayPal and videos from YouTube or Revver to create an enticing offering for your customers.

You might also be interested in a selection of resources that come recommended from sellers who have already set up shop. osCommerce (www.oscommerce.com) offers a selection of open source features that you can use free. It's well worth exploring.

Hire someone

If you're lucky, you already know of a person or business who can build your site. If you're even luckier, you might have a bright spark working for you who can do it. But if you're looking for a developer, what you're really after is a recommendation. I've included a long list of eBay sellers' own websites at the end of the book. Take a look at their sites and how they're hosted and if you see one you like, why not reach out to the seller and discover how it was constructed and by whom?

You might also want to check out Elance (www.elance.com), which is an online space where professionals and businesses like you link up to do jobs for each other. You can easily plug into Elance to find a web developer. The systems the site has in place mean that you have a clear agreement with the service provider regarding the job that needs to be done as well as safety mechanisms to protect your payment. If you go through Elance you need to construct a good brief for your service provider to work from.

You can just as easily get out the phone book and choose someone local. But whoever you select, make sure that you plump for a techie who can communicate with you. In my experience, techies aren't very good at talking to the rest of us. Many of them think that we should speak their language and they are not very good at communicating in any other way. It's often all PHP, Ajax, My SQL and gig this and meg that. If you're having difficulty understanding what they're saying or doing for you, ask them to explain. If you're paying, you're the customer and you should get what you're paying for.

Buy an off-the-shelf package

You'll be spoilt for choice if you decide to go for a ready-made shop: it's a marketplace crowded with thousands of services offering a dizzying array of packages. That's good, but it can be bewildering. Here are some packages that UK PowerSellers have told me they use.

- **Actinic** The most respected and market-leading company offering ecommerce services is Actinic (www.actinic.co.uk). It offers great flexibility for shop owners and developers and charges depending on what you want. It's definitely worth examining.

- **Go Daddy** In the US, Go Daddy (www.godaddy.com) has attracted a lot of attention (not least for its risqué advertising and the exploits of its left-field CEO) and is one of the biggest web hosters. It also offers ecommerce packages that look like good value.

- **BT** For something closer to home try BT (www.btbroad-bandoffice.com/internetapplications/itplanding) and its ecommerce offering, which it claims is eBay and PayPal ready but is more expensive than most at £30 a month.

- **Other services** Opinion is divided about two further services, ekmpowershop (www.ekmpowershop.com) and 1&1 (http://1and1.co.uk). Among the people I have spoken to, it seems like you either love them or loathe them. Have a look at their sites and see what you think.

- **Tidy** One other service that keeps cropping up and is often praised by eBay sellers is TidyEcommerce (www.tidyecommerce.co.uk). The company is run by a British eBay PowerSeller and web developer who knows what sellers need from eBay. Tidy offers custom-built ecommerce sites and aims to make them easy for sellers to plug in to. Check the service out.

Build your own website checklist

- **Do your research** Examine websites you like and analyse what you like about them.

- **Decide what you want** Be very clear in your mind what you want and write a brief that describes your site.

- **Choose a web address that works** Take a scientific approach and choose a web address that will work well in search engines.

- **Choose how to build the site** Will you build it yourself, get someone to build you a custom website or take an off-the-peg product?

- **Build it!** You can't start earning until your website is live. Get to it!

35

Promote Your Website

Once your website is up and running and open for business, it's time to get people through the door. It's a fair bet that your site has fixed costs, so the more sales it makes the better the profits. If your site is built, ready and just sitting there not making sales, it's losing you money.

Market your website to your eBay buyers

The easiest way to market to an engaged, positive and eager customer is to grab their attention when they have just bought from you. That's why your eBay customers are a key target for your marketing. At the very least, include a leaflet or flyer with every eBay despatch to let your buyers know that you're now also selling from your own site. Make the leaflet as good as you can. A print-out is good, but a well-designed printed colour flyer is better. Just check out eBay for sellers of A5 colour printing: you may be surprised how reasonable it is to get 500 or 1000 leaflets printed.

Make sure that your URL or web address is prominent on the leaflet. Also, make sure that your sellers are in no doubt that you're open for business and ready for them to come shopping. You can tempt them to visit by telling them about any special sales or discounts you have available on your site. It's really worth having a popular line that you're selling more cheaply on your own website than on eBay as a draw, so you can say 'Things are cheaper on my website!' with pride.

Additionally, in every email you're sending out via eBay, make sure that you have a link and a call to action: Visit My Website! Consider putting the URL of your site on the exterior of your packaging and anything else you can think of that a customer receives. Be shameless.

Marketing on eBay itself

Marketing your website on eBay is tricky. Needless to say, eBay doesn't want buyers and sellers going elsewhere. You can't, for instance, have your website address as your User ID or eBay Shop name. And when it comes to linking to your own shop, the Links policies that eBay provides (which you can find at http://pages.ebay.co.uk/help/policies/ia/rules_for_sellers.html) do little to explain what's allowed or disallowed. In fact, it's all absurdly confusing.

There's one thing you definitely can do and that's put a link to your shop on your About Me page. You'll get some traffic that way and it's good for search engines too. Do not on any account put links to your own website in your listing pages: that's the fastest way to get kicked off eBay.

Email marketing

A mailing list is an important marketing tool to help you to move forward. Once you have your own site it is a vital means of staying in touch with your customers. In fact, if by the time your site is up and running you haven't already got a mailing list going, you need to get started quickly. Building a mailing list takes time but it's absolutely time well spent.

You might already have experimented with mailing lists and used the facility made available with your eBay Shop. If, however, that list is starting to number more than a few hundred email addresses, it's time to begin administering it yourself. It's too valuable an asset and you need to keep it in your own hands.

The legal regulations for building and maintaining a mailing list are pretty straightforward. You can invite people to join your list and they have to opt in to that list. I repeat: subscribers have to actively join your list. It's not acceptable simply to add an email address you've acquired (maybe it's from an eBay buyer) and then take the person off the list if they ask you to. They have to opt in. And in every email you send out you must provide subscribers with the option to be removed from the list and do that if people ask. You can find out more about the law relating to email marketing at

www.ico.gov.uk/Home/what_we_cover/privacy_and_
electronic_communications/guidance.aspx

In terms of getting people to subscribe, you can simply ask them to email you requesting to be added to your list, or have a special page on your website where people can submit their own email addresses. Make sure that you prominently promote your mailing list on your site and in your general admin emails too. It's worth thinking about adding a tick box in your checkout that people can tick if they want to receive your mailings.

Make the most of your mailing list

Building the mailing list itself is only part of the challenge when it comes to email marketing. You also need to think about what you're actually going to send out. The best way of maximising the value of your mailing list is to send your subscribers emails they want to receive. Sounds easy, but it's surprising how much mail I receive that doesn't have me in mind. A good email could be a case of reminding people that you're still there and doing business. Some successful mail-outs don't even have a sales-driven tone or a specific pitch: they just include news. Others highlight offers, bargains or new lines.

Email marketing pointers

• **The content should be right for your business** You've already spent time building a brand and a website that succinctly represent you and your business. Make sure that these carry through to your marketing emails. Make sure that what you're writing is right and accurate. Emails with text only are fine, but using graphics and images is better and more likely to be compelling.

• **The content should be right for your customer** Targeting the message of your email to the recipient is critical to generating a favourable response. The person who bought a pram last week probably doesn't need another this week. But they might well want something else. You know your customers better than anyone else, so go with your gut.

One seller I know sent a Christmas ecard to his mailing list thanking his past customers for their business over the year and hoping to serve them again in the New Year. It was a well-designed email with a friendly tone. It was completely uncommercial: no offers, no prices and no call to action. It generated more custom than any other email he has sent before or since.

• **Play by the rules** If someone wants to unsubscribe, they want to unsubscribe. No arguments. Make sure you take them off the list promptly and don't email them again. Ever.

• **Don't overuse the list** Have you ever joined a mailing list and subsequently been bombarded by frequent, even daily, pointless email messages? Annoying, isn't it? Don't send too many emails, because it not only alienates subscribers, it dilutes the potency of your emails. It's surely better to generate a big wave of orders from one email rather than five trickles from five emails.

• **Timing is everything** Getting the timing of your emails right can mean two things. If an email is promoting time-sensitive lines (say for Christmas or Valentine's day), make sure that you give subscribers time to size up and respond to your offers. Don't be too late and miss the boat. That said, too early is just as bad, because people won't think what you're promoting is relevant. It's also worth thinking about what day of the week you send your emails out and what time of day they arrive. It's probably best to avoid Monday mornings when people often have overflowing inboxes, but what's right will depend on your customers and you know them best.

Local marketing

Don't neglect the good old-fashioned ways of marketing when it comes to promoting your website. Never leave the house without a small stock of your own flyers, leaflets or business cards emblazoned with your web address to give out or leave in places where people will find them. You might also want to consider getting posters made and asking relevant places to display them. Little things like this can all be an integral part of building the momentum of your new site.

Paying for print advertising is usually expensive and it's difficult to assess its success. So if you want to get in the papers, try to do it for free. Commenting on relevant stories by writing a letter to the editor for publication (including your URL) is worth a try and it's also worth attempting to get featured in articles. You've got a good story to tell – you're a businessperson, branching out, doing something different – and other people will want to hear about your enterprise. Look for opportunities to contact journalists who have written articles that you could have featured in and tell them your story for future reference.

Try to get on the radio as well. Phone-ins are a good means of doing this, and if they are relevant to you as an online seller or eBayer so much the better. It shouldn't be hard to get a plug in and promote your site. It's through lots of little bits of marketing that you build up your site traffic and sales on your website. When you were an eBay seller, eBay did all this. Now you're on your own you have to do it yourself, so take on the challenge with good grace.

Case study: An eBay seller with a website
eBay user ID: Biddybidbidbid
Website: www.allyoubead.com

A timely windfall meant that Sue could pursue her dream of moving to France and taking on an old Breton farmhouse to do up. Running a *gîte* or B&B seemed too much like hard work and her limited French meant that she was unlikely to get a job, so she decided to have a go at making a living on eBay.

Sue had previous experience of eBay and she started experimenting with products she could sell. She settled on beads by accident. She put some of her own collection up for sale and was stunned by how quickly they sold: she even got bids on Christmas Day! She started sourcing more stock and her business quickly took off.

Sue gets her beads from all over the world. Whether it's European wholesalers or direct from manufacturers in India and China, she takes pride in constantly updating her inventory and giving her buyers 'new things to look at'. She ascribes her success to her ever-changing range of beads, making things as easy as possible for buyers and actively encouraging multiple and repeat purchases.

'I have flat shipping fees,' says Sue, 'because if someone has to use a calculator to figure out the P&P, they're not going to want to buy. I keep the communication personal [she writes all her own emails rather than use the eBay templates] and if I mess something up, I admit it, apologise and put it right without leaving my buyers out of pocket. I try to treat them better than I would expect to be treated myself.'

Recently Sue decided to expand her operations and launch a website. It hasn't proved difficult because she is technically minded and has experience in web design. 'A website allows me to reach those customers who, for whatever reason, don't want to buy through eBay,' she says. 'It's also true that certain suppliers see a website as serious or professional in a way that they don't hold to be the case for eBay. As it costs virtually nothing to run the site, there's no reason not to have it.'

She considers there to be two major benefits from running an independent website. Having a shopping cart seems to increase the number of purchases an individual buyer makes and a website can be personalised to her buyers' needs. Sue reckons that that the average eBay buyer buys 4.9 items per visit and the average website buyer buys 6.5.

The website is an add-on to her existing eBay business and not a replacement. According to Sue, 'When you run a website, you soon begin to appreciate the traffic eBay has sent your way. When you have to pay for advertising and marketing for your own site, you do start to see that eBay fees are actually pretty good value for money!'

And ditching eBay would mean losing customers: 'Buyers definitely feel safer buying from eBay and they like to get feedback. I'd never expect to get all my buyers to move to my website. Nor would I want to – eBay is a fun place to sell, and I really, *really* want my shooting star!'

Promote your website checklist

- **Market your site to your eBay buyers** Make the most of your existing customers and alert them to your site.

- **Build a mailing list** Start gathering email addresses and building a mailing list as soon as possible: it takes time.

- **Unleash your emails** Reach out to those on your mailing list in a structured, respectful way to drive sales.

- **Don't neglect old-fashioned marketing** Make the most of your story and the people you know to promote your new site.

36

Search Engine Marketing

One of the reasons your own website is so potentially lucrative and vital to a professional seller is the astonishing number of people who start their online shopping with a search engine.

When a shopper starts with Google, they may not necessarily have a destination in mind. That means that they're ripe for the picking. They could be your customers.

There are two ways of making the most of this opportunity and ensuring you have a profile in search engines. The first is to ensure that your site is the most relevant in relation to what people are searching for, so that it appears at the top of the search results. This is called 'natural' or 'organic' search. The second option is to get your wallet out and use the 'paid for' options and enhance your visibility with sponsored links.

What's the goal?

For your business the ideal outcome is good placement of your website on the search engines. You definitely want to see your website in the first page of search results, and ideally you want to be one of the first three results on the page, up at the top before the point when searchers need to scroll. Depending on the keywords you want to be found with, this is eminently possible.

Of course, the big companies all know this too and destinations like Amazon, eBay and the comparison shopping sites spend astonishing amounts of time and effort optimising their websites and outlay vast amounts on search engine advertising. You may not have the same budgets or the person power as the big boys, but here's the good news: you can do the same.

Optimising your site for search engines is relatively straightforward, especially if you build the requirements in to your original brief and construct a website that search engines will like. Making a start on paid-for search engine advertising is also pleasingly easy, but requires management over time and you need to develop some expertise. You can't afford to let the obstacles put you off: harnessing the power of search engines is critical to your success. It's an absolute 'must do'.

Let me state the bleeding obvious: Google dominates the internet search market. As a result, I've centred this section around the services that Google offers. But there are other significant search engines, such as Yahoo!, Ask, Microsoft and AOL. None is as big as Google, but all of them are worth investigating and all of them have similar services that you can plug in to. Nevertheless, start with Google.

Search engine optimisation

The idea of search engine optimisation (SEO) is a straightforward one: making your website as accessible and attractive as possible to search engines. This in turn enhances your natural search performance and you will show up nicely in search results without paying for that profile. The idea itself is a simple one and most of the techniques laid out here are simple too, but it's astonishing how many sites haven't been adequately optimised. Once you know the tricks, it's easy enough to spot the mistakes that people are making. An unoptimised website is a terrible waste because it means that people who want to find you can't.

Tip: Don't pay extra
> When you're deciding on a website package or service provider, don't pay extra for SEO. It's often peddled like snake oil and that should be enough to get your antennae bristling. If someone asks you to add SEO on to a standard package, the chances are that they're not the best person for your job. It's like buying a car and the car dealer asking you to pay extra for the steering wheel. Request search engine optimisation as standard. Full stop.

Make sure that your site can be read
The first step of search engine optimisation is making sure that your site can be easily read by the spiders that search engines send

out to catalogue and index all the sites on the internet. Ensure that your site is free of 'frames' that block the spiders. Try to use HTML wherever possible rather than images. Sometimes when building a site, a developer uses blocks of images that fit together and look lovely to readers. This tactic is often employed for glossy, glitzy headings on websites. The spiders can read the 'alt text' on an image (the text that displays if the image won't load), but they prefer normal, readable HTML text, so help them out. It's in your best interests, after all.

Help the spiders

The way in which your site is crafted is important in the sense that there are ways of telling the spiders what they want to know in a form that's beneficial to you. You can help the spiders understand what your site is about so that they in turn can categorise it properly. If you're not familiar with HTML or coding this may all seem a bit bewildering, but do try to get your head around it. Even if you're not going to code your site yourself, it's worth knowing about and it'll mean you can communicate your needs to your developer.

How Google works is a secret. Much of what people talk about as being best practice in the field of search engine optimisation is speculation and educated guesswork based on testing and trial and error. But there is still a great deal of argument about what's important and what's just froth and nonsense. The best advice is to cover all the bases and do everything that might have a bearing on your success.

- **URL** We've looked at the importance of your URL already, but the web address of your site is important to the spiders, so make sure that it's working with the other aspects and includes your top keywords where possible.

- **Title** The title of your page is what you see at the top of the browser window. It's just a short description of the site and page you're on. It's an opportunity to describe your page again with your keywords.

In HTML it's something like this:

<TITLE>Put your keyword rich title here. It appears right at the top of the browser window.</TITLE>

- **Meta tags** You have another opportunity to describe your business in the site's meta tags. These descriptions are not visible to people viewing your site, but can be read by spiders (although opinion is divided about what importance the search engines imbue them with).

The HTML for your meta tags will look something like this:

<META NAME="DESCRIPTION" CONTENT="Put a few descriptive sentences here describing the page. Don't forget the keywords!">

<META NAME="KEYWORDS" CONTENT="you,put,your, keywords,here,separated,by,commas,not,spaces">

• **Headers** Just like in a book, you organise your site text with headers that signal to readers what certain sections are about. How you code those headings helps the spiders understand what sections are about too. Using the H1, H2 header tags in your HTML tells the spiders that the text they are reading is a header and therefore more important than the other words, so they can pay more attention to it.

• **Alt text** The alt text describes what a picture is about. It's good practice to use it, because people with visibility problems who use page readers to surf the net go to the alt text to discover what an image is. Spiders also use the alt text to understand what an image is because they can't see pictures and therefore they do attach importance to it. Make sure that you fill the alt text field in and don't leave it empty.

Build keyword-rich content

Search engines love the written word. They love reading your site and understanding what it's about and when they should offer it to searchers. So provide plenty of what internet folk call 'content'. However, reams of pointless ramblings aren't going to do you much good. What you need is keyword-rich content that's relevant to what you're selling.

Keywords are the search terms that searchers use to find the site they want. Your task is to match the words that people are searching for to the ones you have on your site. It's a fact that if you don't include the word 'dalek' on your site, people using the word 'dalek' to search won't find you. We looked earlier in the book at researching your keywords, understanding which were the most popular and making sure that you use them. The same principle applies here.

Get to know your keywords by using the research tools available (noted earlier), and make sure that you have a site that is rich in content including these keywords. Obviously, the pages describing your goods will include lots of lovely keywords, but think about other options. A blog (an online diary) can easily be slotted into a site and it's a great way of making sure that you're regularly adding more content (search engines also reward recently and regularly updated sites), but think too about writing articles about relevant topics and adding pages about you, your business and sales. It all adds up.

But don't overdo it!

If your content is good prose crafted as genuine copy for the benefit of your users, you'll never have a problem. But some website owners try to game the system by disingenuously cramming their sites full of relevant keywords. This could mean concealing long lists of words in their pages, repeating keywords with unnatural frequency or just building pages containing pointless text. It's not looked on kindly by Google. In fact, you sometimes hear about sites being delisted from Google altogether if they do this, which is not good for attracting customers.

Get linked in

The other things that search engine sites love are links: links from your sites to other sites, links in to your site from other websites, and also the links within your site that help the spiders navigate around and understand what the site is about. A key aspect of optimising your site is making sure that you have as many links in and out of your site as possible.

The number of links isn't the only aspect that matters. Google also takes into account what it considers to be the importance of the site.

Tip: Link text

Don't neglect your link text, as the spiders use the actual text to understand what the destination of the link is about.

Make sure that you have an acceptable link from eBay to your site, maybe from your About Me page or shop as a first step. Then start building other links in from anywhere you can. In fact, it's an opportunity for which you should always have your eyes open.

Five ways of building links are:

- **Link exchange** Build a page on your site that is a list of links to other websites. Start with your friends and colleagues and offer to put a link in your list to their website in exchange for a link on their site. Soon you'll be able to build up a good long list and have lots of links in to your site too.

- **Comment on blogs** Bloggers usually welcome comments and responses to their blog posts and when you post you're usually allowed to add a website link that other readers can click on. It's well worth spending a few minutes now and again posting comments on blogs and getting more links coming in. It's also not a bad way of marketing in general: other people on the blog can see your link, follow it and maybe buy something. Choose popular, relevant blogs and comment on as wide a selection as possible.

- **Build profiles** There are squillions of sites that allow you to build a profile and tell the world about you and your business. Most of them are free and in the most part they only take a few moments to establish. Check out BT Tradespace (www.bttradespace.com), Squidoo (www.squidoo.com), Ecademy (www.ecademy.com) and Ziki (www.ziki.com) for starters. Don't forget social bookmarking sites such as del.icio.us (http://del.icio.us). The value you get out of these profiles depends on the energy you put into building them, but it's a good way of boosting your 'link equity'.

- **Join communities and networks** MySpace, YouTube, chat boards, discussion boards and any online community forum that permits you to make a contribution are opportunities to get a link in to your site. But be careful that you don't fall foul of any rules that ban advertising. Lots of sites don't let you blatantly plug your own site, but you can often find ways of doing it legitimately: see what other people are doing and emulate their tactics. On some chat boards, for instance, you are not permitted to link to your site in posts, but you are allowed a personalised 'signature' that can include a website link.

• **Join directories** Don't forget to ensure that your web address is included in as many online directories as possible. They come in all shapes and sizes. Some are the online versions of the phone book or Yellow Pages and you should include your web address in these. Others are local or centred around a theme or interest area, such as parenting or angling. Start with Google and see what exists that's relevant to you. Don't forget that links from classified sites count too, so seek out Gumtree, craigslist, LinkedIn and others and add your links where it's permitted.

Tip: Google toolbar

Download the Google toolbar to see how you're doing. It sits at the top of your browser wherever you are on the web. The toolbar includes a service called 'page rank', which is a speedy way of seeing how Google rates your site. The higher the page rank, the greater the importance of your site in Google's eyes. It also has lots of handy features, so it's well worth getting hold of. You can find it at http://toolbar.google.co.uk.

Search engine advertising

An eBay seller once wistfully told me that advertising with Google was 'a good way to make a small fortune'. I was surprised and asked if he meant it. He said, 'Oh yes, out of a big one.' He wasn't joking.

The last section examined how you can optimise your website to ensure that as much free traffic as possible comes your way from search engines. You don't pay the search engine a penny for 'natural search' traffic. Needless to say, you can also buy advertising. By paying you can ensure that your site is at the top of the list and visible to buyers. It can take weeks and months for your site to even show up and start performing naturally, but with advertising you can achieve an instant presence.

Google sells advertising space and people buy it – people buy it in droves, which is why Google's founders are billionaires. It's been said that of all the money spent worldwide on advertising, 1% is spent with the search giant.

If you've ever searched Google you'll have seen the adverts. They appear in two places in Google search results: at the top and

on the righthand side. Google is also greatly expanding where it display the ads that people pay for. For instance, if you use Google mail, you often see paid-for ads in your inbox, relevant to the emails you've been sending and receiving. Google also has map services that show ads on them.

But probably the most innovative and clever thing that Google does to distribute its advertising is to allow people to display Google ads on their own sites. Any time someone clicks an ad that a website owner is showing, the website owner gets paid. The programme is called Adsense and you can discover all about it at

www.google.co.uk/intl/en/ads

It's pay per click

One of the reasons Google can feel expensive to people more used to the eBay model is that you don't pay per sale but rather per click. If someone clicks a link you're paying for, you have to cough up, regardless of whether that person goes on to buy something. It means that you can spend money and not get any additional sales, which grates. That's something that sellers might have to deal with themselves. If your model is based around the price and sales per item, you might need to change your system. One way of doing that might be setting up and spending a marketing budget that can be used generally to promote your business and is kept separate from 'per item' spending.

From that budget you can allocate some spending to Google Adwords. Even though you can't directly attribute the spend to sales, you can limit your spend to budget accordingly and prevent your costs spiralling out of control. But before you start thinking about spending money, make sure that you've cracked natural search. Spending on advertising before that's all sorted is rather like opening a shop on the high street and only letting people in who've got an invitation, while not opening the doors to allow passers-by to enter.

Google Adwords
Setting up an account with Adwords is pretty easy and getting your ads on Google shouldn't take long. You create your own adverts with the information you want to present to searchers and then choose the keywords with which you want your ads to be associated. You agree what you're willing to spend and then Google displays the ad when it's relevant to a search result. The placement of your ad is determined by Google and by how relevant it is to the search in question.

Set up an account
Set up your Adwords account at https://adwords.google.co.uk. You need to provide some personal details so that Google can keep in touch with you. Next, choose whether you want the starter version of the programme or the standard version. Go with the Starter Edition if you're completely new to Adwords; don't worry, because you can upgrade whenever you want.

Create your advert
Once you're set up, you need to build your advert. First, express a preference about who will see your ad. Will you make it visible to all international viewers or will you opt to limit it to local searchers? For a business that has graduated from eBay it's probably not sensible to limit your viewers to those who are local; that's an option better suited to businesses such as restaurants or services that make the majority of their business from customers close by.

You then have to craft your advert. There are three text fields that you need to fill in to build your ad and you can see what it will look like as you go along. Think about the message you want to put across and craft a tight few lines of text that will attract clickers.

You're not limited to just advertising your shop homepage. You have complete flexibility over what you promote: it could be a certain section of your website or even an individual product that you know sells well and will attract traffic.

Tip: Your budget

Google advises that it's unlikely you'll have much success with a budget of less than £30 a week. However, you can set a budget as low or as high as you like and Google won't exceed that limit. Even £10 a week can help you understand your keywords and what's effective.

Choose your keywords

When do you want your advert to show up? What words will someone be searching for to get your ad? You'll doubtless have lots of ideas of what you want, but Google can also provide you with ideas and suggestions based on what people have searched for in the past. Take a moment or two to validate your ideas and hone your keywords. Don't just select your business name or a narrow interpretation; try to include relevant keywords that relate to your sales in a broader sense.

There's little doubt that one of the reasons Google advertising is so successful is the relevance of the ads to what people search for. People click on the ads because they are linked to what they want to find out. It's the keywords you choose that make sure that your ad is relevant, so it's critical to get them right.

How is it priced?

The keywords you choose also determine the price you pay to Google for your clicks. But it's not as simple as keyword x costing y pence per click. The price is determined by an auction where you compete with the other people who want to buy the same keywords. If you bid higher than other people, you'll more than likely get your ad to appear at the top of the sponsored link section.

So if you set your maximum bid for the word 'gramophone' at 35p and the nearest other bid is 24p, you'll get priority over other ads when people search for 'gramophone'. Google won't charge you 35p when someone clicks, they'll charge you 25p, a penny more than the next highest bidder. Even if you're not the highest bidder, or even the second highest bidder, your ad will still show up. It just won't show up as often or as high up the list as people who are bidding more.

What's particularly smart about Adwords is that money's not the only deciding option. Google's integrity relies on the relevance of the results and ads it shows to searchers. Because relevance is key, low bidders can still enjoy visibility by being a popular ad that lots of people have clicked on in the past. This means that a well-framed, successful advert can knock the socks off ads placed by bidders with more money.

Before you send your advert live you have to provide payment details so that Google can bill you.

Tip: Keywords
You can't bid for or buy the keyword 'eBay'.

Manage your campaign
You can manage your ad from a console on the Google website. You can see how it's performing, how many clicks you're getting, where those clicks are coming from, which keywords are working best and what you're spending. You can also make the changes and corrections to ensure better performance here.

If you want to manage multiple ads, you need to upgrade to the standard version of Adwords. Sate your hunger for information about how your ads are doing with the information that Google provides. It might be tempting to search for your ads to make sure they're appearing and then click on the link to ensure that they're working correctly, but try not to: you still have to pay for the clicks you make yourself.

Keep at it
There's little doubt that Adwords is a potentially powerful way of advertising. Google is the biggest thing on the net, attracting millions of searchers a day, and you need to plug into that potent powerhouse to succeed. But Adwords can be a time-consuming and difficult beast to tame. Start slowly, learn the ropes, ramp up and keep at it. The rewards are potentially worth it.

Measure your site's performance
As with eBay, making the most of Google demands that you spend some time analysing the statistics and performance numbers. Google provides an amazing free tool to help you keep track of your website called Google Analytics (www.google.com/analytics/en-GB), which

can really help you understand who's visiting your site, where they're coming from and how they're finding you.

Search engine marketing checklist

- **Optimise your website for search engines** Help the spiders to catalogue and index your site by optimising it for search engines.

- **Build links and content** Make your site as attractive as possible by developing lots of links in and out and producing keyword-rich content.

- **Experiment with Adwords** Take the plunge and see what results you can get with Google Adwords.

- **Know the numbers** Understand where your traffic is coming from with Google Analytics.

37

Affiliate Schemes

Once your website is up and running and you're getting clicks, traffic and customers, you might want to think about signing up to some affiliate schemes. Affiliate schemes are a way of making money out of the traffic you have by sending people to other websites. When it comes to the internet the most valuable commodity is traffic: the people coming to your site. Lots of big companies are willing to pay good money if you send some of your traffic their way. It's not necessarily going to make you a pile of cash and it's not really easy money, but it could be a good way of adding a few quid to the bottom line.

You may think that you'd be mad to promote other websites, and you might have a point. After all, you've worked hard to build up your traffic and sending it away might seem like madness. But doing it right won't mean losing your hard-won traffic. Rather, it will be about sending people who aren't going to buy from you elsewhere and making some money out of them anyway. You can promote things that you don't stock or even push things that bear no relation to what you're selling. You'll probably be amazed by the variety of businesses you can promote using affiliate schemes.

How does it work?

Different affiliate schemes work in different ways, but all are based around the same principles. You include on your website a banner, link or other ad for another site. Then when someone follows the link to the site and does what they're supposed to do, you get some recompense. Some schemes are only looking for traffic, others are looking to acquire customers and only cough up when you send someone who actually joins the site, while others will reward you if you send people who buy something.

You'll be rewarded in different ways. Sometimes you get a few pence a click, or maybe a little more for a longer visit. The bounty for helping a business acquire a new customer will usually be more, maybe a few pounds (or more for potentially very valuable customers). If you're paid based on sales made by people you send, then that could be a percentage of sales or a revenue-sharing model.

Sign up to an affiliate scheme

Some companies administer their own affiliate schemes (Amazon for instance). eBay's scheme can be found here:

https://publisher.ebaypartnernetwork.com

Many also outsource their programmes to third parties. The two biggest and most respected agencies in the field are Commission Junction (www.cj.com) and TradeDoubler (www.tradedoubler.com). You can sign up to these services and they keep you up to date with the latest offers and promotions.

Tip: The eBay affiliate programme

> Do join eBay's own affiliate programme and ensure that when you link from your site to eBay you use an affiliate link. If someone you send to eBay bids or buys, you'll earn.

For inspiration, take a look at these sites that use the eBay affiliate scheme to make money:

- www.preloved.co.uk

- www.babycentre.co.uk

- www.doyouremember.co.uk

38
What's Next?

My aim as I've been writing this book has been to boil down everything I have learnt about eBay since 1999 and to craft it into a roadmap that will help you use eBay first as a great way to start buying and selling, and then as a springboard for building an online business. Whatever you choose to do with eBay (there are no rules!), I hope that this book has given you a useful introduction to one of the most amazing opportunities to come out of the internet.

It really is possible to embark on a new career as an internet merchant and it could change your life. It won't necessarily be easy and you'll have a great deal of work to do, but the rewards could be wonderful. The sellers I meet rave about the freedom that being your own boss affords you and many have been able to improve their quality of life dramatically. You could do the same.

I hope you found this book useful and inspiring. There is no reason anyone with a modicum of computer knowledge and a bit of get up and go can't make a success of it. Don't forget: I'd love to hear from you and learn how you're doing. Visit my website at www.wilsondan.co.uk/ebay to keep up to date and get in touch.

As I write, the UK (and indeed much of the world) is in the depths of a serious and painful economic crisis. The news is full of doom and gloom. Unemployment's up. The national debt grows daily. But who knows, by the time you read this it may well be over.

In the middle of these economic woes, it's nevertheless extraordinary to report that ecommerce sales are up. The High Street is suffering, consumer spending has decreased, but people are spending more online this year than ever before. Even more astonishingly, experts predict that ecommerce will grow year on year right through until 2012. So, if you're worried about taking the plunge because the economy is faltering, don't be. There isn't a recession online.

In lots of ways, online trading is still in its infancy. Just under half of British businesses don't even have a website. If you take the leap you'll be a pioneer. The ecommerce frontier has hardly been opened and you'll often be charting new territory as you go. You'll always be learning and you'll sometimes be solving problems that have never needed to be solved before, so you'll have to have your wits about you. Keep an eye out for emerging trends and new ideas that you can exploit and take the opportunity to experiment. There are so many opportunities to succeed on the net that a calculated risk could really pay off.

But one thing is certain: eBay will be different. In many ways it stands at a crossroads now and faces many challenges, not least from Google and the changing nature of the internet. Just take comfort from that song by the Carpenters: We've only just begun. eBay is only in its second decade. It's a young company and it still has plenty of room to grow – and there's almost unimaginable scope for you to grow with it.

Some sellers have been gloomy about recent changes, but it seems to me that without change, eBay would fade a little. It would cease to dominate ecommerce. Change is always hard to swallow: sometimes it will be wrong, but it is absolutely necessary.

In fact, the shape eBay takes is up to you. The eBay community charts the course of the business and what the marketplace looks like in ten years will depend on how you, and I, and the millions of other people in the world decide to use it. There is no eBay without the community of buyers and sellers. This feels like where I began, stressing the importance of community: we are eBay.

Online Resources

There's a wealth of further reading available and it pays to keep up with the latest news and developments, not just on eBay but regarding the net and ecommerce in general.

First, you can find my own blog at www.wilsondan.co.uk. It looks at eBay and other online communities and, well, just about anything else I fancy. Pop by and take a look.

All the eBay and ecommerce-related information on my blog can be found at www.wilsondan.co.uk/ebay and I've linked to this part of my site throughout the book. Whether it's up-to-date information on fees, rules, emerging trends or my latest rant on some eBay topic, you'll find it there. You can also contact me direct via my blog. If you have a subject you'd like to cover or a question you want answered, why not ask it there and I'll also publish the response to help others.

Other very useful blogs include Tamebay (www.tamebay.com), which is run by some British Powersellers. I also recommend Trevor Ginn's blog (www.trevorginn.com) as a useful source of insights.

ChannelAdvisor, an eBay services company, has a triumvirate of blogs that I frequently turn to for views and comment:

- **General company blog** http://blog.channeladvisor.com
- **Scot Wingo's blog** http://ebaystrategies.blogs.com
- **A blog about comparison shopping engines** http://www.csestrategies.com

eBay has numerous sources of information that you should take a few moments now and again to keep abreast of. eBay's official blog, eBay Ink, is authored by Richard Brewer-Hay. He's a Brit based at eBay HQ in California and it's entertaining reading. You can find it at: http://www.ebayinkblog.com.

For hard news check out the announcements on eBay's three biggest national sites, eBays US, Germany and UK:

- www2.ebay.com/aw/marketing.shtml
- www2.ebay.com/aw/de-marktplatz.shtml
- www2.ebay.com/aw/marketing-uk.shtml

For a US perspective, take a look at Auctionbytes (www.auction bytes.com), which is a useful repository of knowledge and articles about eBay and other marketplaces as well as a blog.

There's a lot of comment and theorising about Google, but for reliable considered comment I like Search Engine Watch (http://blog.searchenginewatch.com) and John Battelle's blog (http://battellemedia.com).

For the lighter side of eBay, some sites take pride in gathering together the weird and the wonderful items that are being sold. Bayraider (www.bayraider.tv), Oddball Auction (www.oddball auctions.com) and Bizarre Bids (www.bizarrebids.com) are all good for a laugh.

For general small business advice, expertise, news and views I can heartily recommend two superb resources, both based in Britain. Emma Jones is the brains behind Enterprise Nation (www.enterprisenation.com) and she provides energetic and inspirational perspectives on small businesses and home-based enterprises. You'll love it.

Alex Bellinger produces a regular podcast and blog called SmallBizPod at www.smallbizpod.co.uk. If you want some intelligent and varied listening for your iPod there's none better.

eBay Sellers' Websites

If you need inspiration from other sellers who have websites, check out the list below. All these sites are run by businesses that are also selling on eBay.

www.baronbros.co.uk

www.btrdirect.co.uk

www.cablestar.co.uk

www.cdlmicro.co.uk

www.cellpacksolutions.com

www.cheaperbatteries.co.uk

http://cockywrappers.com

www.cvbmedia.co.uk

www.dbits.co.uk

www.everythingipod.co.uk

www.flashdirect.co.uk

www.gadgetsandgiftsuk.com

www.gardenerscottage.com

www.girlyshop.co.uk

www.javaslublu.com

www.jokesbypost.co.uk

www.jons-all-sorts.co.uk

www.lilacandcream.co.uk

www.mhpcomputerservices.com

www.moretonalarms.com

www.mount-and-blade.co.uk

www.peninsulajewellery.co.uk

www.service-champions.co.uk

www.shredacademy.com

www.solentcables.co.uk

www.speckyfoureyes.com

www.thecharmworks.com

www.uk-surplus.com

www.watercooled-pcs.co.uk

www.westroen-spheres.co.uk

www.weldedbliss.com

Glossary

About Me page A page created by an eBay member that tells the community more about him or her.

Announcement Board Where eBay informs the community about changes to the site.

Answer Centre A community facility where you can pose an eBay-related question and receive an answer from other eBayers.

Auction Buy It Now An auction with a Buy It Now option too. The Buy It Now option disappears when the first bid is placed.

Auction format The traditional eBay selling format, where members bid against each other and the highest bidder wins the item.

AuctionWeb The original name of eBay.

Best Match The system eBay uses to determine the order of search results, which takes into account a seller's Feedback and DSRs.

Best Offer When you're selling at a fixed price, a buyer can make you an offer lower than your Buy it Now price. It's up to the seller to decide whether to accept the offer or reject it.

Bid increments The steps by which bids increase.

Blog An online diary or journal. From 'weblog'.

Browsing Finding items to buy by looking through categories.

Buy It Now (BIN) A way of buying and selling that doesn't require bidding, but where an item can be purchased instantly at a fixed price determined by the seller.

ChannelAdvisor A third-party service provider that can advise business sellers about improving their operations.

Checkout The largely automated process through which a buyer passes at the end of a listing that enables them to pay the seller and pass on their contact details.

Community The collective term for all the members of eBay.

Community Boards Chat boards provided by eBay so that the members of the community can interact with one another and with eBay staff.

craigslist A popular online classified service.

Deadbeat bidder Someone who bids on an item but doesn't pay.

Detailed Seller Ratings Part of the Feedback system, buyers leave DSRs to rate a seller's performance in terms of describing an item, quality of communication and shipping.

Donahoe, John President and CEO of eBay, Inc. from 2008. Formerly CEO of Bain.

eBay My World A feature that aggregates a member's on-eBay content such as reviews, guides and feedback in one place.

eBay Shop A personalisable ecommerce shop that an eBay seller can choose to operate.

Elance An online service that helps professionals come together and do business. Ideal for finding a web developer.

Escrow A service that help buyers and sellers by acting as an intermediary. The money and the goods aren't released until both parties are satisfied.

Etsy.com A marketplace dedicated to the trade of crafts.

Feedback Reviews left by eBay members about and for other members.

Final Value Fee The commission that sellers pay to eBay for a successful sale, based on a percentage of the final price achieved.

Fixed price Another name for Buy It Now, where there is no bidding and buyers pay a price fixed by the seller.

Gallery A listing enhancement that allows buyers to catch a glimpse of an item on a listings page before clicking on the Item Title.

Google Adsense Google's advertising service that allows you to buy keywords and pay for the clicks you get through to your website.

Google Adwords A service that enables you to incorporate Google Ads into your website and get a share of the revenue when someone clicks on an ad.

Google Analytics A free service from Google that helps you track a website's traffic and visitors.

Gumtree An online classified ads site owned by eBay.

HTML Hyper Text Markup Language.

Insertion fees Another name for Listing Fees: the fees for placing an item for sale on eBay.

Item Description The written description that a seller gives an item.

Item Specifics Information about an item (such as size, brand or condition) that a seller can choose when listing an item that allows buyers to locate it using the Product Finder.

Item Title The one-line description a seller gives an item to attract buyers.

Kelkoo.com A shopping comparison site owned by Yahoo.

Keyword A word that people search for that is used to return relevant results.

Keyword spamming The practice of including irrelevant keywords in listings to attract searchers, which is banned by eBay.

Listing An advert on eBay.

Listing Designer Template A service offered by eBay on the Sell Your Item form that allows sellers to make their listings more attractive.

Listing Enhancement A paid-for option to make your listing more prominent in Listings pages.

Listing Fees The fees for placing an item for sale on eBay.

Listings pages Pages where the items that match a buyer's Search or Browse requirements are displayed.

Markdown Manager An eBay Shops facility that allows you to reduce items and hold sales.

Member Profile A detailed digest of a member's feedback and history on eBay. Accessed by clicking on the member's feedback score (the number next to his or her User ID).

My eBay A personalised list of your eBay buying and selling activities that is automatically updated. You can also use My eBay to access your account details and leave feedback.

NARU Not A Registered User: eBay slang for someone who has been suspended from the site.

Navigation bar The links at the top of a page that you use to get to other parts of the eBay site.

Negative feedback An unfavourable review of another eBay member after a trade. Negative feedback can only be left for sellers by buyers.

Neutral feedback A neither favourable nor unfavourable review of another member, but considered by many eBay members to be nearly as bad as negative feedback. Neutral feedback can only be left for sellers by buyers.

Omidyar, Pierre eBay's founder.

PayPal An online payment system integrated with the eBay site.

Positive feedback A favourable review of an eBay member.

PowerSeller A seller recognised by eBay for making a significant number of sales and maintaining high standards of conduct.

Pre-filled Item Information A service for sellers that provides catalogue information and stock images if you enter a barcode or EAN. Only available in certain categories.

Privacy policy eBay's promises to you that govern how it manages the personal details you submit when you register.

Product Finder The tool that a buyer uses on listings pages to sort items by values assigned to them by sellers, such as brand, size and condition.

Proxy bidding The automatic bidding system that means eBay bids on your behalf up to your maximum, depending on the other bids placed.

Pulse An information service that allows buyers and sellers to see what the most popular search terms are by category.

Scheduled Listings The option to create a listing but request that eBay delays making it live on the site until a time of your choosing.

Search engine optimisation Making your website attractive to search engines.

Searching Finding items on eBay by putting keywords into the site's Search engine.

Second Chance Offer A service for sellers that allows you to offer items to under bidders at their highest bid.

Sell Your Item form The online form where you enter information about your item so that eBay can build your listing.

Seller Information Box A section on the View Item page that summarises a selling member's details.

Selling Manager An advanced, free version of My eBay that is useful if you are selling numerous items.

Selling Manager Pro More advanced than Selling Manager and charged for, a listing and management tool for high-volume sellers.

SEO Search engine optimisation: making your website attractive to search engines.

Shill bidding When a seller bids up their own item to inflate the price, prohibited on eBay.

Shopping.com A shopping comparison site owned by eBay.

Site Map Accessed from the Navigation Bar, an index of the pages on eBay.

Skype An internet telephony company that allows users to call each other for free over the net using VoIP (Voice over Internet Protocol).

Sniping Bidding in the final seconds of a listing.

Spoof emails Emails that appear to come from eBay and aim to trick you into revealing your personal information.

Starting Price The price bidding starts at on a listing.

Subtitle A listing enhancement that allows a seller to add more detail to an Item Title.

Turbo Lister An offline program that eBay provides to help sellers create listings in bulk and upload them to eBay in one go without using the Sell Your Item form.

Under bidder The buyer who made the bid before the winning bid, and so did not win.

URL Uniform Resources Locator, a web address, such as http://www.ebay.co.uk.

User Agreement The contract between a member and eBay that you agree to when you join eBay.

User ID The unique name that you are identified by on eBay.

View Item page An eBay listing or advert.

vzaar A service that makes it easy to add videos to your eBay listings.

Watch List A buyer can add an item to their Watch List and the item will be stored in My eBay so they can monitor the progress of the listing and bid at a later date if they wish.

Whitman, Meg President and CEO of eBay from 1998 to 2008. She was succeeded by John Donahoe.

Also from Nicholas Brealey Publishing

THE SEARCH
How Google and Its Rivals Rewrote the Rules of Business and Transformed Our Culture

JOHN BATTELLE

"John Battelle has written a brilliant business book, but he's also done something more: he's used the amazing saga of Google to explore what it means to search. All searchers should read it."
Walter Isaacson, CEO of the Aspen Institute, former editor of Time

Jumping into the game long after Yahoo, Excite and the other pioneers, Google offered a radical new approach to search and redefined the idea of viral marketing. In *The Search* John Battelle lucidly reveals how search technology actually works, explores the amazing power of targeted advertising, and explains the implications of what he calls Google's Database of Intentions.

The Search offers much more than the inside story of Google's triumph. It's also a big-picture book about the past, present and future of search technology and its enormous impact on marketing, media, pop culture, dating, job hunting, international law, civil liberties, and just about every other sphere of human interest.

For anyone who wants to understand how Google really succeeded – and the implications of a world in which every click can be preserved for ever – *The Search* is an eye-opening and indispensable read.

John Battelle is a co-founding editor of *Wired* and the founder of *The Industry Standard*, as well as TheStandard.com. He is currently program chair for the Web 2.0 conference, a columnist for *Business 2.0*, and the founder of Federated Media Publishing, Inc.
www.battellemedia.com

PB £10.99 978-1-85788-362-6
www.nicholasbrealey.com